SIGNS OF MURDER

A DANA DEMETER MYSTERY

A. F. WHITEHOUSE

FOR FRAN.

SHE LOVED GOD, HER CHILDREN, AND
BOOKS.

1

Only a deaf person would lean on my doorbell without let-up for such a long time. I feel dizzy with the sudden jump from sleep to not quite awake. From the window of my third floor studio apartment, I look down and see my father at the locked entrance giving the intercom a workout. I buzz him in and search the mess of moving boxes in the main room for some sweatpants. While I pull them on, I hear his methodical trudge on the steps.

John Josef Demeter rounds the second floor staircase and I stomp twice to get his attention. He gives me a quick glance and short wave. I watch the top of his head as he gets closer, black hair combed neatly in place and sealed with pomade, until he reaches the top step and stands in front of me. His hands tremble when he signs good morning. We hug.

"There's only one chair," I sign, clearing it for him. He smiles at me and sits, his back to the studio's only windows lining the long wall to the right in the rectangular room. I don't like the chalky color of his face

—he doesn't do ghostly well. At sixty-six, JJ has the build of a former football player, though he never played sports.

"It's pretty early, JJ. I'm not having a housewarming party for a while." I gesture at the mess from moving in over the previous weekend. *"And when I do, it won't be Tuesday morning at,"* I grab his wrist to look at his watch, *"seven a.m."* I sign this last bit with exaggeration, my eyes wide open, mostly to tease him about waking me early on my day off.

No response, except for a morose look. Damn, his hands are still shaking. I ask him to tell me why the early visit as I sidle over to the toy kitchen embedded in the short wall adjacent to the windows. Extra grounds go into the Mr. Coffee with the hope a stronger brew will burn away the fog behind my eyes.

"What're you—is something wrong with Evie?"

"No, no. Your mother's fine. You remember my old friend T-O-B-Y?" JJ then uses a common shorthand and taps his upper arm at his bicep with the letter "T" to show me Toby's sign name: the first initial of his name connected to something memorable about him. *"We used to work together at ARC."*

I frown at JJ, his features darkened in silhouette against the window. I hold up my index finger so he'll wait a moment. I pour two cups of coffee and hand one to JJ, then sit on the end of my futon snugged up underneath the windows. No other furniture yet.

"Turn your chair so I can see you better," I sign. Not an easy feat with the clutter, but at least now we can see each other's faces as we talk. I give myself another mental slap to get this place in some kind of order, then pick up the conversation thread.

"Sure, I remember Toby." I tap the letter "T" on my upper arm to mimic the name sign JJ created for Toby instead of fingerspelling the name again. *"He's short, strong, built like a weight-lifter. You met him at ARC a long time ago."* Allen Rehabilitation Center trains people with disabili-

ties for jobs in the community. My father received services there for six months and then got a real job. Toby never left ARC.

"Right, right. Toby saved my life."

To myself, I smile at JJ's hyperbole. Thirty years ago, Toby saved my father's hands. I heard the story countless times growing up.

The two men were shrink-wrapping industrial-sized packages of detergent, sending them through a laminating machine. A malfunction caused the hot iron jaws to snag JJ's arms. Surprised and in pain, he tried to pull away but that burned his forearms and hands even more. Toby saw it happen. He pulled on his rawhide gloves and pried apart the clamped bars, using only his brute strength. His quick action saved JJ from permanent disability.

My father's arms and hands still bear scars the color of raw meat from second- and third-degree burns. But if he'd lost the use of his hands he would have lost much more—his ability to communicate. Maybe Toby did save his life after all.

"Did something happen to Toby? Is that why you're here?" It doesn't seem possible but JJ's face turns even paler.

"Yesterday I was going to take Toby out to dinner. I waited outside ARC to pick him up after work."

I nod, knowing my father did that from time to time.

"But Toby wasn't there. I was surprised because he never misses work. I remember the supervisor always had to take away his work gloves at lunchtime, or Toby wouldn't even stop to eat." JJ smiles and shakes his head.

I scrunch my nose up and down a few times, quick movements that cue JJ I'm paying attention but also urging him to get on with it. It won't do much good. My father never takes the direct path when telling a story. A headache parks behind my eyes.

"When Toby didn't show up at four o'clock, I went inside to see his case manager, J-A-N M-A-R-I-E." JJ lands the letters "JM" on the back of his hand in a staccato movement, establishing her initials in the same location that "work" is normally signed. *"She told me he had called in sick."*

I pull my head back and squint at him. *"Can he use the TTY or VP?"* My recollection of my father's friend is of a deaf man with very limited signing ability. As kids, my sibs and I made fun of Toby behind his back when he visited our house. We thought he was stupid because he knew exactly three signs: Work. Money. Toilet. Most of the time he simply watched us play, smiling and clapping his hands for reasons we couldn't fathom. That he gained the skills to use the teletype-writer or videophone to call in sick was beyond imaginable.

JJ leans over and places his coffee cup on a carton marked "kitchen," his hands still trembling. *"Toby didn't make the call. Someone from the group home called his case manager."* He rubs his thick, powerful hands. The red scar tissue from the old burns deepens, loudly pronouncing the calluses and ridges on his pale skin.

I get up for more coffee and use it to down three ibuprofen, my headache now elevated to persistent throb mode. My father declines a refill so I shut off the coffeemaker and return to the futon. *"I still don't understand why you're so upset. Is Toby sick?"*

JJ holds up his index finger signaling me to wait. God forbid I should want him to cut to the chase.

"I went to his apartment, the group home."

I nod as he spells out Campbell House, named after the Chicago street where it stands, familiar with the already-established sign JJ uses next: he makes the sign for house but both hands form the letter "C" to make it specific to Campbell House.

"I thought I would at least see him, tell him we could go out another night instead."

I wonder how JJ could relay the nuances of that information, considering Toby's limitations. But deaf people always seem able to make other deaf people understand. My entire head aches and nausea has kicked in because of the coffee. But on second thought, it must be JJ's tortuous rendition.

Time to be blunt. I exaggerate my signs, making them large and almost aggressive. *"JJ! What happened?"*

He sits back in his chair and blinks in a slow, deliberate way.

"At Campbell House the manager wouldn't let me in to see Toby. He kept telling me Toby was S-I-C-K, S-I-C-K." JJ fingerspells the last two words in a laborious way, mimicking a person with inept signing ability. *"I tried to ask what was wrong with Toby but he kept spelling S-I-C-K right in my face."* Again, he mimes this for me, spelling the word two inches from his nose, which lets me know the manager has no idea how invasive this is to a deaf person. *"As if I was blind."*

JJ looks despondent and grouses to himself with quick, small movements. *"Why does a group home for deaf people hire a manager who can't sign?"*

"Because hearing people can be stupid," I answer. Not the first time we've had this particular conversation.

"Then he shut the door in my face."

Well, that message was clear.

"I didn't sleep much last night. I kept worrying. Something didn't seem right. I got up early this morning to go back to Campbell House to see Toby before he went to work. When I got there a large white truck, like an ambulance, blocked the street so I couldn't park. I sat there trying to decide whether to back out of the one-way street or wait. Then the manager came out of Campbell House followed by two men carrying a black bag." JJ's hands circumscribe a large area.

"They struggled putting the bag into the truck. Then they drove away."

A body bag? In a flash I understand why JJ's hands shake and his face remains a sickly white. *"Toby?"* I sign, registering my shock with my jaw dropped, and point to the space JJ used to describe the body bag.

JJ nods. His pale face creases into tears. Holding his scarred hands in front of his body, one palm toward the ceiling and one palm toward the floor, he flips them over in one smooth motion.

"Dead."

2

10:00

I curse the morning sun, having lost my sunglasses someplace between my vacated home and new studio apartment during the recent weekend move. I head south on Lake Shore Drive, the remnants of rush hour causing traffic to slow approaching downtown Chicago. A glance to my left at the lake makes my stomach roil, matching the choppy, lurching motion of the water. The sunlight intensifies my headache, which persisted throughout JJ's earlier visit in spite of the ibuprofen.

Traffic comes to a predictable halt as I near the Michigan Avenue exit, giving me a second chance to contact my partner, Detective Felice Abandonato. But I get only voicemail. While JJ was at my place, I got a text that Abandonato caught the call for Campbell House, ARC falling within our district's catchment area. He confirmed Toby's death a homicide. I withheld from JJ the grim news his friend died of multiple stab wounds. Even though it's my day off, I promised JJ I'd get whatever information I could.

Traffic moves suddenly, so I toss my cell onto the passenger seat and head for the QuickLoss Clinic on Dearborn Parkway.

After a fifteen-minute search for a parking place, I sit in an examining room waiting for the doctor. The blue paper gown barely covers my ass. I make one more call, this time to the squad room where I work as a homicide detective, and wait to be routed to the first responders at Campbell House. JJ's sad story replays in my mind, the irony not lost on me that Toby died in a place established to protect folks like him.

"Detective? Sorry to make you wait," says the voice of the desk sergeant. "I can't find the guys who were there. Don't know if they're still out or what. Want I should have 'em call you?"

"Yes. Wait, no. I'm coming in. Give me an hour." So today won't be my day off. "Can you tell me what they found? Anything?"

"The ID, but barely. Guy's name is Toby "X", no last name. Multiple stab wounds. Abandonato's got the details. He's lead."

Nothing I don't already know. "That's it?"

"Only been a couple three hours, Detective."

"Right." I disconnect, wanting more than the scant detail offered but having to wait to talk with Abandonato. A bleeder case. It will be hard to tell my father how his friend died. I send a quick text to my brother and sister telling them about Toby's death, encouraging them to contact JJ to express their sympathy.

A sharp rap on the door and my doc enters. I put the phone on my clothes heap and stand to climb onto the exam table, grabbing the back of my gown but trying with no luck to close the wide gap.

"Morning, Dana."

"Morning, Dr. Hwang." I see from the frown on her face when she scans my computerized chart that this won't be an easy conversation.

"You can sit up on the table."

I do what she asks. She rechecks my vitals even though the tech has already given me the once-over. The short, wiry woman completes my brief physical and looks up to meet my eyes.

"Okay. No sugar coating. Since your visit eight weeks ago your stats are worse." She draws my attention to the computer where my medical life glows on the screen. "Your blood pressure's up, you've gained eight pounds." She wrinkles her nose. "And you obviously haven't stopped smoking."

Nope, no sugar coating. "Yeah. That patch didn't do much for the craving." I look down at her. A tiny woman, really; feline-shaped face and delicate makeup. I'm uncomfortable around women like her who seem so sure about putting all the feminine pieces together. My gut trembles.

"This is your last visit. You've used up your six months with us on the Department's dime. I'll have to report this to your Lieutenant, uh..." she searches for the name.

"Kozlowski," I finish for her.

"Right. You're not alone in trying to do this. Every officer has to follow the new regs."

As if that's supposed to make me feel better. Not all officers are dealing with their spouses going AWOL, jerking them around from a thousand miles away.

"Dana, what I can do at this point is offer my services to you privately. We could get you in compliance by the January deadline, but you'd have to work really, really hard."

"Lose forty pounds in two months? Is that even possible?" I know the answer even as I ask the question of a woman who, judging by her size, has never eaten an entire package of Oreos in one sitting.

"Koz will put me on desk duty for now," I say. But the thought of being taken off active duty status as a detective rocks me hard. I won't cry in front of this woman. I won't.

Dr. Hwang sits on a small stool with wheels and scoots up close to me, eye-level with my kneecaps. I look down at her.

"I'm concerned about you, Dana. You can't get away with what you're doing to your body. Maybe you could've when you were twenty. But not thirty. Smoking on top of your other...issues," her voice drops a notch, "makes you a candidate for heart disease and stroke."

I'd never heard her use these threats before.

"Stroke? Are you purposely trying to scare me so I'll stop drinking, walk the straight and narrow?" My anger forms a physical lump, high in my chest. God, I want a cigarette.

Dr. Hwang looks puzzled, then has the nerve to grin at me. "Well, as long as you bring it up, how much are you drinking?"

Shit. "Not much." The lie flutters in my stomach. "When I want to unwind."

"You shouldn't be drinking at all right now. Liquor equals empty calories, it increases your blood pressure—"

I hold up my hand to stop her litany. "I get it."

"Right. I'll stop lecturing you." She pushes away from the exam table and walks to a small sink behind me to wash her hands. The noise of running water almost causes me to miss what the doctor says next.

Almost.

"And if you and your husband are trying again, drinking could, ah, maybe cause another miscarriage. It's something to be aware of." I hear her yank a paper towel from the dispenser.

Her words jolt loose a momentary clip from my personal slideshow: Driving myself to the emergency room, the cramps coming low down in repeated fist-pumping thumps, sitting in the warm wetness as it spreads and soaks through my coat to stain the driver's seat.

"You can pick up your final report at the desk. I'll email a copy to your lieutenant. You can get dressed now."

In the mirror on the back of the door, Dr. Hwang checks her haircut and dye job, which cost three hundred bucks easy. We lock eyes in the reflection. "Dana, seriously. I can help you. Think about coming to see me as a private client."

For what? To obliterate my last bit of self-esteem? Not fucking likely.

The doctor closes the door and I slip off the blue gown, my naked self staring back in the same full-length mirror the doctor recently vacated: disgusting.

I'd have to lose forty pounds to get back to my normal one-forty. I flex my arms in a mock bodybuilding pose. They still look strong, a remnant of lifting weights and working out with Jimmy—when we were together.

After donning my clothes I take a closer look in the mirror, hand-combing my otherwise unstyled short hair. Maybe I'll ask the doc where she gets her hair done.

I leave the office without waiting for the report. I don't want to see it. But the receptionist catches up with me at the elevator to deliver it anyway, sure I had forgotten.

In the parking lot I tear off any identifying information, rip the rest of the report to bits, and toss it in the garbage.

3

Noon

Parking is a bitch because only the brass have the reserved spaces. The rest of us are relegated to the vagaries of the street. I pull my well-used Corolla into an illegal spot and flip the sun visor to display an official "Police Business" placard.

Entering the District Office, built from crusty-looking Indiana limestone a hundred years ago and consuming the entire block, I wait for the ancient elevator in the six-story monstrosity.

I exit on the fifth floor and cross to my desk on the opposite side of the squad room. Newly installed wall-to-wall carpeting exudes a chemical smell, not helping my iffy stomach. It does reduce the raucous banter echoing throughout the large open area to a quiet, dull drone.

After stowing my backpack under my desk, I scan the room for Abandonato. His text to me on the way over said he'd be here by now. Nada. I re-adjust my computer monitor so I'm not facing the bright sun flooding the room through tall arched windows. I check all the mails: e-, voice, snail, and inter-office. As expected, a terse note from Koz takes me off detective rotation and remands me to desk duty effective tomorrow. Just for now, I tell myself, just for now.

In the break room I scrounge around for a jolt of caffeine and spy my partner of three years crossing the area to our desks. He carries two foam cups from Dunkin' Donuts and a bag with the same logo looped over his wrist. On the street Abandonato's short stature and wiry frame turns no heads, but as I watch him move I wish, not for the first time, that I had his dedication to running. He trains year-round for marathons he tackles around the country.

An unpleasant realization hits me. With the news from the doc this morning, I probably out-weigh Abandonato by thirty pounds.

Back at my desk I accept the large, black coffee and pry off the lid. Bliss. I eye the plastic bag on my partner's desk. "That guy'll go out of business the way he pushes those freebies on you almost every day."

Abandonato rolls his eyes and pushes the bag onto my desk. "They're all yours." He never eats the kind of crap I love.

The other doughnut hounds see the doughnut logo and immediately leave their desks to crowd around me, emptying the box in short order. A young rookie, a good-looking guy whose name I don't know, stops and peers into the empty box as some of the others drift toward the break room for coffee.

"Jeez. Can't you text me with a nine-one-one when you get here so I have half a chance against these vultures?"

A smile plays at the corners of Abandonato's mouth. "Happens every day around this time, Marty. If you're gonna be a detective you got to figure these things out."

I laugh and break off half of my double chocolate, handing it to the young cop. "Here. I shouldn't even be eating this shit."

Looking at Marty I feel old at thirty. He's somewhere in his early twenties, not that much younger than me but with an eager quality new recruits always seem to project. It shows in his carefully matched attire, hair slicked into place, and shoes that gleam. He also looks healthy and well rested.

"How long you been around, Marty?" I ask.

Because he'd put the entire half doughnut I'd given him in his mouth, it made responding awkward.

"He transferred over from the Emergency Communications Center," says Nick, now acting as Marty's unofficial mentor. Nick works his way through a Bismarck, and jelly leaks out the side of his mouth as he talks. "Been with them two years, wanted to make a change, took the test and vi-ola, here he is."

Marty nods at Nick's recitation but doesn't add anything to his résumé.

"OEMC's loss is our gain. Welcome to Homicide," says Abandonato. Marty actually blushes at this.

Nick gestures at the empty doughnut box, then nods at my partner. "Nuts here won't even touch doughnuts."

A genuine look of surprise lights Marty's face. "I never knew anyone doesn't like doughnuts."

"Where you think he got the nickname?" Nick says. "Anybody doesn't like doughnuts is nuts." The two walk away and I hear Nick give Marty chapter and verse: "Guy who owns the DD thinks he's getting protection from us with this bribe. He ain't. He's only making us tubs of lard. But you never, ever let him know that."

"Speaking of tubs of lard, I'm on desk duty starting tomorrow." I toss Koz's note onto Abandonato's desk.

He picks up my note but doesn't read it. "I know. I heard it from Carrera." A frown creases his face when he says the name.

"Jesus, how'd he find out? I got the word myself about two hours ago."

"Yeah? He seems to have a direct line to Koz. Get this: I caught the call this morning on our guy, did some prelim on the scene. Then the Prick arrives telling me how he's in charge and I'm his gofer."

This is news. "Koz took you off lead and put that asshole on?"

"I thought you and I'd be talking about a game plan right about now but Carrera thinks he's already got it figured out." Abandonato pulls the tea bag out of his tall cup and tosses it in the trash, then snaps the lid back on and takes a drink.

"What've you got so far?" I ask.

"When you called this morning I'd just finished with the house manager. That's when Carrera came in and ordered me to check the other buildings in the neighborhood."

My partner pulls out a small, spiral bound notebook from his jacket, leans back in his chair and puts his feet up on the desk. After flipping through some pages he looks at me and says, "No one saw anything unusual."

"Big surprise."

"I got a list of the people who live at the home. They're all deaf. I figure you'll either interpret for me or interview them yourself. We waited until they went to work to move the body."

"My father had the bad luck of seeing Toby being loaded onto the ME's truck." I tell Abandonato about JJ's early morning visit. "Toby and my dad go back a long way." I sketch out what little I know about Toby's background.

"Your guy was stabbed at least twenty times. Looks like he was attacked in his sleep. The bed was soaked."

"Shit. It's going to be hard telling JJ how Toby died."

"So keep it general."

I shake my head. "I could try. But he'll keep pressing me for details, wanting the whole story so he can visualize it."

I push aside thoughts of the grim duty. "So what did you get from the house manager? Anything before Carrera barged in?"

Abandonato flips forward a couple of pages in his notes.

"Walter Washington. He said Toby's roommate, Sarah Gilbert, reported Toby sick yesterday morning. Washington called ARC's sheltered workshop to notify them. Later that evening Toby didn't come out of his room to help make dinner for the people on their floor. Sarah was worried and told Washington, but he didn't check on Toby until this morning. That's when he found the body."

"So Carrera's going to need me to interpret at the group home when everyone gets back when? Around five?" I check my phone.

"Yeah, but you're talking like Koz is going to okay you running around. Technically you're off today and on desk starting tomorrow."

I pull a cigarette from my backpack and roll it between my index finger and thumb, then hold it between my first two fingers. The familiar pose produces calm. Matches in hand, I stand and point toward the elevator.

Abandonato and I stand in the alley abutting the old building. It's still lined with cobblestone pavers from over a century ago. I scratch a light to my cigarette and inhale, letting the smoke linger in my lungs before exhaling in the cold air. Abandonato watches me and shakes his head but says nothing.

"What? I smoke. Get over it." I take a hard drag on the butt and try to put a damper on my irritation, knowing my reassignment affects Abandonato the most. "Look. It's not like this'll go on forever. We'll partner up again as soon as I lose the weight."

Still nothing but one arched eyebrow and a pointed look at my cigarette.

"I *will* lose it, Nuts. I can't give up the smokes right now. I'm too edgy about money and not knowing when Jimmy's coming back." Or if.

"Still no word?"

I shake my head. Flicking the half-spent butt at a dumpster across the alley sends sparks showering to the ground. I cross my arms against the cold.

I don't want to talk about my husband staying in L.A. for four months when the training there on gangs took only three. The last time we spoke on the phone ended in an argument about my drinking. Since then we've been waiting each other out to see who would make the first move.

Abandonato squints at me. "I never took Jimmy Gennaro for a coward."

I acknowledge his support with a smile, but want the attention off me. "So you're working with Carrera. Try not to commit suicide."

"I might. Unless he gets me killed first."

"No, no. That's not how it went. When Carrera didn't provide backup his partner was only paralyzed, not killed. You'll be fine."

Abandonato laughs outright and we start back into the building.

"Why don't you talk to Koz about the Prick," I say, "see if he'll assign you another temp until we're back together."

"I did. Problem is, with the new regs a lot of the dicks are suspended. There's nobody else right now. Carrera may be an asshole but he's a fit and healthy asshole."

"And lately a much better-dressed asshole. Have you noticed he's wearing suits now?"

Abandonato looks around the hallway before speaking again. "I think the union is pushing Koz to put Carrera back on the street, give him the lead."

"Crap." After Carrera put his partner in a wheelchair for life the other detectives refused to work with him, although they didn't openly show this to Koz. Instead, they went about their investigations solo, relegating the Prick to paperwork and minor detail bullshit so he'd be off the streets and out of their way.

"While I'm on desk I'll do whatever I can to help you. You know that, right?" The elevator opens for us but Abandonato heads for the stairs, so I follow.

"Lose the weight, Dane. Do that. Get back to what we had."

He takes the stairs two at a time and I lose sight of him as I slog my way to the fifth floor—one step at a time. Once there, I get my back-pack and head out to my car, determined to empty the packing boxes in my studio and get things in order.

I can't control Koz's orders for me and I will miss working directly with my partner—the two of us have the best solve rate in the district. Working homicide is all I ever wanted, starting ten years ago when Jimmy and I were newlyweds attending the police academy together.

No doubt about it, the next few months will be hard. And although Carrera is the lead on Toby's case, he has about as much chance of finding the killer as I have kicking nicotine. I trust Abandonato to penetrate the mystery of who murdered my father's friend, this harm-less deaf man with no last name.

4

2:00 p.m.

Entering my studio, I toss the few pieces of mail I received onto a small corner desk. The forty-watt bulb in the overhead fixture near the front door does little to cut the gloom. Among the boxes stacked waiting for my attention since Saturday, I discover the one with my lamps, but instead of brightening the room's pall their light seems to heighten the shadows and dark spaces.

After this small effort I stop trying to organize the room any further because the task I thought I could easily complete has left me overwhelmed.

Even though it's late for lunch I make something to eat, since I want to get over to Campbell House in a couple of hours to interpret for Carrera. But my stomach is still queasy from this morning. I crack open a beer and surprisingly it settles my stomach. The persistent headache I've had since JJ's morning visit disappears too. I promise myself I'll only drink this one.

I sit at my little desk to smoke a cigarette and think of Koz's terse message taking me off active detective duty. I know that working the desk, pushing papers, and processing incoming suspects will bore me out of my mind. I chide myself with the thought—the hope, really—that motivation comes in all forms, including boredom. I will lose the weight. I *will*.

With that I feel a surge of adrenaline and decide to at least get my home paperwork in order. I hunt through a few boxes, find my calendar, and tape it to the wall in front of me. October will be over in a week, which pushes my thoughts to payday on the thirty-first.

I unload piles of paperwork onto my desk and sort it into stacks, ranking bills in order of due date. It's then I realize Jimmy's check for half the mortgage on our now-vacated home didn't arrive in today's mail. If I don't pay that on time we'll get slapped with a huge penalty. There's not enough in my own account to cover his half.

I pull his name up in the directory of my cell phone. Dread. We haven't spoken for a month and that conversation ended in an argument about my drinking.

I light another cigarette and hit the call icon. His line rings several times. As I'm about to hang up he answers, sounding out of breath.

"Yeah. Gennaro."

No recognition in his voice. I realize I'm not even on his caller ID.

"Hey, it's me. Dana." Your wife.

"Hey." A pause. "How *are* you?"

I can hear the thinly veiled concern in his voice and resent it. Don't ask me about my drinking. Don't you dare.

"Listen, Jimmy. I need your half of the mortgage. It's due in a few days."

"Sent it to you last week. You should have it by now."

Damn. I didn't figure in the extra time consumed by mail forwarding to my new address.

"Right, okay. It'll probably show up tomorrow. Sorry I bothered you."

"Dana, wait! What's going on with the house, the renovation?"

"Nothing, Jimmy. I'm not there. I moved last week." I can't deal with staying in the house without you, can't deal with watching them build an addition for a useless nursery.

"Moved? Why didn't you tell me? Or is it a big secret?"

His sarcasm boots my sadness away with a clean kick.

"You know, this phone system works both ways, Jimmy. I can call you —and guess what? You can call me too. And speaking of secrets, your three-month training ended a month ago. Any chance you're going to tell me when you're coming back?" Or if.

I take a deep drag on my cigarette and exhale loudly.

"Still smoking. Has anything changed besides your address, D?"

"Oh, I see. You're going to stay in L.A. until I'm smoke-free and forty pounds lighter?" Damn. I hadn't wanted the weight thing to slip out. Whenever I feel hopeless, which I do when we argue, my anger kicks in. "Nice knowing what our marriage really means to you."

I punch the end button on my cell and hold it in a tight grip until the screen light dies, then turn off the phone. Times like this I miss having a landline, complete with a receiver I can slam into the cradle with a gratifying crash.

I pace around the stacks of boxes in the small room, berating myself for my outburst at Jimmy. Two photos pinned to the refrigerator distract me and I stop: my parents smile at me from their forty-fifth wedding anniversary party last year. They stand with their arms around each other, Evie a half-pint and JJ a long drink of water. The difference in their heights coaxes a smile from me.

My gaze shifts to the second photo: Jimmy and me decked out in our dress blues on graduation day from the academy. We hold hands. Jimmy grins at someone on his left and I face the lens with an impatient look on my face, my then-long hair pulled back in a tight bun.

I like this shot. Jimmy looks impossibly young, an impression enhanced by his cadet-style buzz cut. My own expression reminds me of how anxious yet eager I was to start our new lives together. Ten years ago.

I look back at my parents, who seem happy and content with each other, and wonder if Jimmy and I will be together thirty-five years from now. Hell, I wonder if we'll be together *one* year from now.

The earlier hopeless feeling when talking to Jimmy returns. But instead of becoming angry again about my rocky marriage, I feel sad and can't figure out what to do about it.

Half an hour later, I return from the liquor store with two bottles of Greek wine and a six-pack, which I stow in the fridge. My anger at Jimmy has dissipated, replaced with a deeper sadness than I felt when I headed to the store. I want what my parents have, a stable, long-lasting marriage—with children. Alone, I'm unable to achieve it.

I uncork the retsina wine and pour a generous splash in my empty coffee cup from this morning. Sitting on the futon with my back against the wall, I turn on my cell phone to find a text from JJ and voicemail from Jimmy.

Hi Dana. Dad here. Any news about Toby? Mom wants you come dinner tmw. Pls call me

I have nothing to tell him about Toby, plenty to tell him about me: I'm not an active detective anymore, my life is in a bunch of boxes stuffed in a cramped, dingy room, and my husband is two thousand miles away, probably for good. But my father doesn't need to hear his thirty-year-old daughter complain about her failures—they're mine, not his.

I delete JJ's text but stare at Jimmy's voicemail icon for a minute, then take a gulp of retsina. The wine's earthy pine taste blooms in the back of my throat and burns on the way down. Whoever called booze liquid courage didn't know anything. If I called my husband now, I wouldn't know how to begin from where we ended. I turn off my phone, leaving his message unheard until tomorrow.

5

Wednesday, 6:00 a.m.

Early the next morning I hustle into the shower and freeze my ass off. For some reason the hot water is not working and I make a mental note to chew out the manager. Breakfast is burnt toast because no matter how low I turn the knob on my old toaster, it continues to scorch the bread. Then I run out of bread before I can manage a piece with dark brown instead of burnt black.

But my meager breakfast is plenty for my stomach, which feels queasy from drinking early into this morning. I clear two empty wine bottles and several beer cans from the kitchenette's counter and scoop them into a plastic bag, stowing it in my neighbor's trashcan on our shared back porch. When the building manager empties the trashcans from each floor, he'll think my neighbor parties instead of me.

I jog to my car, turning on my cell phone to see I have fifteen minutes to make the seven-to-three shift. The message from Jimmy I ignored last night remains. I fire up the car's ignition and put the phone to my ear for Jimmy's message.

"Don't you ever fucking hang up on me again!"

I jerk the phone away for a second, his voice in full anger mode.

I put the phone back to my ear, his voice not as loud but clearly still angry.

"This isn't about me, Dana. And it isn't even about us! It's about what *you're* going to do! I stuck with you after you lost the baby. I thought we should give it another go, get back on the horse. Hell, the doc thought so too. But *you* didn't. Okay—I get that. But I couldn't stand the drinking anymore."

I cradle the phone in my lap thinking he's done, but in a voice so quiet it is unintelligible, he continues. I have to replay part of his tirade to get to these final words.

"I'm not the one who left, D."

This last sentence echoes, dredging up a dream that's recurred since my miscarriage and Jimmy leaving for L.A.

I'm swelling with our child. We go for a boat ride on a large lake. Jimmy rows and I face him, watching the oars plop into the water, dance a circle and disappear, only to rise again. We are both naked. I look at his beautiful, contoured arms. Sweat pops on his muscles. In American Sign Language he asks me if I'm all right, which puzzles me because he doesn't know how to sign. I shake my head, grab my stomach and press my knees together. I look down. Bright red clots of blood drip down my legs and plash on the silver bottom of the boat. Jimmy sees it and jumps over the side of the boat, swims away. I slide to the bloody bottom and hug my knees to my chest. He's gone. He's gone and never coming back.

~

I PULL into an almost legal spot at work and narrowly miss hitting a black cat as it darts across the street. I begin to make a sign of the cross but stop. That's my mother's superstition, not mine. A cold wind hurries me through the building's entrance, the chill driving my over-active imagination to serve up this picture: Jimmy lounges on an L.A. beach in the hot sun—and he's not alone. A bikini-clad woman lies next to him, languorously sliding oil onto her perfect skin.

I shake my head to clear the unwelcome thought and open the door to the stairwell. In a nod to Abandonato's healthy habits, I again climb the stairs to the fifth floor, where I stop to catch my breath before heading to the break room for coffee and ibuprofen. My woozy feeling persists.

At Lieutenant Kozlowski's office I stop by his administrative assistant's desk. "Hey, Veda."

She gives me a long once-over. "You better not let Koz see you like that." She tilts her nose up and sniffs the air. "You smell like my ex trying to clean up from one of his drunks."

"See me like what?" I ask this of a woman whose mini-skirt and fishnet stockings plant her fashion sense squarely in the sixties. I look down at my clothes. No way could she know I'm wearing maternity slacks. And okay, I have on a man's sweater—but it's mohair. I think it looks acceptable. But what really riles me is the crack about how I smell.

"Didn't ask and don't want your opinion, Veda. Just want to talk to Koz about starting on desk today." When I say this Koz sticks his head out of his office.

"Demeter. Come see me at eight." I nod and he shuts his door.

Veda sings low enough so only I can hear. "Ooooh, sounds like trouble to me."

"Easy to see why you're stuck in a shitty civil service job, what, twenty years now?" I rap my knuckles on her desk to punctuate my sarcasm. "People skills, Veda. People skills."

She inhales audibly and gives me the slow burn stare. "I'm gonna ignore that on account you ain't feeling so good, Detective. I was you? I'd get my ass out of here and go clean up." She inclines her head toward Koz's door. "Know what I'm saying?"

No snappy comeback occurs to me and I resist the urge to flip her off, showing her my back instead, intent on stoking up on caffeine and nicotine for the next hour before meeting with Koz. I have to be coherent to convince him to let me interpret at Campbell House, even though I'm relegated to desk duty.

When I approach Koz's door at eight Veda raises her eyebrows at me but says nothing. I ignore her and rap on my boss's door, entering without waiting for consent.

Stacks of manila folders thick with administrative minutiae and back-logged work are piled on Koz's desk, rendering him almost invisible. I can barely see the top of his head, his ragged comb-over helmeted into submission with hairspray.

"Sit."

He doesn't look up from writing on a yellow legal pad wedged between two piles of folders. I sit on a hard leather chair opposite him, two tiny breath mints lingering on my tongue.

The bright morning sun breaks through a heavy cloud cover and streams through the window behind his desk, ratcheting up my hangover several notches. I turn my chair sideways to escape the direct glare. Koz finishes what he's doing and leans back in his chair.

"Haven't seen you for awhile, Koz. Busy?" Social chitchat: never my strong suit.

"Always, always. My daughter is making noises about finally moving out on her own. I've been helping her with condo hunting. I'm afraid I'm finding out exactly how much I've spoiled Caitlyn." He shakes his head.

My recollection of Koz's personal life is that he was widowed early in his marriage and raised his only child, a daughter, alone.

"So it's 'the kitchen's too small' or 'there's no fireplace.' No matter that she likes everything else about the condo. If there's one small problem she walks out the door."

I shrug and commiserate with a smile. "Kids. What're you going to do?" I say this as if I relate to being a long-suffering parent, then feel impatient with myself for being phony.

"She reminds me so much of my wife." Here he pauses and looks at me as if deciding whether to further confide in me.

I point to a two-sided picture frame on his desk with a family portrait on one side and a picture of a young woman in a cap and gown on the other. "That her?"

Koz picks up the frame and hands it to me. "At her graduation from law school."

I look at Caitlyn's graduation picture and see the strong resemblance to Koz's wife. Her self-assured femininity reminds me of Doctor Hwang. The family photo shows a much younger Koz and his wife sitting close together on what looks like a park bench. They hold a young girl between them, maybe four or five years old, their arms encircling her.

"She's very pretty, Koz."

"Well, I want her to be happy, whatever it takes. That's all that matters to me."

He takes the frame back and centers it on what little space exists on his desk. "Enough about my daughter the diva. Haven't had a chance to talk with you since your assignment to desk duty. Adjusting?"

"I guess it's okay. I mean, hard to know since today's my first day." I place my hand on my stomach, willing my body to fight the nausea and stay calm.

"Your partner okay with this?"

Koz comes around from behind the desk and to my side, adjusts the visitor's chair to face me, and sits. His direct gaze is unnerving.

The truth, Koz? No, he's not okay with this. He's pissed as hell at me for being fat and smoking too much, for not having his discipline. And he hates working with Carrera because the Prick's an egomaniac who could get him killed.

"Sure, Lieutenant, he's okay with it."

My head throbs. I direct my gaze at the floor and blink rapidly several times. My eyes are dry and gritty.

"Are you sick, Demeter? You don't look so hot."

God, why is he grilling me? I shake off my irritation at Koz for his unwanted personal attention and remember why I'm in his office.

"Look Koz, I want to talk with you about the case Carrera's handling. He needs me to interpret for him at Campbell House. The people who live there are deaf and there's no way he can interview them." I have a momentary flash of my own lapse yesterday, blowing off my intention to go to Campbell House in the afternoon, instead feeling sorry for myself and getting drunk.

"Dana, look at me."

When I do as he asks, something like pity or recognition radiates from his eyes. He puckers his lips together as his nostrils flare.

"I can smell alcohol on you. Have you been drinking?"

His question is so unexpected that I rush to answer.

"What? No—I mean, yesterday I did feel sick so I drank some sherry. I thought it would help me sleep. I guess I drank more than I should have. I'm a little woozy this morning."

My words sound phony, even to me. A visual flits through my mind of the depleted wine bottles and empty beer cans scattered on my kitchenette counter this morning, now nestled in my neighbor's trashcan.

I break eye contact with Koz. Outside his window choppy clouds race over the sun and create a strobe-like effect in the room. Koz returns to his chair behind the desk.

"I'll be straight with you, Demeter. You haven't met the regs on the weight and smoking. And now you show up for work smelling like alcohol. You understand, don't you, the policy for the department is zero tolerance for alcohol and drugs on the job. Zero."

Koz goes to a filing cabinet and digs around inside a drawer. "I'm required to give you a Breathalyzer test."

What the hell? My stomach lurches. Koz is leaping ahead and I'm stuck behind unable to react to the starter gun.

"Wait, Koz. I don't understand." I twist farther around in my seat and see him unearth a testing kit, which he brings to his desk.

"It's for your benefit as well as the Department's, Dana. Otherwise it would be my word against yours. If you have alcohol in your body—"

I start to protest but he holds up his hand.

"If you still have alcohol in your system from last night it will show."

Koz sits down next to me and places the testing kit on his lap. He pulls out a small silver rectangular device about the size of a cell phone and presses a black button on the front. Three red zeroes light up on the display screen. He holds it out to me.

"You know the drill."

I do know the drill. I take the device from him, inhale deeply, then exhale, careful to turn my head away from him. After another deep breath I blow into the tube for as long as I can. I'm dismayed that numbers actually register.

Koz glances at the display and jots something on a pad on his desk. "It's point zero seven, which is—"

"Just below the legal limit," I finish for him. Shit.

"But that legal limit only applies to the citizens out there driving under the influence, Dana, not you. I can't let you slide on this. CPD's standard is no detectible drugs or alcohol in your system while on the job. Z-E-R-O."

I rub my eyes, understanding how JJ must've felt when the manager of Campbell House kept fingerspelling in his face. Does Koz think I won't get it unless he literally spells it out for me? For any ordinary citizen, driving with the number I just blew wouldn't be grounds for a ticket, but for me it warrants punishment.

"I know what zero means, Koz."

My boss disconnects the disposable mouthpiece and tosses it in the trash, then deposits the Breathalyzer in his filing cabinet. He returns, but instead of sitting behind his desk, he again takes the chair next to mine and adjusts it to face me.

"You have two choices here, Demeter. I can suspend you with pay if you agree to go to the Employee Assistance Program for assessment and follow their recommendations."

I stare straight ahead, not daring to look at him, and watch what is happening outside the window behind Koz's desk. Heavy grey clouds now coat the sun, rendering the fluorescent lighting in the room colder and more intense.

As it darkens outside, I can see the reflection of my face in the window—tired, hung over, worried. He wants me to go to the EAP? Only the stone cold junkies or alkie cops go there. Or the crazy cops, the ones who beat their wives or flip out on the job.

"You said two," I say. "Choices. What's the other one?"

Koz sighs. "If you decide to file a grievance about the charge, you'll be suspended *without* pay until the union brings it up for a hearing. And understand that you may have to wait a while for that to happen."

Koz consults his desk calendar. "So you have some thinking to do."

I must look as confused and devastated as I feel because Koz's next words are spoken kindly.

"To help you with your decision-making process I'm going to give you a grace period of ten days to decide which option you want, Dana. During those ten days you'll be suspended with pay. I'll need an answer from you by November fifth."

My body slumps further down in the chair and I exhale, not realizing until now I've been holding my breath while Koz speaks. Everything he said whirls in my mind and evaporates except one thing, I'll be off the job until November fifth.

"Go home and get some rest, Dana. Turn in your badge and gun to Veda. By the way, did you drive here this morning?"

I nod, afraid my voice will quaver if I speak.

"Well, you can't drive home in your condition. Get someone to pick you up or cab it home. The Department can't be liable."

Koz stands and returns to his seat behind the desk, opens a folder, and begins reading. I try to say something more but his eyes stay focused on the folder and he holds up his hand at me like a crossing guard stopping traffic.

Dismissed.

Veda is not at her desk when I emerge from the inner office. I hurry to my desk and gather a few belongings to take home, embarrassed at flunking the blow test because it registered alcohol in my system. I charge down the five flights and out the door. Rain hits me in the face and obscures my view of the city as I jog to my Corolla.

If he wants my goddam shield and gun, he'll have to take them from me.

6

10:00 a.m.

"Zero tolerance. That's about how much *I* have for this bullshit. How could he suspend me when I haven't touched a drop today?"

I sit in my car in the McDonald's parking lot bitching out loud to myself. A woman walking by notices but quickly averts her gaze when I challenge her with a look. The large black coffee I sip is glorious and helps my queasy stomach. God, first Jimmy and now Koz. This morning isn't shaping up well around my personal failings. I light a cigarette and consider my situation.

The Employee Assistance Program is a non-starter. Koz has jumped to an extreme response for what really amounts to a minor infraction —hell, not an infraction of any sort. In the past I reported for duty with hangovers much worse than the one this morning. He never said anything when I came in sick.

This is the same damn thing. I feel some relief that I'm suspended *with* pay, given my situation with Jimmy. Though the suspended part riles me again. Koz is wrong. But it's obvious I'll have to prove myself with results. Ten days ought to be plenty of time.

The only thing I can do at this point is go over to Campbell House, see if I can help with interpreting for Carrera. Sort of off-the-record. Or maybe interview the residents myself and give the results to my partner. I head north toward the group home.

As I near Western Avenue the caffeine kicks in and I remember Abandonato telling me the residents work at the sheltered workshop at ARC during the day. They won't be back until about five, so no one's home to interview. Except maybe the manager. Williams? Washington?

I find Campbell House on a side street a block long near the dividing line between Chicago and Evanston. The aging red brick four-flat squats in the middle of the block, flanked by other similar apartment buildings. A cemetery spreads out across the street overshadowing the neighborhood.

In the lobby, four cheap mailboxes line the wall next to the locked entryway. The first three boxes list the residents, three to an apartment, by a first initial and last name. The glaring exception is Toby, which shows an "X" as a place marker for his last name.

A slip of paper marked "Walter Washington, Manager," is taped to the fourth box, and I push his buzzer several times before the door yields. Above the entry door a small light flashes when the buzzer sounds, a visual alert for the deaf residents.

The stairs begin below the first floor apartments, adding one more flight for me to conquer, but I remind myself that Abandonato would approve of the added exercise and feel almost virtuous.

As I pause on my way up the final flight to the fourth floor, I notice the entire wooden staircase is dust-free and the carpet freshly vacuumed. The sharp scent of pine cleaner tinges the air. I assume the manager likes to keep things clean, an assumption that holds up until he opens the door to his apartment.

When I glance inside to the right, the living room looks as though someone has broken in and thrown Walter Washington's belongings up, down and around. Clothes drape across chairs and tables and lay on the floor. Old pizza boxes, some containing desiccated food, are scattered around the room. A waist-high stack of newspapers next to the door partially blocks my entry. But my stomach roils again when I spy a thick crust of animal hair collecting along the crevice where the wall meets the floor.

What a slob. Makes me wonder who cleaned the outer stairwell.

I step into his apartment's foyer and see two large German shepherds standing at attention by the empty fireplace. They start for me.

"Stay!" Washington's order comes out a lot louder and deeper than his slight build would suggest. The dogs whimper and slink back to the fireplace.

"I'm Detective Dana Demeter, Chicago Police Department, Homicide. I'm here to follow up with a few questions about Toby." I show him my badge and shut the front door.

"Cop's already here." Washington points over his back at a hallway leading to the rest of the apartment. As if summoned, Alberto Carrera appears at the end of the hallway and saunters toward us.

"Demeter? What are you doing here? You're suspended."

I still want to know how the hell he found out about my suspension so early, but for now I push my annoyance aside.

Standing next to Washington, Carrera's solid build makes the African-American house manager's small frame appear even more fragile than my first impression.

"Mr. Washington," I say, "can you excuse us for a minute? I need to speak to Detective Carrera out here." I open the front door and motion to Carrera.

"Whatever," says Washington. "I ain't got all day. Some new death people are moving in later and I gotta get they room ready."

Death people? I cringe internally. Not the first time I've heard "deaf" mispronounced this way. The guy's a slob *and* needs speech therapy.

"Look, Demeter. I don't know what you think you're doing here." Carrera claps his palm to his chest. "This is my case. I don't need you."

"Out here." I hook my hand around Carrera's arm and coax him onto the third floor landing, fixing him with a straight-on gaze. "You're absolutely right. This is your case. I'm only here because my father and the victim were friends. Do you have any leads, anything I can tell him?"

"You nuts? I just got started on this. I'm busting my ass to solve this thing and I got nothing to tell you. And I wouldn't even if I did because it's none of your fucking business. I'm on lead." As a seeming afterthought Carrera adds, "That goes for Abandonato, too." His face flushes red.

"Don't have a coronary, Carrera."

In his tailored suit paired with a maroon tie and cream-colored shirt, styled hair and manicured nails Carrera looks more like a pharmaceutical sales rep than a cop. A noticeable change in the past few of months from the spandex crap he always wore, as if he was either going to or coming from a workout. A fit asshole, and now a GQ asshole.

"You had a chance to interview any of the residents here?"

"Washington's going to help me talk to these deaf and dumb people." Carrera gives me a suspicious look. "Why?"

The urge to correct his slur almost erupts from me but I stifle myself.

"Look, most of the *deaf* people here use American Sign Language. Washington's not your man if you think he can interpret," I said, remembering JJ's gripe about the manager.

"Oh, but he is my man." Carrera waggles his stubby fingers in my face. "You're not the only one knows that finger alphabet, Demeter. Besides, how much can these people know if they can't hear?"

I want to smack the smirk right off his face. Plenty of deaf people can run circles around his pea brain, and I personally know...but I quash my internal rant and remember my first priority: information I can use.

"Even if Washington can do that finger alphabet," I draw air quotes around this last phrase, "doesn't mean he understands what deaf people are signing *to* him. I do. My whole family is deaf. You need me to interpret for you." I hold my breath, waiting to see if I coerced him.

"How many times do I have to say it? You are not on this case."

His voice has taken to growling, as if he thinks the sound itself will scare me.

"You want to tell your daddy something? Get it from Koz. Now get out of here and go home, Demeter. And if you're bored because you got nothing to do, have a few drinks to pass the time."

He barks a one-syllable laugh, then heads back into Washington's apartment and yells for the manager to hurry up. The door slams in my face before I can follow him in.

"Asshole."

I keep muttering to myself as I head down, pausing on the first floor landing outside Toby's apartment. I puzzle over how Carrera knew about my suspension so soon. Could it be from Veda? He couldn't be getting it straight from Koz. Why would Carrera be favored by our boss, especially when he's reviled by the rest of us?

Above me I hear the two men start down from Washington's apartment. I lower myself into a position on the stairs that lead down to the lobby door. I'm hidden from them but have a perfect view of Toby's front door, which stands ajar in spite of yellow crime scene tape draped across the threshold. I assume Washington is going to show Carrera the crime scene again and I decide to watch, hopeful I might overhear something, anything that would jumpstart my own investigation.

The two men stop at the door to the apartment, their backs to me, but instead of ducking under the tape and entering, Washington pushes the doorbell next to the entrance. No sound results and I assume a light has flashed somewhere within to summon whoever is home.

Sarah Gilbert, a woman I recognize as a friend of my father's, comes to the door, the yellow tape in front of her, facing Carrera and Washington. Her left arm is in a cast from shoulder to fingertips and cradled in a sling.

She spies me on the stairs and I quickly put my index finger to my lips and shake my head. She moves her visual attention smoothly from me to the two men so effortlessly neither of them notices.

The building manager begins a slow, laborious process of fingerspelling every word to her and using his voice at the same time for Carrera. I see my father is right about Walter Washington. How did he get a job here when he doesn't know American Sign Language?

"H-I S-A-R-A-H T-H-I-S M-A-N D-E-T-E-C-T-I-V-E H-E W-A-N-T T-O T-A-L-K T-O Y-O-U A-B-O-U-T TOBY."

Instead of fingerspelling Toby's name, Washington taps the letter "T" several times on the bicep of his opposite arm. I recognize Toby's name sign as does Sarah, or anyone who knew Toby.

I catch Sarah's eye and sign quickly. *"Act like you don't understand him, need interpreter who signs."*

Sarah flares her nostrils in subtle affirmation. She frowns at Washington, scratches her head and fingerspells back to him.

"A-G-A-I-N P-L-E-A-S-E."

What a ham.

"What'd she say?" Carrera pokes Washington's shoulder.

"Uh, she wants me to do it again."

Washington exhales loudly and struggles through the fingerspelling again. With a confused look on her face, Sarah spells out "detective" and asks what that word means. Before Washington can respond, Carrera elbows him out of the way and stands nose-to-nose with Sarah, the yellow crime scene tape crossing in front of his face. He grabs it and pulls it away.

Carrera yells at Sarah, thumping his palm on his chest with each word. "I am from the police. Police! Cops! A man was murdered here! I want to ask you questions!" His voice climbs in volume as he slows and exaggerates his speech.

This time Sarah's puzzled reaction doesn't look like an act.

Show time. I stand and clear my throat.

Carrera and Washington turn toward me as Sarah slips under the crime scene tape and comes out of the apartment, meeting me halfway as I climb the last few stairs to the first floor landing.

"Hi Dana! Good to see you! How's your father? You know, he won a lot at bingo last week. Five hundred dollars!"

I smile at Sarah and look at Carrera and Washington. *"Seems like you could use an interpreter,"* I say, using my voice as I sign.

Sarah nods several times, her curly red hair bouncing in different directions.

"Not so fast, Demeter." Carrera points at Sarah and asks Washington, "What'd she say?"

"Uh, something about bingo, I think. She signs pretty fast, even one-handed. Let me ask her—"

"She asked me how my father was and told me he won five hundred dollars at church bingo last week."

I flash my best smile at Carrera. Then, in an unscripted moment, Sarah grabs my arm and pulls me toward the apartment.

I hear Carrera tell Washington to get upstairs, adding "And don't even think about going anywhere, junior."

Sarah and I slip under the remaining crime scene tape and stand in the foyer, the apartment layout the same as Washington's. To the right, the living room is cordoned off and the first room in the hallway—a bedroom—has crime scene tape across it. I point at it, and to Sarah sign "T" on my arm with a questioning look on my face.

Sarah's expression saddens and she nods.

Carrera follows us in and gets right in my face, pointing his finger for emphasis.

"Just this one time, Demeter. Don't get any ideas you're on this case."

"I get it, Carrera. Give it a rest."

I ask Sarah if the kitchen can be used for the interview and she leads us down the hall from the living room to the back of the apartment. Two more bedrooms follow in a row after Toby's. The middle bedroom is empty. Sarah pauses at the third one and indicates her suitcase on a twin bed. She's in the middle of packing to go stay with her daughter until the apartment is habitable again.

At the kitchen table I sit next to Carrera and across from Sarah. She points to Carrera. *"What's his name?"* she signs.

I repeat the question and Carrera introduces himself and shows his badge, which Sarah takes and studies, as if memorizing its details. She hands it back.

"My name is Sarah Gilbert. Nice to meet you."

I smile as I voice the hackneyed phrase many deaf people use when meeting someone for the first time. Carrera doesn't return the sentiment. Instead, he pulls out a notepad and pen, flipping to a blank page.

"I've got some questions about Toby."

He proceeds to ask Sarah about the last time she saw Toby, where she was over the weekend when he was killed, who Toby's friends are, and his routine in the apartment.

With me continuing to interpret, she reveals that she saw him at work on Friday, which was payday. Later that afternoon, she broke her wrist in a fall at work and spent most of the afternoon and early evening in the emergency room. Her daughter picked her up at the hospital and took her home to Joliet for the weekend. When Sarah returned to the group home Sunday evening around seven Toby wasn't in their shared living spaces and she turned in early because of work the next day.

"But I knew something had happened here. Toby's very neat and always cleans up after himself but the living room was messy, lots of empty beer cans on the table. It smelled like someone had been smoking and residents are supposed to do that outside. Besides, Toby doesn't smoke."

"Anyone else live here?" Carrera asks.

"We had another roommate, C-A-R-O-L, but she moved into her own apartment last week. That's how I knew it was Toby who made the mess."

"So, you and Toby alone in this place?"

I give my facial expression the snide, sexual meaning Carrera's voice carries with this question.

But Sarah's reaction surprises me—she laughs.

"First, I'm at least fifteen years older than Toby. I doubt he'd be interested in me. But you don't understand Campbell House. This is a group home for ARC workers who need some help so we can live on our own. Each apartment has three single bedrooms. There were nine of us until Carol moved out and Toby...."

I see Sarah tear up at Toby's name and hold up my hands in a "time-out" gesture. Sarah goes to the bathroom for some tissues while I explain to Carrera what JJ told me about Campbell House.

"It's like a co-ed dorm. The people who live here don't have much money, probably are on public aid of some kind or Social Security. They make some money working at ARC, but it's not enough to live as independent as you or me."

"Don't mean she and Toby weren't shackin' up."

"Christ, Carrera. Is that all you can come up with?"

I wither a little inside thinking the case is doomed if he continues as lead.

Sarah returns and Carrera turns to a fresh page in his notepad.

"So you didn't see or hear anything from Toby on Sunday night or the next morning?"

Sarah smiles at Carrera. *"Well, I couldn't hear anything from him. I'm pretty deaf."*

With a closed fist, she puts her thumb in her ear and flares four fingers upward, wiggling them. I chuckle as I voice her response, then glance at Carrera. His face is red.

"Answer the question."

"No, I didn't see Toby Sunday night. My wrist hurt so I took a pain pill and went to sleep early in my room. The next morning I got up and ready for work. Toby's usually up before me but his bedroom door was closed so I left

43

without seeing him. But I told the manager that Toby might be sick because he never misses work."

"Did he have any friends?"

Sarah shakes her head.

"Toby was hard to talk to. Mostly he watched T.V. He liked movies with a lot of action or watching nature shows. Sometimes he'd point out animals to me and I'd show him the sign for it. He'd copy me, but later he couldn't remember the sign. Dana's father would come over and take Toby out to dinner but he didn't have any other friends."

Sarah's eyebrows lock together and she looks at the floor.

Carrera slaps his notepad shut and rubs his face, exhaling loudly. "Well, this is useless. She doesn't know anything and no one was here when the vic was killed. I don't think your interpreting helped me at all, Demeter." He gets up to leave.

As if talking to herself, I see Sarah sign that Toby likes candy but I don't voice it out loud, distracted by Carrera's abrupt dismissal of me and quick departure from the apartment.

"Back in a sec," I tell her.

"Hold up, Carrera."

I catch him on the stairs up to Washington's apartment.

"You're going to need me to interview the rest of the residents. Maybe you didn't get anything useful from Sarah, but wasn't it easy to talk to her? Almost like you were talking to her yourself?" I hate the wheedling tone of my voice.

He gives me a suspicious look but says nothing, stuffs his notepad in his pocket and continues up the stairs, me hurrying to catch up.

"Come on. You saw how bad Washington was. Deaf people trust me! My whole family's deaf, you know that."

He turns and looks down at me.

"And what's in it for you, Demeter? Trying to score points with the Lieutenant?"

He mimes tilting his hand to his mouth, flipping it back and forth in a drinking motion.

"Trying to get him to forget about your little problem?"

His insight not only surprises me it pisses me off, but I stuff my angry response and take a deep breath.

"Look, I'm suspended for ten days with nothing to do. Koz might like the fact that I do some volunteering for the department. Can't hurt."

I shrug, hoping he'll bite. No way Koz wants me anywhere near this investigation.

"And why should I help you look good to the Lieutenant?"

He turns to leave but I grab the sleeve of his coat.

"I'm the only one on the squad fluent in ASL. How're you going to solve this if you can't interview the deaf residents? And what about ARC? They have deaf staff. How're you going to interview them?"

Carrera shoves my hand away and smooths the bunched material of the jacket.

"That's my problem, Demeter. Besides, there are other interpreters in this city."

He starts walking up the stairs but I yell after him,

"Yeah, there are. And you have to pay them a lot of money. Koz won't be happy when he finds out I offered to do it for free!"

I walk back to the first floor landing and hear Carrera's cell phone chirp. His tread stops and his voice takes on a noticeable change from the gruff tone he used with me. Curious, I eavesdrop.

"No, I can't right now. No. Because I'm—" a long pause ensues.

This is new. I've never heard Carrera sound like a pleading puppy.

"Maybe I can get away after lunch, Sugar."

Sugar? He's got it bad if he's entered the arena of lovey-dovey nicknames.

"That's not so long from now," he says, but now his voice is starting to sound aggravated. Another long pause.

"Look, Caitlyn, I can't meet you right now. I'm in the middle of a case and that comes first. You go ahead and talk to them and I'll meet you there in an hour."

I hear his feet start up the stairs again. Carrera and Caitlyn? Didn't see *that* coming. But it does explain how he knows stuff about me before everyone else. Koz. I reach the first floor where Sarah stands just outside the doorway of her apartment.

"Tell your parents I said hello." She holds up her good arm for a sideways hug.

I release from our hug and her face shows an expression of pain.

"Oh, Sarah, I'm so sorry. I didn't mean to hurt your arm."

She runs her hand up and down the cast as if it might make her arm feel better.

"No, no. It's not that. I don't like being here alone, no roommates. And the yellow tape..." She gestures at Toby's room, the door closed and roped off with crime scene tape.

"You're staying here? I thought you were going to stay with your daughter."

I tilt my head, puzzled. I understand what she says about being alone. Sarah's a small woman and a go-getter, still working at sixty-five when she could retire. But her arm encased in plaster and supported in a sling adds a layer of vulnerability to her situation.

"I'll be with my daughter for the rest of this week, but I can't miss more work after that. She lives in Joliet and works, too. She can't drive me back and forth. Too far."

"But this is a crime scene. You can't stay here until the police say they're done."

"I know. They let me in today to pack but I have to share a room with a woman friend of mine upstairs until I can come back down here."

We both gaze at the closed bedroom door with crime scene tape across it. I enter the apartment, Sarah following, and at Toby's room slip my hand under the police barrier to open the door, curious to see inside even though it's officially restricted.

The room, unremarkable in every respect, holds only a small chest of drawers, a thirteen-inch T.V., and a twin bed. The mattress lies exposed, bereft of its bedding, a large coffee-colored blood stain in the middle. A pair of battered moccasins, the backs flattened so the wearer could slip into them, are on the floor near Toby's bed, an empty shoebox next to them. The collection efforts of the crime scene techs are evident throughout the small room.

Sarah points to the shoebox. *"I forgot to tell the other detective about the money."* She runs her hand through her hair several times.

"No problem. I can tell him." I can but I won't. *"What money?"*

"Toby didn't have a bank account. On payday he would cash his check and put the money in that shoebox and hide it under his bed. He didn't understand the concept of leaving money in a bank."

"Makes sense. The money's real to him only if he can see it, hold it," I say.

Sarah nods and wipes away tears streaking down her cheeks.

"How safe would his money be here? Do the bedrooms have locks?"

Sarah fingers a lanyard around her neck, several keys dangling at the end. She holds the keys, each one topped in plastic of a different color, and ticks them off for me.

"One for my bedroom, one for the front and back door to the apartment, and one for the building entrance. Everyone has separate keys."

"Does the manager have a master key to the apartments?"

"Yes. For emergencies."

After confirming Sarah has a videophone, I give her my card and tell her she can call me anytime, day or night.

"Especially if you remember something else like the money. Anything. Even if you think it's not important." We gingerly hug again.

"Thanks, Dana. Really, I'm not scared. I'm so sad about Toby. He didn't have much. I'm so lucky to have my daughter."

With her good hand she lightly strokes the cast again. I give her shoulder a squeeze and leave.

On the way out to my car I discover only one cigarette left in my pack. I slide in the driver's side, light up the lone soldier, then crush the empty box and toss it in the back.

There's little to follow up on from this botched attempt at gathering information. Still, I jot down what I can remember from Carrera's interview, knowing anything I interpreted will quickly fade from memory if I don't note it. I add the last bit from Sarah about Toby keeping his cash in his room.

As I smoke I decide to wait and see if Carrera leaves. There's probably not much to gain from talking to Washington but I want to anyway. It's all I have.

Half an hour later the Prick still hasn't shown, my nausea has disappeared and I'm hungry. I'll have to come back later. I drop the car into gear and leave in search of nourishment—food and cigarettes.

7

11:30 a.m.

Not far from my studio I pass Louie's Liquor Palace and backtrack, pulling into the parking lot adjacent to the store. Loud, hand-painted signs decorate the windows with promises of any kind of booze I could possibly want, all at a low, low price.

Inside I snag a bag of pretzels to stave off my hunger until my next stop, promising myself I'll buy some healthy food to prepare at home instead of scoring some greasy take-out. I pause in front of the glassed-in refrigerator where cold six-packs are stacked floor to ceiling, their faces shining at me.

My earlier nausea has evaporated. The thought of a cold beer to go with the pretzels and lunch beckons. Problem is, I won't stop at one, especially if I don't have to get up for work tomorrow. I pass the case and search out a Diet Coke.

As I wait at the end of the line to pay, I notice the cigarette cartons spanning the entire wall behind the counter, every brand and type represented, including some imports like Gauloises, Gold Flake and Sweet Afton.

"Hi, how ya doin'?"

Louie, according to his name tag, greets me with a wink. The man is short and skinny with black hair oiled in place. From forehead to chin his face caves inward, reminding me of decaying fruit.

"I'm okay. Out of Kools." I scan the wall for the familiar green logo. "My boss wants me to quit."

"Yeah? Hard to quit, ain't it? Hardest thing I ever hadda do in my life."

"If you quit, what's with the butt?"

I jut my chin at the cigarette tucked behind his left ear and points at a dime-sized liver spot near his eye.

Louie pulls the cigarette down and conducts an imaginary orchestra with it.

"Well, I smoked for a lotta years—thirty, forty-some—and got the cancer in my lung—just the one, mind you. Hadda go under the knife. So I got one lung left, got outta the hospital, and first thing, I fire up a butt.

So when I go back for follow-up, you know, to the guy who yanked my bad lung, he smells the cigarettes on me. Me? Can't smell worth a damn. What I liked about Camels, you could taste 'em, you know? These others," he waves at the wall of tobacco, "like breathing hot air."

He makes a face and repositions the cigarette behind his ear that sprouts hair, and points the price-scanner at my pretzels and pop.

"So my doc takes one whiff and bawls me out for smoking."

Louis shrugs at me with a silent *what're you gonna do*? "So I got dressed and left outta there. Didn't need him raggin' on me, now did I?"

I grin as he bags my purchases and hands them to me.

"So you gonna keep tryin' for today, or what?" he asks.

I hold up my hand as if stopping traffic.

"Hold on. You made me listen to that whole story and I still don't know what that butt's doing behind your ear."

I open the bag of pretzels and eat a handful.

He touches the cigarette lightly, his hand continuing on to slide over his hair in one smooth movement.

"Oh, right. Well, after the doc got so mad I had a heart-to-heart with myself. I knew I couldn't quit on my own so I joined one of them twelve-step programs—you know, like AA—only with smokin'. So this," he points to his ear, "is so I don't forget: one butt and I'm back to two packs a day. If I wanna go on breathin' I gotta take care of the lung I got."

He winks at me again.

"So how'd you do it? Cold turkey?"

"I tried them other ways: hypno-whosits, patch, the thing with them needles. None of 'em worked for me. You know what did? Sunflower seeds."

"What?"

"Yeah! I know, crazy. The kind with the shells on 'em—kept my hands and mouth busy and after awhile the craving stopped. I ain't smoked for eight years now."

I gaze at the small man with his bright eyes and animated demeanor and feel a small bump of hope. For as shitty as this day started with Koz putting me on suspension and continuing in that vein with Carrera, this chance encounter with someone whose off-handed advice is exactly what I need almost makes me cry with relief. The half-eaten bag of pretzels goes back in the sack and I look around the store.

"You sell them here?"

"Sure, kid. Got a new shipment in this morning. They're in back. Hold on, I'll get ya some."

While Louie is gone I experience a coughing fit so deep it feels as though I've pulled a muscle in my back. Seems my body agrees that it's time to quit smoking. Louie appears holding a bag of sunflower seeds as big as a man's head.

"Put your eyeballs back in their sockets, kid. It's only two pounds. You're gonna be surprised how fast you go through these things. Hell, they're as addictive as the butts. Probably why they work."

Chuckling, he dumps the sunflower seeds into another bag and waves me off when I try to pay him.

"Put your money away, put it away. First bag's on me. You need any more, you know where to come."

"Hey, isn't that how pushers hook new prospects?" We both laugh. "Thanks, Louie." I hold out my hand and we shake. "I'm Dana. I moved near here last weekend and you bet I'll be back."

My inner nag pipes up: But you won't be back in the next ten days, right? It *is* a liquor store. I push away the thought.

"See ya, kid."

I leave the store feeling oddly comforted by the heft of the sack in my arms. At home I unpack the sunflower seeds and open the bag at my little desk, experimenting with cracking open the small gray and black striped shells with my teeth and savoring the salty seed. The thought of not returning to Louie's to buy any booze during my suspension gives me an idea. The next ten days will be my personal test: no smoking, no drinking. Hell, I'll even throw in eating right and exercising.

"But nothing more ambitious than a jog around the block for starters."

I change into a pair of old sweats and some cross-trainers from years ago when Jimmy and I played in the Chicago PD softball league. I head outside and complete one quarter of the distance, my arms hissing as they slide back and forth against my down vest. At the first corner a brisk wind hits me head-on. The cold air shoots ice pellets into my lungs. Immediately, I hate every one of the fourteen years I smoked. Almost half my life.

Another deep, hacking cough causes me to stop and bend over, hands on knees, until I clear out more phlegm. I jog to the next corner and meet jumbled hunks of concrete, the sidewalk jackhammered into oblivion, so I shift to the street and huff to the next corner.

But as I turn into the final stretch toward home a car approaches from behind and honks, startling me. My default reflex is to flip him off, but I do return to the sidewalk.

"Bitch!" He hits the gas, making the tires squeal as he speeds away.

"And proud of it!" I flip him off a second time but he's already out of sight, the smell of burning oil left behind. I slog the last quarter of the block and sit on the front stoop of my apartment building until my breathing returns to normal.

I now understand three things about jogging: it requires less clothing than I have on, it makes me nauseated, and it is totally incompatible with smoking. But mostly I wonder why anyone does this for exercise.

Still, as I drag myself up to the third floor, I feel pleased with my first attempt at exercise in over a year. Since just before I got pregnant. I push this thought away. It reminds me of Dr. Hwang's recent admonition about Jimmy and me "trying" again.

Inside, I decide to track my self-improvement regimen for the next ten days. It will give me something concrete to show Koz. He'll see he's wrong about me. I'm not a burnout.

On a piece of paper I draw a grid and fill in categories across the top: Cigarettes, Food, Booze, Exercise; down the left side I plug in the dates starting with today and ending November fifth, the day I have to give Koz an answer to his ultimatum.

I fill in jogging for my exercise and enter what little I've eaten so far, but the day is still early; I'll have a better lunch and dinner. That means grocery shopping, so I leave the progress chart reckoning for the end of the day.

After a quick shower, a check of my cell shows a message from Abandonato. I hesitate about whether to call him back because I haven't yet figured out a way to tell him about my suspension. My new enthusiasm takes over and I punch in his number, thinking I might tell him about my jogging.

"What's up?" I ask when he answers.

"I got Toby's file from the Prick. Meet me at the Elite for lunch."

8

"Were you going to tell me or did you prefer I heard it from Carrera?"

I make a face at Abandonato. "Oh hell, Nuts, of course I was going to tell you. I had to get out of there when Koz suspended me. I was so pissed."

"I talked to the Prick an hour ago and he knew about your suspension already. It's like he's got a direct line to Koz or something."

"He does. Caitlyn."

Abandonato's surprised expression pleases me. I know something before he does, which is not a common occurrence. He waggles his fingers at me in a beckoning gesture and I lean forward, my arms on the table, my voice low.

"Koz told me Caitlyn's looking to move out of his home and into her own condo. I didn't think anything of it until I overheard Carrera talking to her on his cell. Sounded like she wanted him to condo-shop with her."

"You think they're moving in together?"

"God, who knows? I'm still trying to wrap my mind around them as a couple."

A look of sudden understanding crosses Abandonato's face. "The Prick's clothes—she must be dressing him."

"Yeah. He's so dumb Caitlyn probably even has to do the tie for him. But she's the connection for him and Koz being so chummy. The Prick knew about my suspension when I saw him at Campbell House at ten this morning, not even two hours after I met with Koz."

"I tried to convince Carrera to let you interpret the interviews with the ARC residents later today," he says. "But that was before I knew about your suspension."

"Yeah, I tried to convince the Prick too, but it didn't go anywhere." I fill Abandonato in about my largely unsuccessful trip to the group home.

"He said he's going to solve Toby's murder by himself without any help from me or my lush partner," says Abandonato.

The words sting: first Koz, now Carrera again. By now, gossip about my suspension must be flying through the squad room with cops making jokes at my expense, embellishing their stories about my drinking. I know, because I participated in similar patter about other cops during the last ten years, and over a lot less.

"Asshole," I say, the word nowhere near sufficient to fully express the shame I feel over the reason for my suspension, unfair as it is.

"Look, there's nothing I can do about him," Abandonato says. "But whether the Prick likes it or not, I'm still assisting him on Toby. Only Koz can take me off. But Carrera will make solving this case hell. You've got to get back on board as soon as you can, Dane."

Abandonato pauses but maintains intense eye contact with me. "Lose the booze, okay?"

I hope the look I give him is as bitchy as I feel.

"You too, Nuts? Why is everyone sticking their noses into how much I drink? What I do after hours is none of your fucking business. Save the lecture."

I sit back in the booth and look around the restaurant at the other customers—people having business lunches, moms treating themselves to a mid-day break, college students nursing a cup of coffee in order to utilize the free wi-fi. I feel as out of place here as I feel out of sorts with my partner. That earlier small bump of hope about the possibility of quitting smoking has evaporated and a craving for nicotine surges through me.

The waiter arrives with three plates ascending his left arm and two more in his right hand, momentarily distracting me from my wish for a cigarette. Even though it's lunchtime, we've both opted for Elite's breakfast.

"Denver with hash browns and Greek toast for the lady, side of sausage." He winks at me as he deposits the plates in front of me. "And a feta and spinach egg-white omelet, dry rye with a side of tomatoes for the gentleman. And I'll be right back with your grapefruit juice, sir."

Abandonato stares at the stack of the food in front of me but says nothing.

"Look. I quit smoking. Today. This morning. Haven't had anything to eat until now." I make an elaborate show of opening my napkin and tucking it into my shirt like a bib, earning a small smile from him.

"Okay. Good. It's a start," he says.

High praise from Abandonato. I contemplate telling him about my initial attempt at jogging but now it only seems pathetic, wanting his approval for a quick trip around the block. Instead, I wave my cup at the waiter for more coffee and we chow down.

"The good news about my suspension is I can do a lot of the leg work on Toby myself, assist you, be your invisible partner." I tell him about my missed opportunity to interview Washington.

Abandonato pushes a thin manila folder across the table to me. "Haven't gotten much from my initial work. The photos are in the back."

He frowns, his hand stays on the file. "You going to okay it with Koz? Doing the leg work?"

"Oh, come on. Whatever I get I'm feeding right to you. Koz doesn't have to okay that."

I tug on the folder and although Abandonato is slow about it, he lifts his hand.

"Besides, I'm still on the payroll, still have my badge," I say. Abandonato doesn't have to know I directly disobeyed Koz's order to turn in my badge and gun.

I bypass the short report to look at the pictures. The first shot was taken at the doorway of the messy bedroom I saw this morning, with clothes strewn around the floor, the twin bed against the far wall, and the empty shoebox near the sad slippers.

The only difference is a grey corduroy comforter forming a large, lumpy pile on the bed. The next shot, a close-up of the bed, reveals the fingers of an upturned hand peeking out between the edge of the cover and the headboard.

After that, a series of shots of Toby sans comforter, ripped and bloodied from at least twenty stab wounds, his stocky and muscular body stilled in death. Blood saturates the white sheet beneath his body, a deep red halo outlining my father's friend. I tell Abandonato about Toby keeping his cash in a shoebox, presumably the one in the picture.

"Washington has keys to all of the apartments and all of the bedrooms," I say. "Makes me even more anxious to interview him." I repeat my wish, hoping to sway Abandonato. "I doubt the Prick knows anything about the money."

I gesture at the photos with my coffee cup in hand. "I mean, look at him, Nuts. My god, Toby was savaged. This isn't a stabbing in response to something like a robbery. This is personal."

The graphic photos don't bother me. I've witnessed scenes more horrific as a homicide detective. But when I recall for Abandonato what Sarah said about this deaf man without much in his life, no family, few friends, literally isolated in his own body, I feel the same sadness Sarah and JJ expressed for Toby.

"That's something else bugging me about this. No family," says Abandonato.

"On my father's birthday he'd bring Toby over to our house and my mother would make a cake for both of them, they'd celebrate together. Toby had no way of telling us his real birthday."

I push my plate aside and read the brief report in the file. Some of the details I already knew. For instance, early Tuesday morning Washington found Toby stabbed to death in his bed.

Some of the evidence the techs from the ME's office gathered included pubic hair, a half-full can of 7-up, brown synthetic fibers consistent with a carpet, a steak knife with a bright red plastic handle (the assumed murder weapon pending testing), three used condoms, a trace amount of red glitter, Toby's paycheck stub from the previous Friday, animal hair, a used matchbook from the Lincoln Hotel, and torn up pieces of a black and white photo. Fingernail scrapings were retrieved from Toby and the apartment was dusted for prints.

"Shouldn't the shoebox be part of the evidence?" I ask.

Abandonato takes the report from me, scans it, and hands it back. "The techs goofed. It should be included. I'll have it collected and processed."

Attached to the last page of the report is a photocopy of the torn-up black and white picture someone had pieced together. Evident are two children's dark-skinned calves, their lower bodies clad in cut-off blue jeans, each grasping a fishing pole. The photo bears a hand-printed date of almost fifty years ago.

"Toby and who?" I say.

He shrugs in response. "From the date, probably a picture of Toby when he was a boy."

I pull out my notepad and jot down info about the collected evidence. As I push the file back across the table I remember something Sarah said this morning and flip through my pad to find it.

I tell Abandonato, "Sarah told the manager on *Monday* morning that she thought Toby was sick because he hadn't come out of his room for work. But your report says Washington didn't report the death until early Tuesday morning."

"That's all Carrera would give me. His report on Washington's interview should be done today. I'll email it to you as soon as I have it. In the meantime, you'll do better to talk to Washington yourself."

"Top of my list." I'm happy but puzzled that my partner gives me the leeway to interview the manager. Because of Abandonato's penchant for rigidly following rules, I thought he'd ignore my angling and relegate me to more minor jobs.

"You don't figure Washington for this, right?"

Abandonato shakes his head. "I saw him when The Prick talked to him—the guy's too puny. But I *am* interested in the time gap. And the money." He taps the file. "This is what we got right now. A further complication is Koz assigned me on a call that came in last night—

possible shaken baby death. My time's going to be pretty limited for Toby."

So that's why he needs me. I feel a stab of jealousy, left out of the new case he's pursuing, something we would work together if I weren't suspended.

Abandonato glances at his watch and then at me. "But I've got about an hour right now. Let's go talk with Toby's case manager at ARC's work site. Your unofficial duties start right now. She's deaf," he points at me, "and I need an interpreter." He picks up Toby's file and stands.

And just as fast as my jealousy arrives, it dissipates. I grin at him and grab the check.

9

2:30 p.m.

We enter ARC's mammoth training center through an automatic door at the end of a long wheelchair ramp. A security guard signs us in, we slap on visitor tags, and he tells us how to get to the office of Toby's case manager, Jan Marie.

On the third floor we get lost following a long corridor that dead-ends right after a women's bathroom. As we turn to retrace our steps a tall African-American woman emerges from the bathroom and bumps into me.

"Oh, excuse me. I didn't see you," she says, then laughs.

I don't get the joke until a second later when she unfolds a guide cane and snaps it into place to form a solid white stick with a red tip. She pushes her hand through a leather loop on top of the cane, then holds it an angle in front of her.

"Uh, my fault," I say, my laugh uneasy. "Can you help us? My partner and I are looking for Jan Marie's office and somehow ended up here."

"Follow me. Jan's office is right next to mine."

Abandonato and I exchange looks and hustle to catch up with the woman, who has confidently walked away from us, sliding the cane lightly along the crevice where the floor and wall meet.

"This big old building is nothing but trouble," she confides. "Dozens of nooks and crannies, false starts and stops. Took me forever to map it out."

"It is huge," Abandonato agrees. "What was this building originally?"

"Factory. You know, a hundred years ago this area was full of buildings like this—mainly manufacturing. Gone now, mostly to Mexico or overseas. ARC bought this building cheap during the Depression, set up our work programs here. This neighborhood used to be pretty rough but now it's hip to live here. You've got yuppies and million-dollar condos up and down this corridor. We're the last standing reminder of the past. Kind of like the ugly baby at a Gerber convention."

All three of us laugh. She makes a quick right turn into another hallway that brings us to a series of small offices.

"Here we are," she says, feeling the open doorway to the first office and waving her hand. "Anyone home?"

A petite blond woman working on a computer at her desk looks up and smiles, then rises and comes toward us. Taking the blind woman's free hand in hers, she fingerspells something into her palm that I can't quite make out. The woman responds by signing in the hesitant, exaggerated manner of a novice. *"Visitors for you."*

"Thanks for your help," Abandonato says. I agree, signing at the same time for Jan Marie's benefit.

"No problem. Let me know if you need a guide out of this monster," she says, then turns and leaves.

"Hi. You're J-A-N M-A-R-I-E?" I ask. She nods.

"I'm D-A-N-A D-E-M-E-T-E-R." I quickly show her my name sign, tapping the letter "D" at the dimple on the right side of my face. *"I think you know my father, JJ?"*

Jan's face brightens at JJ's name, motioning us farther into her office and seating us in two folding chairs in front of her desk.

"Are you the hearing or deaf daughter?" Jan asks me.

"Hearing. My sister lives in M-N, works at a Center for Independent Living. My twin brother works at NTID in Rochester, New York. He's deaf, too."

A familiar swell of pride rises when I mention my brother David and his work at the National Technical Institute for the Deaf.

"NTID? What does he do?"

"Teaches in the Communications Department, something with computers that I don't understand!"

She and I both chuckle and I notice Abandonato shifting in his chair.

"What are you saying to her?" he asks.

"Crap, I'm sorry." I forgot I'm his interpreter. I explain our exchange to him after telling Jan what I'm doing, then introduce the two of them to each other.

"We're here to talk to you about Toby," I tell Jan.

"I remember now. You're a detective, right? Your father has bragged about you many times. He's very proud of you."

I summarize this for Abandonato, but I'm embarrassed about JJ's praise and leave that part out.

I smile at Jan and tell her, using my voice while I sign, that JJ is sad and upset about Toby.

"We're shocked at his violent death. Do the police have any information about who did this to Toby?" Jan's blue eyes, set off by eyelashes thick with black mascara, search each of our faces.

Abandonato speaks up. "We have very little information at this point, which is why we want to talk to you." Jan watches my simultaneous interpreting as my partner explains. "Detective Demeter's father said he came here on Monday to pick Toby up after work, but you told him Toby called in sick. Is that correct?"

"Yes. I was very surprised because Toby did not call in sick in the ten years I worked with him."

"Was it Toby who called in?" Abandonato asks.

Jan Marie watches me finish interpreting the question, then shakes her head and shrugs.

"Toby was not able to use the TTY. You need some basic reading and writing skills for that. Really, I don't know who called in on the TTY. I assumed it was the manager of Campbell House. She fingerspells Jacob Washington's name.

I interrupt at this point and ask Jan why she's still using a teletypewriter—pretty old technology—when most deaf people have videophone access and prefer it.

"You're right, Dana. I have a videophone for my use here to do my job." She shows us her computer with a small video cam attached on top. *"But ARC hasn't invested in the technology yet for the clients. It's a financial issue. ARC has a dedicated phone number for the TTY—have for a long time. They figure it's enough."*

While Jan stands and goes to a three-drawer file cabinet to the right of her desk, I explain to Abandonato that ARC is following the letter of the law with the TTY access, but not exactly making it easy for the deaf clients to make phone calls.

Jan Marie returns to her desk with a manila folder at least five inches thick. In it, she unearths a short piece of paper resembling a paper tape from an adding machine and hands it to Abandonato.

"If a client is sick, they are supposed to call by eight a.m. Since the TTY leaves a paper printout of the message, I usually put that in the file. It saves having to write some case notes."

My partner finishes looking at the printout by the time I'm done voicing Jan to him, and he hands it to me. The message is short.

'jan marie here ga'

'TOBY IS SICK TODAY'

'sorry to hear it pls tell him i hope he feels better ga'

'hello q anyone there q'

"What does 'ga' mean?" Abandonato asks. "I get that 'q' means you're asking a question, right?" He takes the slip of paper back from me so I can sign his question.

"Right, right. The older TTYs don't have keys with punctuation marks so the 'q' is shorthand. GA means 'go ahead,' meaning you're done talking and it's the other person's turn. Whoever called didn't use 'ga' after informing me Toby was sick. If the caller was done, he should have also signed off with the letters 'sk.' He didn't. He hung up without saying goodbye, which is why I asked if he was still there."

I mentally picture Walter Washington, not only awkward and inept in ASL, but typing on the TTY and not knowing the basic etiquette for the give and take of a conversation.

"And the date and time stamp on the TTY paper are accurate?" asks Abandonato.

"Yes. He called in Monday morning at eight a.m."

"What time do the clients start work?"

"They start at eight-thirty and end at four. Toby was always early for work, especially on payday. I arrive about eight to avoid traffic and he's usually waiting at the door. The clients are not let in until eight-twenty though, and then they have ten minutes to hang up their coats, stow their

lunches, and arrive at their stations." She takes back the TTY message from my partner and slips it into the folder.

I finish voicing Jan Marie's comment and glance at Abandonato's pad as he makes a note. *Mon. mgr calls work reports vic sick—already dead?*

"When was the last time you saw Toby?" Abandonato asks.

Jan Marie's forehead creases in thought. *"The Friday before he died."*

She consults a large desk calendar and points a perfect French-manicured finger at the date. *"October 21. A little less than a week ago."*

I glance at my ragged fingernails, my current oral fixation, and wish they looked like Jan Marie's.

The case manager looks at both of us with disbelief. *"It seems much longer than..."* she counts on her fingers, *"six days ago."*

Jan Marie stabs her finger on the desk calendar again. *"Last Friday was payday. Toby came to see me right at closing time. We have a little ritual we repeat every Friday when he comes to get his paycheck. I mime working, point to the calendar the five days he's being paid for and give him his check. I always gave him a pat on the back and "thumbs up". He didn't understand much sign language but a few gestures had meaning for him. Toby always put his check in his wallet and then gave me one of his big handshakes, like this."*

Jan stands and sticks out her hand to Abandonato. When he grasps it she gives him an exaggerated shake, her hand flying up as high as her head and then back down to below her waist.

"That was Toby," she says, sitting down.

"How much money did he make?" asks Abandonato.

"Toby was considered a permanent worker instead of a trainee like the other clients, so he earned more than they did. His language barrier made it impossible to place him in a competitive job in the community. His take home check was somewhere around two-fifty a week. We had to be careful

with how much he earned because his Public Aid money would be cut if he went over their cap. Public Aid covered most of his housing costs. Toby contributed about a quarter of his income per check to his room and board. So that left him about seven-fifty a month to pay for his transportation, clothes and other things."

Abandonato takes more notes and I notice he puts a question mark next to Toby's earnings. "Do the other clients he lived with earn a similar wage?"

"It depends," Jan Marie signs, tilting her head to one side and then the other.

"Some of the residents at Campbell House do have competitive jobs in the community, so they earn more than Toby. But some of the residents are in training, so they earn less. Our goal for most of the clients is to use ARC as a bridge to employment and independent living. But Toby was a special case. We were unable to teach Toby how to communicate in a meaningful way beyond some very basic gestures. Since there was no family to care for him, the agency felt ethically obligated to protect Toby, become his G-U-A-R-D-I-A-N A-D L-I-T-E-M."

Abandonato looks at me as I say this last bit and then asks, "I know how that works for kids, but in this case?"

Jan must understand my partner's confusion solely from his expression because she starts signing before I can even interpret his question to her. She spells the Latin phrase and explains that ARC applied for and received permission from the state to act as Toby's guardian.

"And how did he get here? Did he just show up one day?"

"You know, it's been a long time since I read his complete file—it's so thick and I have a large caseload. And Toby was no trouble. What I mean is he was so uncomplicated compared to my other clients who are here for only eight weeks and then leave. They take up most of my time."

She returns to the file cabinet and after rooting through it brings back three more thick manila folders brown with age. She drops them on her desk with a thud.

"These are his original case files with notes of his social history and copies of his initial work eval."

I gesture at the files stuffed with yellow papers and turn to my partner. "I'd like to look at those, check out his early days to see if there's any info on where he's from." I sign the same thing for Jan.

"I'll have to check with my supervisor before I can give them to you, but I don't think it's a problem," she says.

"I'm curious about something else with Toby," Abandonato says. "Did he have a bank account? I mean, if he couldn't read or write, how did he cash his checks?"

"It was difficult—no, it was impossible—to explain the concept of banking to him. I tried to show him he could leave the money there, that it would be safe, that he could come back and get it the next day. But once the check was cashed, he didn't want to let go of his money."

I chimed in, talking and signing at the same time. "Yeah, it makes sense. Leaving money in the bank is a pretty abstract concept."

Jan nods. *"When he had his money in hand it was real to him. ARC has its payroll handled by F-I-R-S-T B-A-N-C. The clients don't need an account to cash their paychecks there, but they do pay a small fee. We're lucky because Fridays—our payday—the bank stays open 'til six."*

I remember seeing a branch office of the bank Jan mentioned in a strip mall across the street. Her comment about Toby not leaving his money in the bank reinforces what Sarah told me about Toby keeping his cash in a shoebox under his bed.

"So you gave Toby his check on Friday. What did he do after that?" Abandonato asks.

Jan shrugs and shakes her head. *"I don't know. He gave me his customary handshake and left. He looked very happy but that wasn't unusual for him. In spite of his limitations, he seemed like a happy person."*

"Can you tell me anything about his friends or who he hangs out with from ARC? Does he have a girlfriend, anything like that?"

Jan shakes her head. *"No. Toby was pretty isolated, even from the other deaf clients. They treated him like a kid who didn't understand much. If he had a girlfriend, it wasn't anyone here. And believe me, I would know. The clients are shameless in gossiping about each other. Toby was a nice man, but it's hard to interact in depth with someone who can't communicate. Other than Dana's father, I don't know of anyone he spent much time with."*

Abandonato jots a few more notes, closes his pad and turns to me. "Anything you want to ask?"

I think about Jan's description of Toby's closed, limited life and feel a rush of shame at how my brother, sister, and I made fun of him when we were kids. *"Do you have any idea why someone would want to kill Toby?"*

"Toby was such a harmless man. He came here, did his work, and went home. For him to die in such a horrible way, it seems like someone was very angry at him. But who? I have no idea." Jan crosses her arms and hunches her shoulders as if to ward off a chill.

We stand to go. I thank Jan for talking with us and Abandonato gives her his card. She grasps it with one hand and signs with the other.

"I hope you find who did this. Toby did not deserve to die like that." Her eyes squint and imbue her signs with fear. Jan Marie's use of large, stabbing motions when describing Toby's death tells me the deaf grapevine has lost none of its efficiency.

Jan leaves us in the office while she goes to talk with her supervisor about the files.

"It's not much," Abandonato says, flipping through his notepad. I take it from him and quickly copy his notes into my own notepad.

"The files might give me something. I'd also like to follow up with the bank, see if there's anything there. I haven't given up on talking to the residents at Campbell House, either."

Abandonato regards me with a bemused smile, one I've grown used to. It says he knows I won't give up. As he slides his notepad into his jacket pocket Jan Marie arrives with a shopping bag and piles the four heavy manila folders into it.

"They're yours for as long as you need them but when you're finished, we'd like them back."

"Of course," I say. *"Thanks."*

Abandonato and I take our leave and walk to the staircase. At the second floor landing I point to a sign indicating the work center training area.

"This is where my father received his training. It's also where Toby worked."

I beckon for him to follow me around the corner to a large room flooded with light from generous windows flanking one end. A variety of stations positioned around the room provide accessible work areas for the trainees. A loud noise, like a giant branch cracking in two, causes the floor to shudder under our feet every few seconds, the result of a mechanical press punching holes in sheet metal. The two men working the press wear ear protection, but none of the other workers do and seem oblivious to the sound.

Abandonato wrinkles his nose. "What's that smell?"

"I don't see it but I know it's the," I spy what I'm looking for, "over there," I say, pointing at the other end of the room. "That's the same kind of laminating machine that burned JJ."

A guy with no discernable disability feeds a box into the large maw of the machine, which then clamps shut and produces a film of steam, the source of the stink. When the maw opens the box emerges encased in plastic wrap. Another guy in a wheelchair pulls the finished product out of the machine and loads it on a wood pallet as the first guy feeds in another box. A different machine emits a screaming whine as it starts, forcing me to shout at Abandonato. "Melting plastic. A lovely odor."

My partner winces at the noise and waves me away from the room and toward the staircase. "Give me a dead body any day," he says as we descend to the first floor. "I'm used to the smell and they're a lot quieter."

We find our way out of the giant maze with none of our initial fumbling. Just outside the exit we have to thread through a small group of ARC trainees who huddle together smoking cigarettes. Several of the men wear navy pants and light blue shirts with a logo on the pocket for ARC Maintenance Training Program. Their afternoon smoke break. I'm gripped by a mixture of envy and loathing—mostly envy.

Once through the mushroom cloud, we stand at our cars parked next to each other behind the weathered structure. I stow the shopping bag on the passenger seat of my car.

"I'm on the three-to-eleven tonight," Abandonato says, checking his watch. "Got to go check in with Koz every step of the way about this shaken baby thing."

His new case. Even though I'm again angry at not being involved, my curiosity wins out. I tap my watch. "Twenty-five or less."

"Boyfriend takes care of kid while mom's at work." He ticks the words on his fingers as he talks. "She comes home, baby's dead, boyfriend's gone." He looks at his hands. "Sixteen."

I whistle, not at his feat of brevity but at the sad repetition of this particular crime in Chicago. How ignorant do you have to be to not know shaking an infant is deadly?

"Autopsy shows shaken baby?" I ask.

"Not in yet, still need the confirmation. But I'm going to beat the streets looking for the boyfriend."

"Why every step with Koz?"

"The mom, Crystal, has a brother who's a big-shot alderman on the City Council. Johnny Diamond?"

I nod my head, recognizing the name.

"He's been all over the news today threatening Crystal's boyfriend. 'I find you, you a dead muthafucka!'"

I laugh at Abandonato's impression. "Maybe it's not a threat, maybe it's a political promise."

Abandonato grins at me. "And of course Johnny and Crystal are upset with CPD because we haven't found the baby-killer yet. Koz doesn't want this to turn into a PR nightmare but I'd say it already has."

"Yeah." I open the door to my faded black Corolla and get in. Abandonato drapes his arm over the open door frame and I look up at him.

"Go," I tell him. "Do your duty against the relentless crime in Chicago. Me? I'm going to plow through Toby's files, see what I can find. I'll call you if anything turns up."

"Right. I'll needle the Prick and see if he's got anything new or useful. But we both know that's highly doubtful."

I chuckle and shut my door. Abandonato gives my hood a reassuring thump and then slides into his red Prius, which looks freshly detailed. I watch as he pulls out of the lot and merges into traffic, quickly disappearing from view. Not a minute later my cell rings: Abandonato.

"One more thing," he says.

"Yeah?"

"As long as we're partners, what you do after hours *is* my fucking business."

10

5:00 p.m.

The radio warns me to stay off the Dan Ryan because rush hour is in full swing, so I head south on Lake Shore Drive instead. It's not much better. My walk through the cigarette cloud at ARC has triggered in me a fierce urge to smoke, so I tear into Louie's bag of sunflower seeds and work on extracting a small nut from each shell. These are hard to manipulate, especially while driving, but I get the hang of it by the time I reach my parents' house. The seeds have done nothing for my hunger, but as Louie promised, they kept me occupied until the urge passed.

My parents have lived on the south side their entire married life. Neat, three-bedroom brick bungalows hunker down along their street reflecting the solid, working-class strength of the neighborhood. It's remarkably unchanged from when I grew up here. I park and walk around the side of the house to the back door.

Unlocked.

I walk directly into the kitchen. Evie comes in from the living room and sees me.

Using both of my hands I shove the door hard so that it rattles shut. I point to the deadbolt lock and use my entire body and face to shout at her in Sign.

"How many times do I have to tell you to lock this door?"

She dismisses me with a wave of her hand and a sarcastic glance, her signs quick and abbreviated.

"You worry too much. I trust my neighbors."

"I'm not worried about your neighbors! Anybody could walk in here and you'd never know it—you're deaf!"

I ram the deadbolt into the locked position. Evie approaches me and gives me a visual once-over, head to toe.

"Is that why you came over? To tell me I'm deaf and yell at me?"

I stop and look down at the diminutive woman. Evie's white hair is pulled back in a long braid that ends at her waist. Her face, still tan, reflects a summer spent outdoors gardening, walking and spending time at the beach. I feel like a mature tree trunk next to a sapling as I loom over her, yet she still manages to convey being in charge. I sigh and let go of my anger at her.

"No. You asked me over for dinner, remember? What are we having?" I look around the kitchen but see no sign of any preparations.

"Leftovers. You can help me heat it up in about a half hour. I'm still finishing my work outside."

"Where's dad?"

Evie rolls her eyes at my question, points toward the living room, then conveys her disgust with one sign.

"Football."

She slides back the deadbolt, glances at me over her shoulder, and opens the door to carry a box into the back yard. She leaves the door wide open. I get the message. Outside, security lights my husband installed for my parents a few years ago allow no shadows in the evening dusk.

The television dimly lights the living room where JJ sits enthroned on a blue, fake-velvet lounge chair. I flip on the overhead fixture to get his attention. He lowers the elevated footrest and greets me with a hug, then turns off the set. Seeing how easily my entrance into the living room went unnoticed by my father until I made it obvious by switching on the light, my anger returns. My stubborn deaf mother, whom I love, scares the crap out of me sometimes. I start in on JJ.

"You've got to keep that back door locked. Evie is too stubborn and won't listen to me."

One cocked eyebrow from JJ shows me this is old news.

"I installed the deadbolt. But your mother wants to walk in and out to the back yard without having to lock it every time. She's busy getting ready for Halloween. You know: the fake cemetery with cobwebs and ghosts she makes every year."

I do know. My mother's flair for the dramatic thrilled me when I was a little girl, dressing up for Halloween a major event in our home. My twin David and younger sister Daphne also loved how scary the back yard looked after its transformation into a graveyard. Bats hung from the trees, cobwebs crisscrossed the bushes, and luminaria lined the path to the back door where the neighborhood kids flocked for candy. We had the scariest house on the block.

Now the scariest thing about the house is my stubborn mother.

"What have you and Abandonato found out about Toby?" JJ taps the initials "FA" over his heart, my partner's name sign.

"We're assisting another detective named C-A-R-R-E-R-A." In my mind, I combine the "C" hand-shape and the sign for inept to form the

perfect name sign for the Prick. But for JJ I dismiss my snarky invention and instead make up a generic name sign, a "C" hand-shape placed on the chest in the same area as the sign for police.

"We do the field work and Carrera directs everything."

Pretty close to the truth. I don't want to lie outright to JJ but I don't want to tell him about my suspension, either. I steer the conversation away from the reason I'm not in charge and ask JJ about Toby's social life, if he had any friends.

My father looks out the window behind where I sit and gives my question some thought before he answers, his large hands sawing slowly in the air.

"Toby didn't have many friends, really. He couldn't sit down and talk about sports or tell me what he had for dinner the night before. He didn't know how to read or write, or have any regular way of interacting with people. Most of the time people at ARC would smile at him and he would smile back and give his big handshake. But not much more than that."

JJ stands to render a quick, unerring impression of Toby, lumbering over to me with Toby's same muscle-bound gait, smiling while nodding his head, and pumping my hand. It echoes what Jan Marie showed Abandonato and me earlier.

"Like that," he says, returning to his chair. I smile at my father's dead-on mimicry.

"Toby ate lunch separately from the other deaf at ARC. We had a half hour to eat and the deaf usually sat together, you know, to talk and catch up on the latest news. Toby always sat at a table alone, ate his lunch quickly—five or ten minutes—then went back to the work floor to wait for the supervisor so he could get started again. He loved to work."

JJ's face seems pensive as he stares at his hands, rubbing his thumb along the shiny scars ridging his knuckles. I lean forward, touching his knee to get his attention.

"Okay, so he didn't have friends of any depth. What about women? Did he have a girlfriend?"

"No. The deaf women at ARC knew Toby was limited. He couldn't communicate, he was black, and had no education. That cut down on the number of women who might have been interested. But really, most people stayed only eight weeks at ARC for training. Toby was too much of a challenge to get to know. There wasn't enough time." JJ stops and looks at the ceiling for a moment.

"It's funny you ask about women, though. Last year, when I picked him up for our birthday dinner, there was a woman standing by the el near ARC. When we drove past her Toby made a crude gesture." JJ inserts his right index finger into a hole shaped with his left fist, pushing it in and out. "Toby pointed to himself and then the woman. I thought he was making a remark about what he'd like to do. But maybe he knew her."

Well. Add *that* to the three signs Toby knew.

I jot down the information in my notepad with a reminder to ask Walter Washington if Toby had a girlfriend.

"Can you tell me about how much money Toby had?" I fill him in on what Sarah and Jan Marie told me about Toby and his cash.

"I'm surprised Toby kept his money in his room," JJ signed. "Sarah told me once that Campbell House has a large safe for the residents. I thought the manager was in charge of it."

I would try to see Washington tomorrow. Alone. There couldn't be a more logical motive for murder than money, whether Toby kept it in his room or the safe. The branch bank where the ARC clients cash their checks might turn up something, too. I ask JJ if there's anything else he can think of that might help me but he shakes his head.

"Nothing."

Each of his hands, shaped like an "O", push away from his chest in resignation. I go over, bend down and hug him, the angle awkward.

As I straighten up he pulls a photo from the breast pocket of his shirt and hands it to me.

"Last year at Toby's birthday. Your mother made him a small cake."

Toby grins up at me from my parents' kitchen table. A small birthday cake sits in front of him topped with candles that form the shape of a heart. One of his muscular forearms crosses his chest and ends with his hand over his heart, as if poised to say the Pledge of Allegiance.

"He had a way of showing something was meaningful to him. He's doing it here, see? He would put his hand over his heart and pat it a few times."

JJ's scarred hand echoes Toby's movement. *"He was so happy about the cake. And in his own way I think he understood what it meant."*

"You were a good friend to him. I promise you we will find whoever did this to Toby."

I start to hand the photo back but my father shakes his head and waves his index finger at me. I need no further explanation. JJ wants me to keep the memory of his friend—alive and happy—in front of me as motivation.

He asks, *"Can you call me, let me know what you find out?"*

My father does know how to text but isn't up to speed with the technology of a tablet or smart phone for communicating directly with me in sign. David promised to set my parents up with a videophone when he visits at Christmas, but in the meantime if I want to have an extended conversation with JJ I have to take an hour to drive over here. I assure JJ I'll keep him informed, give him another hug, and make my way out through the kitchen.

In the yard, Evie is on her hands and knees digging up some leggy annuals that expired, an open bag of mulch on the ground next to her. I tap her on the shoulder and she startles a bit, which gives me some satisfaction.

"I'm going home," I sign.

Evie sits back on her heels and squints up at me. *"I thought you were staying for dinner."*

"Changed my mind. I need to buy some groceries and get the moving boxes unpacked. My studio's a mess."

"You look pale and tired. What's wrong, are you sick?"

God, she doesn't miss a thing.

"I've been working late and need some sleep." I try not to squirm as her brown eyes scrutinize me.

"Why don't you take better care of yourself? Like Daphne?"

Evie proceeds to describe my younger sister's assets to me in minute, enviable detail, ending with the fact that Daphne is slender.

Unlike your other daughter who wears her husband's extra large sweatshirts, has a crappy haircut and is fat. Thanks, Mom. My stomach growls and a strong craving for nicotine follows. Before I can muster a smart-ass answer she arrives at her real point.

"When is Jimmy coming back?"

I want to shout "Probably never!"

But I take a deep breath instead and respond, my signs stiff and formal. *"I don't know. I haven't talked to him for awhile."*

Before my mother can continue I hurry from the back yard and its faux cemetery. But then I stop at the corner of the house under the glare of a security light and turn back to see Evie looking at me.

I semaphore: *"Lock the door!"*

11

Thursday, 10:00 a.m.

Damn near twenty-four hours without a cigarette. But before I can congratulate myself further the urge to light up hits hard. I pack a sandwich baggy full of sunflower seeds for the road, then duly note my healthy breakfast on my ten-day progress chart.

I deliberately park four blocks from the branch bank so I can hike to the small building directly across the street from ARC's training facility. The short walk has me panting, but at least it's exercise. Abandonato tipped me off to go slow, build small bouts of physical exertion into my day, and use any opportunity that presents itself to move my body—no long periods of sitting. He also promised to show me how to start a serious running program. Later. I think he means once he sees I've really quit smoking.

Because I don't have a warrant, the branch manager is polite but unbudging about discussing anything more than general information about her customers. I ask a few questions about the ARC clients cashing their checks, and the manager supports Jan Marie's description—because the ARC payroll checks are produced by the main bank, no account is needed to cash them. I leave, disappointed at having no new information and walk back—huffing—to my car.

The shopping bag bulging with Toby's files sits in the passenger seat like a sullen child who wants attention. The lure of a deeply satisfying cigarette tugs at me but I placate my craving with the idea of finding a Starbucks to stoke up on caffeine instead, and yes, read the neglected files. I don't have far to look. As I drive past ARC I spy a Starbucks directly across the street from the branch bank and facing the side of ARC's building where the loitering Maintenance Training clients smoked their cigarettes yesterday.

With a venti coffee and an additional cup of hot chocolate, I park myself at an outdoor table and arrange the files in chronological order in front of me. Before I can begin, my phone signals an incoming text—my sister Daphne.

"thnx for news about T. Sad. Sent dad card."

"good girl," I text back. "JJ's upset. FA, me, working on it."

"Jimmy back yet?"

I'm unsure how to respond to her question. I want to confide in Daphne. But Jimmy's message yesterday left me feeling guilty about my drinking and angry that he's unwilling to work things out by returning home. I doubt my single, carefree sister will understand.

"Still in L.A. gotta go. xoxo D." I add an emoji of a smiling sun. Her response is a bouquet of flowers.

The sun is out. Even though it's late October, the weather is exquisite and lifts my spirits. Dust irritates my nose when I open the first file, the smell of mildew radiating from its pages. Probably hasn't been opened in twenty years.

The file has a semblance of order: the left side holds a social history, a physical exam report, an audiology report along with an audiogram documenting Toby's deafness, and a voucher for a work evaluation from the Illinois Department of Vocational Rehabilitation Services.

The audiogram provides a visual map of Toby's profound hearing loss. He's Deaf with a capital "D," not even a modicum of residual, usable hearing. I picture Evie gaily signing this concept with pride, her thumb in her ear and fingers flaring upwards and spreading out in a fan.

The work eval states that Toby had a positive attitude toward work, was punctual in his attendance, and had no absences. However, at the end of his eight-week training the report recommended placing Toby in a sheltered workshop environment permanently because of his inability to communicate. Otherwise, his physical health was superb.

The social history, such as it is, garners my interest the most. The only thing filled in is Toby's first name followed by an "X" in lieu of a last name. This otherwise empty form has a brief, typewritten report stapled to it:

August 14, 1968

Client referred by Heaven on Earth Mission (Cynthia Mason, CA4-2800) for eight-week work evaluation study (DVR voucher attached). Client is profoundly deaf, has no spoken or written language and doesn't seem to understand or use American Sign Language, according to audiologist at Chicago Hearing Society (Mary Cassin, CA5-9121). Case manager could not complete social history with client as a result.

I smile and pull out the sunflower seeds, cracking them open one by one between my teeth and chewing the savory nuts. So Toby had been at the Heaven on Earth Mission prior to starting at ARC. One small end of a thread to pull, a lead I know Carrera does not have.

The right side of the file holds a sheaf of lined papers with hand-written notes, the dates chronological, starting with Toby's first day at ARC and continuing for the next five years.

The three remaining files are a continuation of the case manager's notes for the next thirty years of Toby's work life. Once Toby became a permanent worker at ARC, his case came up for discussion only every six months, the notes perfunctory, mostly the date and declaration of no changes. I assume that at the end of this paper trail his files are computerized.

I pull out my notepad, find where I left off yesterday, and jot down some notes from the files. Money is the main thrust I want to follow and wonder if Toby's murder is no more than a robbery gone bad. Because he didn't put his money in the bank, he either kept it in his room or carried it with him.

I review the evidence list: three condoms, a knife with a red plastic handle, a 7-Up can, pubic hair, fibers, red glitter, animal hair, the stub from Toby's paycheck, part of a torn black and white photo, and matches from the Lincoln Motel. No cash.

My coffee cup is half empty so I pour the hot chocolate in and swirl the mixture, considering my next move. I can't rule out the other residents at Campbell House as suspects until I interview them or have some kind of report from Carrera. Even if Toby had only his current paycheck cash with him, a couple hundred dollars is a lot of money to someone who has little or none. People have shot each other over ten dollars. I make a note to check with Walter Washington about the safe and Toby's routine.

People from the surrounding neighborhood as well as ARC begin to fill the sidewalk and strip mall where I sit thinking about Toby, his money, and the way he died. The viciousness of the stabbing shows one thing—a personal attack, one filled with rage. The pictures in Abandonato's file of Toby's bed soaked with blood support my theory.

The sun spreads a patina of cheer over the hulking ARC building as I watch the clients emerge through the side door facing me, cigarette packs at the ready. I check my phone and see it is lunchtime.

A red sports car pulls into the side street separating the Starbucks from the side of the ARC building where the clients are milling around. A young woman in impossibly tall stiletto heels, fishnet stockings, and a skirt barely covering her ass emerges from a knot of people gathered just beyond the ARC building. The young woman unzips her short jacket and leans into the driver's side window. A few seconds later she stutter-steps around the front of the car and lowers herself into the passenger seat and the car peels away. Bought and sold.

A circle of deaf men almost directly across the street from me, near ARC's side entrance, are in deep discussion, but I can't read their signs because most of their bodies are turned away or blocked from my view. Three of the six men wear the navy blue pants and light blue shirts of the Maintenance Training Program.

I stuff Toby's files in the shopping bag, grab my notes, and pitch my coffee cup in the trash on my way toward the men.

12

Noon

When I cross the side street, the group of deaf men begins to shift farther away from me and head for the same knot of people that produced the stiletto-shoed hooker. I follow the men and see the reason for their interest: four more hookers lean against an abandoned garage behind ARC. The women smoke cigarettes in a lazy way while they eye the advancing group of deaf men.

I hurry to intercept the group of six before they reach their target, crossing in front of them and waving my free arm in a large flapping motion. The men's faces display assorted expressions of interest and puzzlement.

"Hey! Excuse me," I sign. *"Sorry to interrupt! You guys work here at ARC, right?"* I point to the building now behind us.

The group stops and a few men respond to my question by nodding or signing yes. While I lower the bag with the files to the ground to free up both my hands, the men form a rough circle so we can comfortably see each other sign.

"I need to talk with you for a short time about Toby, all right?"

I reiterate the last part of my question in a continuous motion around the circle, making eye contact with each man. Some nod, some still look puzzled. Standing directly across from me is the largest man in the group, a burly African-American with a bald head and a small gold stud in his left ear. He takes one step forward and raises his hands, his signs bold and aggressive.

"Who are you? Why do you want to know about Toby?"

The other deaf men watch him, then look at each other, eyebrows raised, hands thrust in pants pockets. Heads swivel toward me for my response.

"I'm a cop. I'm investigating Toby's murder. I need your help."

Two of the men, each taking sips from a shared brown paper bag, freeze at my signs. One of them begins to slowly hide the bottle behind his back but I give him a shrug and quick shake of the head to let him know I'm here for information, not a bust.

"Are you deaf or hearing?"

Baldy's hands accentuate the last sign, his index finger looping in exaggeration at his chin as his face pulls a sneer.

"Hearing. But my parents, my twin brother and my sister are deaf." My explanation seems to pass muster with this sentry but his size puts me on my guard.

A small Latino guy standing next to Baldy touches the larger man's arm for his attention. *"She's fine. Let's hurry up and answer her questions so we can go."*

He jerks his head toward the clutch of hookers. Baldy surveys the others, who add their own wishes for him to hurry, and he steps back into the group.

"Thanks." I nod my appreciation at him.

All had known Toby and repeat a now-familiar theme: Toby kept to himself, he had no real friends, sometimes he sat at their lunch table but never participated in the conversation, ate his lunch quickly and returned to the work floor eager to start again.

"Did Toby have a girlfriend?"

I re-tell JJ's story about Toby and his crude gesture. The men laugh and elbow each other.

"There is a woman Toby dated," the Latino guy tells me, accompanying his last sign with a sly glance to project a more salacious meaning. *"Only one."*

He fingerspells the name K-A-N-D-Y. After he fingerspells the woman's name he makes the generic sign for candy, the tip of his index finger twisting against his cheek.

I feel a rush of excitement but then dismay as I recall Sarah telling me that Toby liked "candy." I misunderstood the sign to mean the confection, not realizing it might be someone's name. But I never voiced Sarah's observation to Carrera because he abruptly left the apartment. So my mistake is actually a stroke of luck. I have a strong lead and the Prick is left in the dark.

"Really, none of the others." The Latino guy glances at the small group of hookers to indicate who he's talking about, then looks at me. *"None of them would go with Toby. Only Kandy."*

The other men nod or sign their agreement.

I glance at the group of women and then back at him. *"Is Kandy over there?"*

"No, she's not here today." He shrugs as he signs this. *"She was here last Friday. She and Toby partied after work."*

"When's the last time you saw Toby?" I ask Baldy.

His hands form incomplete signs as he thinks for a minute, considering my question.

"Last Friday after work. We waited at the bus stop." He points toward the street that fronts the building. *"Most of the time Toby gets on the bus with us to go home. But a guy picked him up."*

I feel another surge of adrenaline at this new information. But worry kicks in at the thought that Carrera might somehow uncover this too. I take down a vague description of the man and the car. None of the deaf men had ever seen him before or since and don't remember much. One thought the car was white and another thought it was black, so not much help. I thank them for their help, pick up the shopping bag of files, and head toward the four hookers.

The women confirm this new information about Toby and Kandy.

"Does Kandy have a last name?" I ask.

The women laugh. They look at each other and one steps forward.

"Yeah, it's Kane, and believe it or not that's her real name. Her parents must've been real dopes naming a kid like that. Know what I mean?"

The woman who says this is young, maybe eighteen or nineteen. Given her profession she wears little makeup, especially in contrast with her sisters, the only exception being fake black eyelashes. They stand out against her milky white skin, giving the effect of wide-eyed innocence.

"And you haven't seen Kandy since she and Toby got together last Friday?"

All the women shake their heads.

"You know, she hangs with Rameeka," says Wide-eyed. "Meeka's been sick this past week. Pneumonia. She's staying by her sister's. Anybody'd know where Kandy is, it's Meeka."

"You happen to know where her sister lives or Meeka's phone number?"

The woman gives me a long gaze and drops her cigarette on the ground, crushing it with a twist of her high heel. "Maybe I do. What you got for me?"

I sigh. Her makeup may look innocent but her response is street-worthy. Having to wheedle, scratch and barter for information heads the list of Things That Annoy Me as a Cop.

I step back from the group and give them the once-over, then address the woman. "Here's what I've got: I don't bust your ass for solicitation, along with your friends here. That work for you?"

The other women groan and crowd around the one holding out. "Come on, Lala," says one of them. "Tell the lady what she wants to know so's we can get on with it." She shoves one hand out to indicate the deaf men who stand behind me watching our exchange. "Lunch break almost over."

Lala lights another cigarette and gives me a bored look. "Rhonda Hartman. She's a big-shot lawyer, always bailing Meeka outta jail. Lives in the Hancock building."

I jot this down and thank Lala for her help.

"I'd like twenty bucks better'n your thanks."

Lala actually bats her eyelashes at me and I laugh. The other women titter and tell her to leave it alone. "Maybe next time," I say, and turn to shoulder past the deaf men. The Latino guy grins at me, then thrusts out both fists in front of him, thumbs up, in a farewell gesture.

13

1:30 p.m.

"Well, it *is* my life's work, Detective, not merely a job in the conventional sense," Cynthia Mason draws air quotes around the word "job." She sits behind her desk at the Heaven on Earth Mission, smiling at me over her reading glasses.

"I'm astounded you're still here, thirty-seven years later? But it helps me understand why you've never left. And this, this is, what?"

I can't come up with the right word. Amazing? Sad? I gesture at a piece of paper on her desk, yellow with age, showing a crude pencil drawing of a stick figure on what looks like a bus. The name "TOBY" is emblazoned at the top.

"I met him my first year here. He lined up with everyone outside the mission for a meal and then our fellowship. I tried to talk with him but found out quickly he couldn't hear. You can see from this paper," she turns it over, "that I thought I could communicate with Toby by writing back and forth." A few questions had been scribbled on the back of the picture.

"Instead, he drew this and wrote his name, and that's as far as we got. Toby had no other ID."

"Did he stay here?"

"Yes. He returned night after night. I tried to find someone who knew something about deaf people. The Chicago Public Schools steered me to the Office of Rehabilitation Services—DVR back then—and I took Toby to see them.

People there knew American Sign Language and tried to talk with him but it was no use. They gave me the name of an agency for hand-icapped people." She snaps her fingers several times as if to hasten her recollection.

"It's Allen Rehabilitation Center now," I say. "Back then, I don't know."

Cynthia Mason smiles in recognition. "Yes. Yes, that's it. ARC. I felt the Lord was testing me to see what I would do."

I frown. "You felt..." I don't finish my sentence hoping she senses my confusion.

"What I mean is, I was nineteen years old, a white girl from the privi-leged North Shore. Most of my friends were trying to find themselves, but I wanted to find faith. You have to understand, Detective, it was a difficult time in our country. Viet Nam. Martin Luther King and Bobby Kennedy both murdered. Then Kent State. And my parents were stout Nixon supporters.

"My only brother enlisted and was killed in Viet Nam. Nothing made sense to me after that. I dropped out of college and came here to work with the people society forgot." She smiles again. "And never regretted it."

"So you don't know any of Toby's history prior to his coming here?"

"No. Today we keep better statistics about those who attend, but back then I just prayed I was doing the right thing for him when I took him to ARC."

"You did. He was in the right place there. He worked, had a place to stay and even had a social life of sorts."

Thinking of Kandy, I don't delve into what sort.

"Toby did something for me, though, and I think this is what the Lord had in mind for me when He sent Toby my way." She lifts her hands and begins signing fluently in American Sign Language.

I nod. "The Lord's Prayer."

Cynthia Mason looks pleased though she doesn't complete the prayer and folds her hands in her lap. "It wasn't easy to find ASL classes back then. A woman at St. Patrick's Church signed the mass on Sundays and offered to tutor me. I'll never forget Mary Mulcrone. Anyway, today we can serve deaf people who show up because Toby opened the door." She points at the drawing.

I gaze at the stick figure riding the bus. Finding no new information about Toby is disappointing. He had been a homeless person on the streets, one of hundreds the mission sheltered every night. But his drawing of himself gives me a curious feeling of connection, as though he is beckoning me to continue the search for his killer.

Cynthia Mason picks up the picture and begins to slip it back into the plastic frame on her desk—until I stay her hand.

"Would you mind making a copy for me?"

14

3:30 p.m.

Outside the Mission I get into my car and search the Internet for Rhonda Hartman's work number, but when I call, she's not there. I do another search for her home number but get only voice mail. Instead of leaving a message I decide to head over to the Hancock Building, a short hop south on Lake Shore Drive.

First, I call Abandonato and leave him a message about what I've found and ask him to run priors on Kandy Kane and Rameeka.

I park in the lot of the brown skyscraper with the distinctive criss-cross pattern climbing its facade. In the lobby the guard tips his gold cap at me and I ask for Rhonda Hartman.

"Is she expecting you?"

I pull out my shield and show it to him. He recoils as if I'm going to bite him.

"Call her. Please."

The guard does as I ask but turns his back on me as he speaks into the phone in tones so low I can't hear what he's saying. Then he hangs up.

"She'll be down in a few minutes to escort you up. In the meantime, I need to take your picture for a tag." I pull a face at him but he tells me it's required for everyone going into the private residences, so I capitulate and clip the awful result onto my jacket.

"Should've combed my hair," I say to the guard but he's already busy with someone else.

After a few minutes, a diminutive African-American woman steps from the elevator and walks toward the guard desk. She wears an expensive-looking silk suit of deep maroon with a cream-colored camisole peeking out between the jacket lapels. On her feet, in direct contrast to the outfit, are athletic socks and cross-trainers. Rhonda Hartman's tired eyes appraise me as she nears. I hold up my badge and introduce myself, explaining I'm looking for Rameeka.

"What exactly is this about, Detective?"

I glance at the guard and see he's busy pretending he doesn't hear every word we're saying. I indicate a small group of chairs near the public elevators and motion the woman to follow me. Once seated, I bring out JJ's photo of Toby with his birthday cake and show it to Rhonda Hartman.

"I'm investigating the murder of this man, Ms. Hartman, and I need your sister's help. She might have been one of the last people to see him alive."

She takes the photo and stares at it, then hands it back.

"I'm a lawyer. My firm deals with insurance, mostly fraud. I have seen the worst of human greed and deception, but it rarely ends in murder. My sister," she tells me with a doleful look, "my sister is a good woman, Detective. But she has problems and I try to help her as much as I can. She is a drug addict. Not a new story to you, I'm sure."

Rhonda Hartman uses both hands to rub her makeup-free face with a rough washing movement.

I regard the woman's tired demeanor. "I need to talk with your sister for only a few minutes. Is she staying with you?"

"She gets clean and starts to do better, then gets dragged back into the life. When she is using, I will not give her a dime. Not one. So she goes back to the street to earn the money. This last time, Rameeka told me she traded sex directly for the drugs." She randomly plucks at short ringlets of hair springing from her scalp, then crosses her arms tightly.

"Ms. Hartman?"

"Rameeka is very sick. That is how I try to think of her, as a sick person who needs to get well. Otherwise, it overwhelms me."

I hum with the urge to hurry this woman along so I can talk to Rameeka, but her body language is clear. I wait.

"Is my sister a suspect in this murder?"

"At this point I'm only gathering information. Rameeka is the first real lead I've had on this case and I'm hopeful she can give me something substantial about what actually happened. I'll spare you the details but this man," I tap Toby's photo, "was killed in a gruesome way. I'm betting your sister can help me find who did this."

Rhonda Hartman uncrosses her arms and stands, showing me the way to the private residential elevators. As the high-speed car whisks us upward, the lawyer clutches my arm.

"Is my sister in immediate danger? Is the person who did this going to come after her?"

I take a deep breath and let it escape from my mouth in a rush. "Look, I don't know if it was a man, a woman, or a group of people who did this. I also have no idea what even happened when Toby was killed. Your sister's already in danger if she's out there trading sex for drugs.

On the street that's near the bottom of the food chain. But to answer your question, yes, she's in danger if she witnessed what happened."

We cruise to a whisper stop and the door opens, my ears feeling the pressure from the elevator's quick ascension.

Rhonda Hartman mutters under her breath as we exit the elevator and walk down a hallway with deep blue carpeting that mutes any extraneous sounds. At the door to her condo she stops and turns to me.

"Rameeka has pneumonia. She has been on antibiotics for five days and is not contagious anymore, but she is weak from coughing. Please do your best to limit the time you spend with her. Do not upset her."

I nod my understanding but don't promise anything of the sort.

We enter the residence and I have the sense of entering another world. Every available space is devoted to art. Statues from Greek to avant-garde dot the large living room, paintings in miniature cluster in groups on the wall, and black and white photographs are matted and mounted on easels. Southwestern pottery perches on shelves that ascend along a wall.

"Wow," I say, then gasp involuntarily when I look up to see pieces of art suspended from the ceiling. The two photos pinned to my fridge in my one-room studio appear and disappear in a moment's thought. How vacant and dingy my life feels in comparison with this woman's.

"I am a collector," she says, seemingly unaware of her understatement.

I follow her down a hall where the walls are lined with antique wind instruments of the smaller variety. I recognize a flute, a clarinet, and assorted pennywhistles, but am mystified by a black tubular instrument that ends in a twisted mess. I can't see how any music can escape in order to be heard.

In a back room set up as an office the art is limited to framed family photos on a desk. Rhonda Hartman approaches a door at the back of the room and knocks as she opens it. "Meeka? You awake in there?"

She holds up her palm at me, goes inside and closes the door, so I sit at the desk and wait, listening to the low murmur of their voices.

Through a window opposite me I see the sun is setting and the street-lights have come on. The computer on the desk reads 4:45 and I wish I had the sunflower seeds with me, and not only to keep my hands busy. I missed lunch and I'm starving.

Ms. Hartman beckons me from the door and I enter an ultra-feminine guest room with rose-colored carpeting, white French Provincial furniture, and wallpaper with the faintest cream and pink stripes. Although the face of the young woman in the bed is visible, it almost gets lost among the stacks of pillows and a comforter pulled up to her neck. Only a shock of magenta hair signals her presence, like a buoy on open water.

Rameeka looks at me, her eyes red-rimmed and bloodshot, while her sister drags a chair for me to the side of the bed. "Please, only a few minutes with her. She's had a rough day."

I sit down and Rhonda Hartman hovers behind me, her hands on the back of the chair. I identify myself and explain the reason for my visit.

"Start with Friday night, Rameeka."

The young woman pushes herself into more of a sitting position but avoids my eyes and looks at the comforter as she speaks.

"Kandy called me on my cell. Her and Toby party almost every Friday. Said Toby had a friend who wanted to meet me."

"Where'd you party?"

I draw air quotes around the last word and my sarcasm isn't lost on Rameeka. She jerks her head up, angry.

"I don't got to talk to you, you know." She pulls the covers up high around her shoulders and turns her face away from me toward the wall. "Gettin' all fresh with her attitude about my business."

"Let's get something straight, Rameeka. You do have to talk to me."

I lean over her and shove Toby's picture two inches in front of her nose. "Because you're one of the last people to see this guy alive."

A thin vapor stream escapes from a humidifier on the opposite night table, infusing the air close to her with the sharp stink of camphor. I lean back in my chair.

"So that makes you a possible suspect in his death. And if you want to call what you do partying, that's fine. But don't expect me to go along with your little fantasy. Now, where did you all meet?"

I hear her mumble the name of a hotel.

"Again, please. Louder."

"Lincoln Hotel."

"Who's the guy you hooked up with? Toby's friend."

"All I know's his name's CW."

My heart skips a beat. Finally, hard information. I pull out my notepad and begin jotting down her answers. "What do his initials stand for? Who is he?"

Rameeka shakes her fuchsia head and squints at me. "Don't know. Him and Toby seemed like friends."

"Describe him for me."

"He's black, dark skin, taller than me but not much. I'm four-eight but he's short like Washington, probably only five-five or five-six. Fine looking man, lot of muscle like he work out a lot."

"What else do you remember about how he looked?"

Rameeka squeezes her eyes shut and puckers her eyebrows.

"Got a retro afro out to here," her hands describe an arc almost a foot away from her head, "and there's a tattoo across his chest says 'fearless.'"

After I write this down I say, "That's good. You have a good memory. So you partied at the Lincoln Hotel, the four of you? Then what?"

She nods at the number. "CW give me a ride back to my, uh, area," she says, glancing up at her sister who stands behind me. "I needed to make some more money. But he took my phone number, said he might call again. And he did. The next night."

Rameeka suddenly sits forward and descends into a hacking cough, and even though she uses the comforter to cover her mouth, the sound is deep and wet. Breathless from the effort, she flops back against the pillows and Rhonda administers orange juice. When they are done I ask Rameeka about CW's car.

"I don't know the name but it was fancy. A white sports car, the kind with the top down. I thought that's crazy 'cause it's cold at night, too cold for that. Car was real nice, though. Leather seats, CD player, even had a TV. We watched *Jeopardy!* I want to be on that show. You can win a lot of money." She blows her nose in a loud raspberry.

"Any chance you can remember his license plate number, or even part of it?"

"Unh-unh," she says.

Well, worth a try.

"He didn't have one, I mean. His car had that yellow cardboard thing. You know, temporary."

I give her a look that must convey how impressed I am because she raises her chin and actually preens a bit.

"Doin' what I do, you notice things."

"I'll bet," I say.

She goes on about Saturday night, another party, this time at Campbell House. Toby and Kandy stay in his room while Rameeka and CW smoke pot in the living room. Walter Washington, the group home manager, shows up and gets high with them.

Then, casually, Rameeka adds that she and the two men had a three-way. At this, I hear Rhonda Hartman take a deep breath and slowly exhale. I imagine her silently counting to ten.

I turn around part-way. "Ms. Hartman, could I bother you for a cup of coffee? I quit smoking yesterday and the caffeine seems to help my withdrawal." I hope my smile looks sincere.

"Oh, of course, Detective. It will take a few minutes. Meeka, you want anything else to drink?"

"Some hot tea, Rhon? Throat's all raw from coughing."

After Rhonda leaves the room I ask Rameeka to tell me more about the three-way, whose idea it was.

"CW. He's bossy that way. Friday night at the hotel CW wouldn't leave Toby and Kandy alone. He wanted to watch 'em even while he was goin' at me. Saturday night he wanted to watch again but Toby took Kandy into his room and closed the door. Kinda made CW mad.

So me and that little skinny manager was his show instead. He arranged us on the floor with big cushions, Washington on his back and me riding him. CW he like that. Starts whoopin' and hollerin' like we was at a rodeo or something. All of a sudden he pulls down his jeans and humps me from behind while I'm riding Washington."

Rameeka shoots me a disgusted look.

"I screamed at that nigger, 'You better pay me good for what you doing to me!'" She burrows down further into the pillows and clutches the comforter around her.

"What happened after that?"

"Ain't that enough? I got my money and left outta there. CW wasn't gonna pay me to stay all night. Hell, didn't even give me a ride back this time." Her lower lip juts out at the remembered mistreatment.

"So when you left, Toby and Kandy were in his bedroom with the door closed and CW and Washington were still in the living room?"

Rameeka nods.

"Have you had any contact with Kandy since Saturday night?"

She sits up and hacks some more into the comforter, then leans back against the pillows and shakes her head. "I started feeling real bad Sunday, got a high fever. My sister took me to the ER and I been here since. Haven't talked to anybody 'cause I lost my cell phone. Rhon won't let me use hers."

Shit. There goes one possibility of retrieving CW's number. I take down her cell phone information for Abandonato to follow up. "If you do hear anything from Kandy or about her, I need to know, I need to talk to her. She's probably one of the last people to see Toby alive."

Rhonda steps into the room and hands us our hot drinks.

"About CW, Rameeka. I want you to describe him to a police artist as soon as you're feeling up to it. You willing to do that?"

"Meeka, if you have any way of helping the police catch a murderer, I hope you will do it," says Rhonda.

"He'll know it was me who tipped on him. What if he comes after me?"

"You're safe here, Meeka. No one can get up here," Rhonda says.

Rameeka studies the tea bag label as she dunks the bag repeatedly into the hot water. "Yeah? And what am I supposed to do? Live here the rest of my life?" She thrusts the cup of tea onto the side table, sloshing the hot liquid, and turns on her side away from us.

I flip my notepad shut and pocket it. Taking a few hot gulps of the fresh brew I stand and glance at Rhonda, indicating the outer room with a slight tip of my head. I thank Rameeka for her help and leave her my card, but she says nothing.

We walk to the front door and Rhonda Hartman apologizes for her sister's stubbornness, but I wave her off.

"She's scared and I don't blame her. We've been trying to find her friend Kandy but so far nothing, which doesn't look good. See if you can persuade Rameeka to change her mind about the sketch artist. It would be a huge help to have a picture to circulate."

I hand Rhonda Hartman my half-full mug of coffee along with my card. "Keep her here as long as you can. I'll update you as much as possible about this CW guy and whether we find him."

Lake Shore Drive is packed with rush hour traffic in both directions and I creep along the Michigan Avenue on-ramp.

My cell rings. Abandonato.

"Got your message," he says. "Both women have the usual sheet— drugs, prostitution. No known address for Rameeka Hartman. She's homeless according to the last arrest, gave a shelter number for where she was staying. Kandy Kane does have an address and I checked it out. She shares it with another, shall we say, co-worker who hasn't seen Kandy in almost a week and is worried. That's all I got."

I give him the specifics about Rameeka ensconced in the Hancock, but hurry to share the real find, feeling a thrill at having solid information to give my partner.

"Kandy and Rameeka partied Friday and Saturday night with Toby and a guy he knew, initials CW, but Rameeka doesn't know his name." I feed him CW's details. "I tried to get her to let one of the guys sketch her description but she refused."

"I'll have to change her mind on that."

"Good. CW's driving a late model sports car, white with leather interior and a TV built into the dash. Car's so new it still has the temp plates but she couldn't remember any of the tag. Anyway, this guy sounds like a control freak with some voyeurism thrown in. He roughed up Rameeka with some back door sex she wasn't too happy about."

"Nice work. You've found out more in twenty-four hours than Carrera has in three days. I'll put out a BOLO on the car and I can run down new car purchases through the tags for the past month, see if we get anything that way."

This pleases me no end, both the compliment from Abandonato and his doing what I can't in my current position. It's as if we're still working partners. And of course, bypassing Carrera.

"One problem with the BOLO. I can order it but Carrera will find out, so sooner or later I'll have to tell him why."

"Shit." I don't want to give anything to the Prick, but I know Abandonato is right. "Okay, no choice there. One more thing, though. CW called Rameeka on her cell but she lost it. Get her records and look up the calls from last weekend. Hold on." The slow traffic has come to a complete stop at Fullerton so I pull out my notepad and give him Rameeka's phone company information.

"She say anything to you about Kandy?"

"Zip. The last time she saw her was Saturday night. Kandy and Toby went into his room for privacy. Rameeka and CW got high in the living room, Washington shows up and smokes with them, they have a three-way, she gets paid and leaves."

Abandonato grunts as though something I said doesn't make sense. "I finally got the Prick's report about his interview with Walter Washington. Everything you told me matches his version of Friday and Saturday but CW doesn't make the cut, he's not in Carrera's report. No three-way, just Washington and Rameeka, Toby and Kandy."

My stomach roils at this news. Traffic begins flowing and I get my car up to thirty. "The report doesn't mention CW at all?"

"Negative."

"So is this the Prick's omission or Washington's?"

"Hold on, I've got another call coming in."

As I wait for him to return I try to understand the glaring discrepancy between Washington's and Rameeka's stories. I realize I've already begun to form a theory about why Toby was killed. CW sounds like the only person with the physical ability to kill a man of Toby's size and strength. His immediate motivation could be that he's mad Toby took Kandy into the bedroom for some privacy. CW's a voyeur and likes to watch others having sex, but Toby nixed this the second night. I also wonder how much cash Toby might have had in his room, maybe a secondary motive for the murder.

Abandonato returns with a rushed voice. "I'll do what I can on my end but my other case is heating up," he says.

"What's going on?"

"Seems Johnny Diamond found Crystal's boyfriend first and beat him senseless in a bar on the west side. Bartender called the cops and they cuffed the alderman. He's in lock-up waiting for his lawyer and arraignment."

"The boyfriend dead?"

"About as close as you can get and still be breathing. He's at Stroger in a coma. I've got to run, Dane. Keep in touch and I'll get on that BOLO."

I disconnect and toss my cell on the passenger seat, then pick it up and speed dial Abandonato but get his voice mail. I ask him to email me Carrera's interview with Washington because I want to see exactly what was said.

Even as I say this I decide the hell with the Prick's report. I want to talk to Walter Washington right now.

15

8:00 p.m.

I push my knees lightly against the two German shepherds who crowd me at the door of Walter Washington's apartment. "Shut the dogs in another room." The small manager of Campbell House is slow about it but complies.

Once inside, I can't help but notice Washington's apartment isn't any cleaner today than yesterday. I shove some papers from the couch to the floor so I can sit down.

The manager comes into the living room and stands over me. "I gotta go fix a toilet downstairs. What you want? I already talked to the other cop, told him everything."

"Have a seat. I have a few questions, Walter. Won't take ten minutes."

He stays planted in front of me—as if his slight build could possibly be threatening—until my glare moves him into a chair across from me.

"I talked with Rameeka Hartman. She said you partied with her in Toby's apartment on Saturday night."

Walter Washington's eyes flick back and forth. He crosses his arms and shrugs but says nothing.

"What's that mean?" I mimic his shrug. "Yes?"

"No. It means no. We smoked a little weed but I didn't do nothing else. CW was all in charge of her, not me."

There's the name I'm hoping to hear.

"Tell me what you know about CW."

Washington shrugs again. "I don't know nothing about him 'cept he's not from here. He talked country, like my cousin."

"Like what? From Mississippi?"

"Yeah. South."

"Okay. Tell me more about Saturday night when you partied in Toby's apartment. What time did it start?"

"I got back here about eleven. Me and my girlfriend had a fight so I came back. I could smell them smoking when I came inside. It made me mad 'cause the people here ain't supposed to be smoking no dope." Washington's face doesn't match his words. He's smiling.

"And?"

"So I knock on Toby's door and CW answers. I see him and Rameeka are the ones smoking."

"Where was Toby?"

"He wasn't there. He was with Kandy in his bedroom."

"Rameeka tells me the two of you were the sex show for CW until he decided to join the fun."

Washington stands up and waves his hands in a crisscrossing motion at me. "No, uh-uh. I don't want no part of that bitch. Yeah, I smoked some weed with them two. But then Shanti showed up and we came up here."

"Shanti your girlfriend?"

He nods.

I jot her personal information in my notepad. "Why would Rameeka lie about having sex with you, Washington? Look, I'm not telling Shanti you hooked up with Rameeka. I don't care about that. I only want to know about Toby and what happened Saturday night."

Washington sits down and shrugs again, trying to act casual. "Don't know. Like I said, I got here about eleven. Shanti came by after awhile. I don't remember what time 'cause I was high, wasn't looking at no damn clock."

"And Toby was alive when you went into his apartment?"

"I could hear him in there, in his room, with Kandy. The two of 'em always gettin' together on weekends."

"And he was there when you left?"

Washington nods.

"Did you ever see CW before or after Saturday?"

"Nope. Just thought he was someone Toby knew."

"How old do you think CW is?"

"Lot older than me. I'm thirty and he gotta be in his fifties. He—"

A sudden banging on the apartment door. Someone yells for Washington to open up. When he does, two uniformed cops catch themselves from falling forward as they stumble into the foyer. Alberto Carrera walks in behind them and thrusts a piece of paper at Washington.

Then he sees me.

"Again, Demeter? I've had it with you. The Lieutenant hears about this."

I try for a pacifying expression. "Hold on, hold on. I'm here following up on a small thing, Carrera. Don't get your back up."

"And don't you fucking tell me what to do."

The Prick gives me what I guess is supposed to be a withering look to go with his tough words but he appears more like someone with heartburn. He orders one of the cops to search the apartment.

"Where are the dogs?" Carrera asks Washington.

"In my bedroom."

"Go get them. Tie them up on the back porch. Go with him," he nods at the other cop, "then bring him back here."

Carrera turns back to me. "Get your ass out of here."

"What're you looking for?" I ask, genuinely curious.

"None of your fucking business, Demeter. The Lieutenant gets an earful from me tomorrow."

"I found it, Detective! I found it!" An excited Uniform rushes into the living room holding up a small block of wood with four red-handled steak knives protruding from it. Two slots are empty.

"Bag it. Keep looking for the other stuff."

The Uniform starts to leave the room but Carrera stops him.

"And don't keep running in here like a little girl telling me what you found, Perino. I'm not your mommy. Do the job. Bag the stuff and let's get the hell out of this stink hole." He shakes his head. "Rookies."

I know from the crime scene list that a red-handled knife was found in the apartment—the probable weapon used to kill Toby. The other cop comes back with Washington.

"Where's the safe?" Carrera asks.

Washington juts his chin toward the hallway leading to the rest of the apartment, the floor plan an exact replica of Toby's place. "Back in my office."

Carrera grabs the manager's arm and frog-marches him down the hallway. The other cop and I follow. We first pass what I assume is Washington's bedroom, then pass a second bedroom turned storage, and land at a third bedroom now outfitted with a desk, filing cabinet, and overflowing trash can. The cop kneels in front of a large safe, the one I assume JJ told me about for the Campbell House residents to store their valuables. Carrera shoves Washington toward the safe.

"Open it," says Carrera.

I'm about to ask Carrera if he's got a search warrant, but of course following protocol isn't on his agenda. I stay mum because I want to give him plenty of rope to hang himself with the way he's handling this investigation.

The cop kneeling at the safe slides aside. Walter Washington bends down, twists the combination lock back and forth several times, then levers the handle to open the door. Empty.

Carrera gestures at the kneeling cop, who jumps up and pushes Washington against the wall, looming over him while handcuffing the skinny manager behind his back and Mirandizing him.

I'm apoplectic when I realize what's happening. "You're arresting Washington for killing Toby?"

Turning toward me, Carrera hitches up his pants in an exaggerated way. "Got the evidence I need, Demeter."

Washington starts to cry. "You got this all wrong. I didn't kill nobody."

"Yeah? Then why's the safe empty? Where's the Vic's money?" Carrera leans in and growls in Washington's face.

Washington jerks his head back but the cops holding him on either side keep him planted in place.

"I—I don't know. He didn't have any," Washington says. "I mean, Toby didn't keep his money in the safe. The rest of them, it's in the bank."

"Get him out of here." Carrera nods toward the door. The cop who cuffed Washington grabs him under the arm and practically lifts him off the floor, then propels him out of the room and down the hallway.

"Carrera, this is crazy. No way Washington could've overpowered Toby. Did you look at him? For god's sake."

"You can't stand it, can you?"

"Can't stand what? That you're incompetent? You're right, I can't stand it."

I want to blast him for his stupidity but don't want to waste what little energy I have left. The Whopper and fries I wolfed down on the way over start repeating on me and I belch. Carrera gives me a disgusted look.

"You think *I'm* incompetent? That's rich, that is, coming from you, Demeter. I've got the proof I need."

"What? The steak knives? Jesus, anybody could've used those knives. There are six other people living in this building you haven't interviewed."

"Don't need to. I got motive." His eyes flash at me, startling in their intensity.

At best, I have always considered Carrera a bumbling idiot, and at worst, a liability to partner with. This is the first time I entertain the notion that he might be mentally unbalanced. I take a step back. "Okay, I'll bite. What's his motive?"

"Money, pure and simple. Washington's maxed out on his credit cards to the tune of twenty thou. Toby had money and Washington stole it. When Toby found out, they fought. Your guy lost."

"So even though Toby outweighed Washington by at least fifty pounds of pure muscle, he was overpowered by the puny guy? Washington gets close enough to stab Toby dozens of times until he kills him? That's the picture?"

"Surprise, Demeter. He caught the vic by surprise in bed."

"And what about the other guy at the scene? CW is a guy powerful enough to really take Toby. A guy who is," I lean in, drawing out the hiss of my final word, "missing."

"That's crap Washington made up. There's no other guy. Washington didn't want his girlfriend to know he was fuckin' a skank, so he made up this CW." He draws air quotes around CW's name. Carrera points at the empty safe. "Follow the money, Demeter. Or in this case, the missing money." He barks a single laugh in my face.

I hurry after him as he heads back to the living room. "So that proves Washington's a thief, not a murderer!"

Carrera sits on the couch that I had cleared, pulls out a small notebook, and jots something down. Then he gives me a long stare before flipping the pad shut. "You can't stand it, can you?"

This is the second time he's said those words and my curiosity gets the better of me. "Can't stand what?"

"Koz trusts me, not you."

Carrera's insight is surprising. The truth of his statement brings me up short. It also pisses me off. "Yeah. Too bad you have to fuck his daughter to make that happen."

The words fly out of my mouth, a lame retort—I know as soon as I say it. But I get the desired reaction. Carrera jumps up from the couch and crosses the room in five quick steps. He thrusts his face so close to mine I can see he shapes his eyebrows.

"You better fuckin' leave Caitlyn out of this. Koz made me lead on this case, not you or your lame partner. Washington killed Toby and that's the end of it." He points to the apartment's entrance. "Now get the hell out of here."

"I know where the front door is."

"Then use it."

"This is really typical of your shitty work, Carrera. You force some of the facts to fit your ridiculous theory, even if it means changing or ignoring other facts altogether. Ah, fuck it."

I slam the door on my way out. Why should I try to persuade him any further? I have my own leads to pursue, my own investigation to continue. Finding CW quickly will be impossible in a city the size of Chicago, assuming he's still here.

But the BOLO Abandonato put out is a start. At least I feel good about how things are still clicking between the two of us. With the list of evidence found at the scene, the missing Kandy to track down, and now Washington's girlfriend to interview, I have plenty to keep me busy. Best to follow these leads on my own to a clearer path.

16

Friday, 9:00 a.m.

I wince at the headache that greets me in the morning. I wish more positive reinforcement coincided with giving up smoking because this painful withdrawal is a sure way to keep me chained to tobacco for the rest of my life. My progress tracker shows I stopped smoking only two days ago. Hard to believe. Seems like a month. More pleasing to note is that I haven't had a drink for two days, either.

It isn't a problem.

My two-pound bag of sunflower seeds, now reduced to one pound, goes on top of a box of clothes I've put together to donate to St. Nick's church for its annual fall rummage sale. I stuff a roll of masking tape in my pocket and balance my commuter cup of coffee next to the sunflower seeds, then hoist the box carefully and descend three flights.

The manager is decorating the lobby with cobwebs, cardboard skeletons and "Happy Halloween!" posters. In the corner by the mailboxes sits a huge, misshapen pumpkin with a devilish grin drawn with black marker. I haven't seen the manager since renting the studio and root around for his name but come up blank. When he sees me, he stops spraying the fake cobwebby stuff.

"Ah, good morning miss. You are liking the apartment?" He is slightly shorter than me and wears olive green work pants with a matching shirt. I put the box down.

"Yes, thanks. My studio's fine. So Halloween's Monday?" I gesture at the decorations.

"Yes, yes. The children they come here for candy. My wife she does not like all the time to answer the door, answer the door, answer the door." He shrugs, takes off his Cubs cap to scratch his head, then pats down his wispy gray hair before again donning the hat.

"This American holiday I like very much, seeing the children in their dress-up. So I sit here," he takes off his reading glasses perched on the end of his nose, using them to point at a small stool next to the pumpkin. "I am with the candy waiting for the children and they thank Sandor. I tell them 'boooo' to be like ghost and they laugh."

I smile, happy that he's given me his name. "I'm glad you'll be handing out candy, Sandor. I don't think the kids will come up to my place on the third floor."

An entire fantasy plays itself out in my mind in a millisecond: Happy together at home on Halloween—our baby dressed in a one-piece bumblebee costume made by Evie—Jimmy and I pass out candy to neighborhood children. We then go door-to-door to trick-or-treat with the baby, basking in a sacred parental moment: the joy of partic-ipating in childhood rituals.

The scene disappears in a snap. "I've got to go. See you later."

"Seeing you later," he says.

Once outside I feel overdressed. Must be at least sixty degrees. I put the coffee cup and sunflower seeds on the passenger side of my car's front seat and stow the box of clothes in my trunk. With my window rolled down and the radio on, I head south for a talk with Washington's girlfriend.

The radio gives me an update about Abandonato's new case. The boyfriend is out of his coma and is being questioned by police in the death of his child. The end of the short report states that the boyfriend is still in critical condition and it is unclear if he will survive the beating from Johnny Diamond.

At a large high-rise facing Lake Shore Drive, I identify myself over the intercom and hold up my ID to the closed-circuit television. Shanti Bennett buzzes me in. A tall, overweight African-American woman in a floor-length bathrobe answers the door. I look at my phone: ten a.m.

"Don't be embarrassed Detective, you didn't wake me. Actually, I'm now getting ready for bed. I work the overnight shift. Please come in." Her voice, quiet and unassuming, contradicts her size. "This is about Walter." A statement instead of a question.

"Yes, that's right."

She indicates a chair for me across from an overstuffed sofa, where she settles. The woman's age is hard to calculate, mid-to-late thirties? Definitely older than Washington. Or maybe it's their size difference.

"I'm sure Detective Carrera has already questioned you but we have a few more things we'd like to clear up." Though I'm ninety-nine percent sure Carrera has not interviewed her, I want to quell the one percent that nags me.

Surprise lights Shanti Bennett's amber eyes. "Why, no one has questioned me about Walter, Detective. He called me after he was arrested last night. I was able to drop off his asthma inhaler and a change of underwear, but nothing else. I picked up his dogs this morning on my way home." She points to her left. "They're in my spare bedroom."

I mentally run through the summary of Washington's story from yesterday, as much as I got anyway, and flip open my notepad.

"Ms. Bennett, we have conflicting information about what happened last Saturday night at Campbell House where, as you know, Walter Washington is manager."

I hand her Toby's birthday cake picture. "This man's name is Toby and he was brutally murdered in his bed at Campbell House. Walter Washington was one of the last people to see him alive. Did you go to Campbell House on Saturday?"

Shanti Bennett studies the photo and then looks at the ceiling, her eyes tracing small trajectories back and forth. She looks oddly regal in her long robe, a light pink hair-wrap surrounding her head. I take the photo of Toby from her.

"Saturday Walter and I went out to eat about one and he was going to give me a ride to work—I was on the three-to-eleven that day—but we had a disagreement at lunch. I wanted to know his intentions for me, for our future. I—I have not had many men in my life, Detective."

Shanti Bennett's fingers worry the top button of her robe.

"My parents were strict, insisting I go to college, and then I continued on with my Master's in nursing. I met Walter a year ago in the Emergency Room where I work. He brought in one of the deaf residents who had a broken leg. We've been together ever since. You see, I want to get married. Walter's younger than I am and I think he feels pressured whenever I talk about marriage."

She gazes at her clasped hands, her complexion bordering on pale ash, and rubs a thumb over her naked ring finger. "I'm thirty-nine my next birthday."

"So you had an argument at the restaurant," I prompt.

She leans back into the couch and crosses her legs, revealing slippers sporting the head of Minnie Mouse over the toes. She crosses her arms.

"I asked him about our future together and he started yelling at me, right there in the restaurant. I was so embarrassed. People were looking at us. I told him to calm down and we could discuss it later. He didn't talk much after that. Then on the drive taking me to work he blew up again, started calling me all kinds of names, said he didn't want to marry '...no old woman.' Really Detective, I felt so hurt. I thought we had a good relationship."

Her eyes tear up. She pulls a cloth hankie from her pocket and blows her nose.

"So he drove you to work and then what happened?"

"Well, no. After he said he didn't want to marry me I couldn't stand being in the same car with him. I was mortified. At a stoplight I got right out of the car and walked to the nearest bus stop, went to work that way. It was hard concentrating on my job after that. I kept thinking about everything we had together. It was strange for Walter to throw our age difference in my face like that. I mean he always told me before how much he appreciated being with me because of my career, how serious I am, that I want a secure future. That's when it hit me, Detective."

She nods her head decisively and looks me in the eye. Since I have no idea what she's talking about, I give her the best "raised eyebrows" inquiring look I can muster.

"Money, of course!"

Shanti Bennett's arms shoot up and out in a large gesture, as if it's such an obvious answer even a child would've guessed it.

"Walter has no money. Only the day before he told me he was deeply in debt and wouldn't be able to continue school for a while, that he was going to find a second job until he could pay off the money he owed. And here I was pressuring him about our future together. That's why he got so angry with me. He didn't really mean those things he said about my age. His ego was bruised because he couldn't be a man without money and give me what he thought I wanted."

I don't know how in the world this woman could come up with such an explanation. I guess love really is blind. And apparently stupid. Irritation with her tangential story makes my next question brusque.

"I'm interested in what happened at Campbell House on Saturday night, Ms. Bennett."

"I was getting to that, Detective."

Her face belies her aggravated tone of voice. She looks beatific, her face awash with a broad smile, her eyes glassy with tears.

"I got off work late on Saturday but decided right then and there to surprise Walter, tell him it was all right that he didn't have any money. I am a habitual saver. There's plenty for us to pay off his debts and get married. He could return to school, get his degree and then get a really good job. We could live here until he finished, then maybe buy a home and—"

I interrupt this flight into the stratosphere, waving Toby's photo. "Ms. Bennett? What happened at Campbell House Saturday night when you got there?"

She emits a nervous laugh and pats her pink turban.

"Oh, I'm sorry, Detective. Where was I? Oh, yes. I went to Campbell House and let myself in—I have my own key—and as I walked up the stairs I could hear Walter's voice in that first floor apartment. So instead of going up to his place I knocked on the apartment door. Walter answered and I explained everything I figured out about us. Sweet man that he is, he agreed that money was a problem for him. He asked me to stay over and we went upstairs to his place right then. We're engaged, you know."

I glance at the bare ring finger of her left hand. It's probably difficult to shop for an engagement ring when your fiancé is in jail. I also have a mean thought: Shanti will probably go buy the ring herself.

"So, Walter Washington came out of the first floor apartment to talk with you. You didn't go into the apartment?"

The pink turban produces a negative shake.

"Who or what did you see in the apartment when you were talking to Walter?"

Shanti Bennett squeezes her eyes shut in concentration and begins to talk in a singsong manner.

"I'm knocking on the door and Walter answers. 'Shanti, what you doing here?' 'I'm here to apologize,' I say. Walter looks surprised. Behind him I see a man sitting on the couch smoking marijuana. He's got hair out to here."

She holds up her hands about a foot apart on each side of her head.

"Then I see another man come out of his bedroom and go into the bathroom. Walter comes out to the hallway with me and we talk and go upstairs to his apartment."

Her eyes pop open. She takes the photo from my hand and stares at it, her voice becoming excited as she waves the photo at me.

"This is the man I saw going into the bathroom! Toby?"

I nod at her.

"Walter's not the last person to see him alive! I am too!"

Shanti's description of the man smoking marijuana in Toby's apartment places CW at the scene and proves it's not a story made up by Washington. Taken together with Washington's and Rameeka's recollections of that night, Shanti is the third witness to corroborate those present in Toby's apartment the night he was murdered.

Discovering CW's motive for killing my father's hapless friend is secondary. My biggest problem is finding CW before Carrera has Washington convicted and sentenced for a crime he didn't commit.

I give Shanti my business card in exchange for Toby's photo and ask her to call me if she thinks of anything else to help exonerate her fiancé.

On the way over to my parents' home I consider the top three reasons most people murder each other: greed, jealousy, and rage. I can't rule out jealousy or rage in this case because women, alcohol, and drugs are part of the mix. But greed often seems the most popular justification in this triangle of human faults.

Even if the manager did steal money from Toby and the other Campbell House residents, Shanti Nightingale had already swooped in *prior to the murder* with the offer to alleviate Washington's financial worries. So money wasn't an issue at that critical point. But for some reason I can't shake the nagging feeling money somehow fuels this entire tragedy. But I can't put order to it. Yet.

My stomach grumbles. Sunflower seeds have kept the tobacco cravings muted and my hands busy but they don't do much for hunger. I see a vendor's pushcart emblazoned with a sign announcing Taquerias, and swerve over a lane. I park illegally to purchase a bag of the original fast food. The car's interior fills with enticing, spicy aromas. I down two beef tamales and one crunchy flautas, then finish with a light piece of dough deep-fried and sprinkled with cinnamon and sugar.

I arrive at my parents' home berating myself about the dubious health benefits of the food I ingested. I'll have to make peace with my progress tracker later. I let myself in the house but no one is home. Leaving a note to Evie on the box of rummage sale clothes, I stow it underneath the kitchen table so the box is out of the way. She'll handle sorting them for the St. Nick's sale.

I head into their home office to try to download and print a version of Carrera's report. Much easier to read a printout than my smart phone. But the attachment doesn't open on Evie's computer, so I'm stuck waiting until I get back home to print a hard copy, or *try* reading it on my phone. Do I really need reading glasses at thirty?

I return to my car and nibble on sunflower seeds, waiting to see if either Evie or JJ returns. My text to Evie asking her whereabouts has gone unanswered, which is unlike her. Probably too involved in talking with her friends about her lame oldest daughter—me.

My cell phone rings. Koz. I almost answer but assume he's got to be calling about my badge and gun, because I haven't turned them in. He'll be angry, so I let it go to voicemail and in a short time hear the message alert tone.

I am right about one thing—Koz is mad. But it isn't about my badge or gun, it's about the Prick. Carrera ran to him like a little punk and complained about me, as he threatened to do back at Campbell House. On the message Koz orders me to cease and desist from any further interference in Toby's case and to lay off Carrera. Yeah? No, that's not going to happen.

On the passenger seat next to me, JJ's photo of Toby peeks out from under the bag of sunflower seeds. I unearth it. The candles on the birthday cake illuminate Toby's bright smile.

For someone who has been my boss for three years, Koz still doesn't know me very well. Cease and desist? Lay off Carrera? Like waving a red cape at a bull. The only thing I heard in his order is a challenge— a challenge to continue.

I dig the masking tape out of my pocket and post Toby's happy memory to my car's dashboard above the radio, a beacon for me as I press on.

17

12:30 p.m.

"I was so upset when she wouldn't give you any information about Toby. That woman! The only thing tighter than her lips is her ass!"

I bark out a laugh, spewing cookie crumbs across the small table where I sit with Franki Cramer. The teller from Toby's branch bank has downed a turkey sandwich and opens a bag of low-fat pretzels. My chocolate chip cookie, originally the size of a steering wheel, is down to only a few broken pieces. I gather up the errant crumbs and sweep them into my empty coffee cup.

"I appreciate you're willing to talk to me, Franki, but your manager's right. I don't have a warrant for the information I need. I want to know if Toby had a bank account, how much money was in it, if there were any recent withdrawals. If I do find something helpful to the case, I can get a warrant to make it official. But your manager doesn't have to provide anything unless by court order."

The young woman selects a pretzel from the bag and sits back in her chair, regarding me with direct appraisal.

"No," she says slowly, "she doesn't have to provide anything. But how about doing the right thing by somebody for once, cooperating instead of stonewalling? I mean, the man's *dead*."

She bites into the pretzel with a deliberate snap and her deep brown eyes challenge me to disagree. I say nothing but hold her gaze until she looks down, closing her eyes for a long moment. When she looks at me again, tears spill down her cheeks.

"I don't understand," I say, handing her one of my napkins. "Are we still talking about Toby?"

The curves of the young woman's ears are lined with diamond studs. Her hairstyle of short, shiny ringlets bounces as she first nods, then shakes her head at my question. Confusion. Franki Cramer dabs the tears on her cheeks.

"Toby reminded me of Carl, my brother. I mean, Toby was much older than Carl, but my brother was deaf too. He graduated from Gallaudet University at the top of his class. Five years ago he came back to look for a job. He and a friend are walking down the street signing to each other. Gang bangers drive by and think my brother's flashing gang signs. Pop, pop, they shoot 'em and leave. Carl dies right there and his friend is paralyzed from the neck down. He's deaf and can't sign. That's got to be worse than dying." She stops and takes a long pull on her water bottle.

The shiny scars on my father's hands and arms loom in my mind. His claim that Toby saved his life gains further traction for me as I consider what Franki says about the paralyzed deaf man. How much can one person suffer and still want to live? I doubt I could be that brave.

"God. I'm so sorry about your brother and his friend. The city can be a vicious place." My words sound inadequate even to me. "My whole family is deaf," I offer, hoping to show understanding but also to build rapport. I'm still uncertain why Franki is relating this story about her brother. Her face looks spiteful and she folds her arms across her chest.

"They were shot in the middle of the day. People all around but all they'd say to the police was..." Franki thrusts her head back and forth in a mock imitation of the witnesses, "...'I didn't see nothing' and 'bruthas musta had it coming.' No one, not *one* person would step up and do the right thing by my brother. I swore that day if I ever had a chance to help in a similar situation, I would. Carl deserved better, a lot better." She uses the napkin to blow her nose.

"So, Toby," Franki says.

Here we go. I scoot my chair closer to the table and lean in.

"He didn't have an account with us but he could cash his check at the bank because we handle ARC's payroll. We charge a small fee to cash their checks. Toby liked to come in right after work on Fridays with his check and get his money."

"So, no account," I say.

She shakes her head. This checks out with what Jan Marie already told me, but good to know directly from the bank in case Toby did somehow manage to open an account without anyone else knowing. But no account also means no way for me to check if money was withdrawn either before—or more importantly—after Toby's death.

"Franki, Toby didn't know much American Sign Language, couldn't really communicate in a meaningful way. How did you understand what he wanted? I mean, was he able to tell you whether he wanted large or small bills, that kind of thing?"

Franki Cramer smiles at me. "I know, I know. But I think we communicated pretty well, had a little friendship. He always came to my window to do his banking and the routine was always the same. His check was two-fifty a week. I'd give him a one hundred dollar bill, five twenties and then ten fives for his uh, girlfriend."

She shifts in her seat and crosses her legs.

"Kandy? He came in the bank with Kandy?" I picture the hookers lining up on the side street next to ARC's training facility, the group of maintenance guys checking them out. So Kandy must've waited for Toby to finish work, then went with him from there.

"You know about her, huh? Don't take this the wrong way, Detective, but she gives white trash a whole new meaning. I didn't like Toby hanging with her. And that red glitter she sprinkles on her face? Cool —if you're maybe eleven or twelve." She shakes her head and rolls her eyes at the memory. "Kandy *Kane*. Seriously?"

We both grin at each other for a moment. I make a quick note about the red glitter, no longer a curiosity on the evidence list.

"We haven't been able to track down Ms. *Kane* so far and she's an important potential witness. If you do see her, would you contact me immediately?" I pass her my business card and she studies it, then slips it into her purse. "So Toby would pay Kandy fifty dollars, all in fives?"

"Mmm-hmm. He'd give it to her standing right there and she'd count it out every time."

Franki uses one hand to pull an imaginary bill from an imaginary stack of money in the other hand: "Five, ten, fifteen, twenty...like I was going to cheat her or something. Toby would put the rest of his cash in his wallet. So this was every Friday until the last Friday of the month. Then he'd get his money orders."

This is new. I straighten up in my chair. "What were the money orders for?"

"You know, with regular people it wouldn't be my business. I make out the amount and the customer fills in the details. But Toby, he couldn't really read or write. He would put his name on two blank envelopes and give them to me. Then he'd hand over the cash that he'd saved during the month. So one money order was for two hundred fifty and the other was for four hundred dollars."

Jan Marie had said Toby's portion of his rent was two-fifty, so that made sense. My excitement rises as I realize what Franki is telling me.

"You filled out *who* the money orders were for. So Campbell House got the two-fifty?"

She leans forward when I make the connection.

"Right. And the four hundred went to a woman in Marietta, Georgia. Toby had an old leather luggage tag with her name and address on it. It was always the same thing. I didn't really need the tag because I memorized it pretty quick, but I'd copy her name and address on the money order and envelope and give it back to him, along with the tag. He'd stuff the envelope and seal it, then pat his hand over his heart a couple of times and smile at me when he was done. It was like our little ritual."

Her smile turns sad.

Suddenly Franki Cramer looks at her watch and swears. "I'm late. I've got to get back or you know who will write me up." She pushes out of her chair, stuffs her unfinished pretzels in the trash next to our table and grabs her water bottle.

"Wait! Can you give me the woman's name and address?"

I push my notepad across the table and hand her my pen. She scribbles the information quickly and shrugs into her jacket as I stand and shake hands with her.

"I have a good feeling about this, Franki. If you think of anything else, anything at all, please call me as soon as possible. Thank you for stepping up."

She bobs her head once, ringlets swaying in response, and hurries back to work.

Outside I stand at my black Corolla and survey ARC's hulking presence across the street. The century-old former factory looks sinister. Its edifice has modern ramps allowing access for wheelchairs, but otherwise the structure's mammoth limestone blocks seem to brood in silence.

I read Franki Cramer's hasty scribble: Otha Lee Worthy, Marietta, GA.

So maybe Toby has family after all.

18

2:00 p.m.

"Hey."

I answer my partner's call as I drive south back to my parents' house. A text from Evie much earlier in the day arrives on my phone, inviting me to dinner. I guess she's gotten over my bawling her out over not locking the back door.

"We found Kandy," he says.

"Great. How did you—"

"No. She's face down, not far from the river, north branch over by Goose Island."

"Shit. How long?" I pull over and park.

"The ME says at least twenty-four hours but maybe as high as forty-eight. Here's the capper: she's got a red-handled steak knife sticking out of her back. It's a match from the set at Washington's apartment. Same as—"

"Toby," I finish for him. I pinch the bridge of my nose, trying to stave off a headache insinuating itself behind my eyes. "Don't tell me. Carrera thinks that proves Washington did it, so he's charging him with Kandy's murder too."

Abandonato snorts on the other end. "Hey, you're good. That's exactly what happened after Carrera found out. The Prick is doubly proud of his detective skills. I almost feel sorry for Washington. A double murder charge, a lousy public defender, he's broke. Guy's going away for a long, long time."

I recap my run-in with Carrera last night at Campbell House. "The Prick arrested Washington on pretty flimsy grounds to begin with. Carrera thinks Toby found out Washington stole his money, they fought about it, and Toby lost."

"You know, that money angle isn't completely off target," says Abandonato.

I start to protest but he stops me.

"Wait. The Prick is right about Washington being in deep debt. Remember when Jan Marie said Washington reported Toby as being sick on *Monday*? That kept nagging at me, because he didn't report finding Toby's body until *Tuesday* morning."

"Right. I forgot about that."

Abandonato's remark reflects his scrupulous attention to detail, something I envy at times—like now. I pull out my notepad and flip to the notes from Sarah Gilbert's interview.

I read from my notes. "Sarah Gilbert said she didn't see Toby on Sunday night when she got back home but she went to bed early. She didn't see him Monday morning either, and told Washington she thought Toby was sick."

"So if Washington took Sarah's word for it instead of checking on Toby himself, and then called in for him," Abandonato says, "he wouldn't have known Toby was dead. But suppose on Saturday Washington and his girlfriend hook up at his place. After she leaves, he goes back to Toby's apartment to party some more? But when he goes in everyone's gone except for Toby, who's already dead. Washington knows about the shoebox and steals the money."

I chime in. "So he avoids Toby's place on Sunday and doesn't see Sarah until Monday morning. By then he's jittery because he knows CW killed Toby but doesn't have proof, he's waited two days to report it, and thinks he'll be charged instead."

"Which is exactly what the Prick has done," says Abandonato. "Washington is in our holding until he can be processed for County on Monday. I'm going to question him again, see if our theory is credible."

"Good. Wait 'til you hear what else I've got," I say. "And it will put Carrera's theories up his ass."

"No room. His head's already up there."

I laugh as I rifle through my notepad to Shanti Bennett's interview, then fill him in on the details, including Shanti's ability to place CW at the scene Saturday night and actually seeing Toby alive before she went upstairs with Washington.

"Shanti offered to solve Washington's money problems while Toby was still alive. When the two lovebirds went upstairs, that left CW with Toby and Kandy in the first floor apartment. CW kills Toby, and that means Kandy's an accessory or a witness. It follows he'd kill her too. I know CW's our guy, Nuts."

I hear him acknowledge my thought process with a grunt, then he adds, "Here's some good news. I convinced Rameeka to describe CW to the sketch artist. They Skyped. I emailed it to you."

I hear my phone ping signaling the email's arrival. I'm eager to see a sketch of the mysterious CW. "I'm on my way to Evie and JJ's. I'll print it there. Has Carrera seen the sketch?"

"Yeah, he saw it. Says Washington made up CW as the murderer, paid off Rameeka to back up his story, and got his girlfriend to give him an alibi. Washington's his guy and he's sticking to it."

"I heard the same song last night. Come on, Nuts. Talk to Koz, make him see Carrera's got this all wrong." I can't keep my voice from sounding harried and insistent.

Silence on the other end.

"Look Dane, what you got right now is hearsay and it *is* compelling. But there's no hard evidence to make the finger point away from Washington. Not yet, anyway. If I go to Koz now trying to dispute Carrera's slam-dunk, it'll only cause problems for me. Koz'll think I'm trying to get the Prick in trouble. Besides, I'm working overtime on the Diamond case. Koz'll think I'm skimping on that if I had the time to do all the work you've actually done. Is that what you want?"

I start to interrupt.

"No, save it. Get me something solid I can take to Koz and show up the Prick. Got to go. The boyfriend's out of his coma and it's time to get his side of the story."

He clicks off without a goodbye.

I clench my cell phone and punch the "end" button, wishing Abandonato had at least heard me out. When I finally loosen my hold and slide my cell into my jacket pocket, I realize I didn't tell him about Franki Cramer and the luggage tag with Otha Lee Worthy's name on it.

I pull out my phone to call him back but stop. He wants hard information. The luggage tag proves nothing. It's a detail, a clue to massage and digest along with the other accumulated information.

Then a sneaky thought rears its ugly head. Did I withhold the Franki Cramer information from Abandonato, and by extension, Carrera, so

I alone could investigate it? I pull into traffic and consider the idea but dismiss it. I forgot, that's all. I was shocked at Kandy's murder and excited about putting a face to CW. Besides, if the Prick would actually follow real leads, interview everyone involved, and apply some thought to the process, he'd have the same information I now hoard. Instead, he arrests Washington on nothing but the most superficial evidence. Nope. Otha Lee Worthy belongs to me.

I pull into traffic and continue south. I call Rhonda Hartman, thinking I can get away with leaving a voice message, but she answers. I tell her about Kandy and encourage her to keep Rameeka under wraps—literally and figuratively.

"I wish I could do that, Detective. My sister chose to leave this morning and didn't even say goodbye."

Or thank you, I bet. "Any idea where she'd go?"

"Out on the street. She slept at a shelter over on Harrison, near the university, before she came here. But their services are strictly for overnight. Everyone is up and out by seven the next morning."

"I think I might know where she is," I say, once again picturing the hookers near ARC. My phone says three-thirty. The timing is almost perfect.

"Are you any closer to catching this, this killer?" She chokes out the last word. "Is he going to go after Meeka?"

"I've got some strong leads I'm following now, Ms. Hartman. I'll try to find your sister to warn her. I have to go."

I click off, frustrated with Rameeka's stupidity and not knowing a good thing when she has it. Or maybe she does know but can't stop from self-destructing.

I'm near the Field Museum so I exit there, then turn right around and head back north on Lake Shore Drive. Before I get to ARC I make a quick stop at the Fullerton branch of the Chicago Public Library to download and print ten copies of CW's sketch. As I near ARC's training facility I see Rameeka's troll-doll magenta hair beckoning me from almost a block away. I pull up across the street.

"Rameeka!" I yell at her, motioning her over to my car.

She takes her sweet time. A large red and white striped Kate Spade bag is slung over her shoulder, which I imagine carries all of her possessions. She leans against my door, hip jutting out, her stature so short she looks at me eye-to-eye through my lowered window.

"My sister tell you to come get me?" Her voice is exasperated and her bottom lip sticks out like a little kid not getting her way.

"Rhonda is a saint for putting up with you."

"There you go again." Hand on hip, chin challenging me. "Why you do that? You got no right to—"

"Kandy's dead, Rameeka."

That shuts her up. For a second anyway. Then she starts crying, leaning against my door and hugging her short jacket close to her body. I let her go on for a minute.

"Come on, get in." I lean over and open the passenger side door and she climbs in, now coughing more than crying. I leave my window down, unconvinced she's not contagious.

"God, you don't sound any better than when I saw you yesterday. Why'd you leave your sister's place? You're in no shape to be out here."

"Ain't like I got no sick time or nothing. I got to make some money."

Point taken.

"What's gonna happen to me? CW killed Kandy 'cause she was there. And I was there before. He's gonna come after me next." She starts crying again, making an agitated, gulping noise as she tries to breathe between sobs.

"Calm down, Rameeka. Listen to me."

I raise my voice to make myself heard over her rising hysteria, then grab her arm to get her attention.

"We've got cops out looking for CW's car but nothing's come in yet. I'm thinking he's gone. He's already killed two people," but before I can finish she starts shrieking and crying louder. I push myself to wait and let her wail for a minute.

"Listen to me! He's killed two people and isn't hanging around for us to find him. He's long gone."

I grab my backpack from the back seat and pull out the folder with the copies of the description she gave of CW. I hold out half of them.

"Here. You did a great job on this sketch."

CW's billowing afro is the most striking difference between him and Toby, otherwise the two men could easily be related based on their facial similarities.

"Take these and pass them out to the other women. They can watch for him too. But like I said, I don't think he's still in Chicago."

Rameeka takes a long minute to blow her nose and repair her makeup, then takes the copies and stares at the sketch of CW.

"That your phone number?" She points at the information I added below the sketch.

"Yeah. Call me anytime, day or night. And think hard about going back to your sister's place. You're safe there."

"Rhonda don't want me around. She act all nice when you there. But she keeps trying to haul me to church with her, telling me to get right with Jesus. Wears me out with her attitude, judging me."

Rhonda's preaching sounds similar to Jimmy's rant about my drinking. I'm vaguely annoyed that I side with Rameeka on this.

"I guess people don't always pick the right way to show how they feel about us."

She ignores my psychological analysis with a toss of her head.

"Whatever."

Waving the sheaf of papers with CW's sketch, she asks, "You really think this muthafucka's gone? Not gonna come after me?"

I shake my head. "But stick with your friends. Check out every guy before you get into his car. Common sense, Rameeka."

It's dark by the time I get to my parents' bungalow and I hurry through the side yard and around to the back door, anxious to get at their computer to track information about Otha Lee Worthy. I find my key but don't need it. The back door yields.

"Evie, what the hell am I going to do with you?"

I mentally award my mother the gold medal in the Stubborn Olympics. I love her, but I'm pissed she ignores my repeated warnings. Does something bad have to happen before she'll acknowledge I have a point?

I keep muttering as I pass through the empty kitchen to the den where they keep their computer. Before I settle at the desk I need to pee.

This means going upstairs to the bathroom off my parents' bedroom, my father's plumbing efforts in the downstairs john making it necessary to call in the professionals. So it's temporarily off limits.

Their bedroom door is closed. Thinking they might be inside resting, I pause a moment before cracking it open. A glimpse of the bed tells me it's not occupied, so I try to swing the door open further. But it thuds into something blocking the way. I put my shoulder into it and shove harder, creating at least enough space to poke my head in for a look-around.

Evie's body lies on the other side.

19

Late Friday night

It's almost midnight when I bring Evie back from the hospital and put her to bed. A concussion and five stitches closing the gash on the back of her head are the remaining evidence of an intruder who surprised Evie in her bedroom. Her wedding ring and purse are gone.

"I could've stopped him. He'd never get past me."

My father repeatedly flexes and clenches his hands into fists. I haven't seen JJ this angry since the time I was ten and an older kid in the neighborhood beat up my twin.

"Stop blaming yourself for not being here," I tell him. *"She'll be okay. She'll have to take it easy for a few days."*

My confidence is purely for show. Seeing Evie crumpled up like a dead dog on the side of the road caused my heart to jackhammer and I froze, only able to stare at her inert shape.

For a long minute my inner voice screamed, *she's dead, she's dead.*

Then my training kicked in and the paramedics responded in under two minutes, bless them. Now JJ wants to rehash the incident for the fifth time but I'm tired and hungry.

"Look. You and I know she wouldn't keep the damn door locked. Now she will."

My anger at Evie surfaces again for her stubborn refusal to listen. But the sad and scared look on JJ's face tells me to tone it down, not take it out on him. I give him a quick hug and step back slightly to sign.

"I'm staying here with you and mom tonight. Why don't you go to bed?" I point to the computer. *"I still have work to do tonight, so I'll be awake for awhile."*

"Work? About Toby?"

"Yeah."

I pull a photocopy of Rameeka's sketch from the folder in my backpack and hand it to him. *"That man? He's the one who killed Toby."*

JJ studies the grainy printout. *"Strange. He looks a little like Toby."*

I nod. JJ notes Toby didn't have an afro like CW, instead wearing his hair cut close to his scalp and showing me the general shapes of their heads are similar.

My father's normally mild features harden into anger and he crushes the paper into a tiny ball.

"Why did he kill Toby? Toby never did anything to anybody." He throws the wad into the trash.

"I don't know why yet, JJ, but I'll find out. I promise. He won't get away."

I reach out my arms again and enfold my father, this time in a strong embrace. When we part, he pulls out a handkerchief and wipes his eyes.

"You use the computer. I'm going to make some tea. Want some?"

"Hot chocolate? And a sandwich?"

"Sure, sure." He gives me a gruff pat on the back and goes into the kitchen.

At JJ's desk I boot up the computer. The monitor resembles a boulder from the Neolithic Period. The machine whirs, grunts, and after an eternity lets out a grinding moan.

On the monitor, the desktop picture slowly fills in—a picture of our family at a deaf club picnic sometime in the past. In it, Evie signs "I love you" with one hand and beams at the photographer, happy to be in her element with other deaf people and surrounded by her family. Tears well up unexpectedly and I cover my face, cry into my hands.

My short outburst reminds me of what I usually suppress—how much I love my infuriating mother. Even though it's late, I text my brother and sister about what happened to Evie. David—ever the night owl—responds immediately, and I reassure him that Mom's okay.

I wait for a minute to see if Daphne will respond, but she doesn't, so I dry my tears and return to the job at hand—Otha Lee Worthy. I click on the Internet icon and wait for what feels like several minutes before the home page eventually appears.

I re-check the spelling of Otha Lee Worthy's name, enter it into the search engine, and wait.

Otha as a first name has umpteen references and appears to apply to males or females. It's also a vernacular spelling for the word "other." I try her name in Georgia's phone listings for Marietta but come up empty. Could she be dead? It would explain the absent phone listing. I wish I could check with DMV for a current license but am locked out of the resource because of my suspension. And I won't ask Abandonato for help on this, not until I produce what he wants—something "solid" for him to take to Koz.

I go through the evidence list from the scene of Toby's murder but see nothing to indicate a luggage tag. I make a note to call Franki Cramer tomorrow at the branch bank to get the exact address in Marietta where Toby sent his money orders. For now, it seems like the direct method might be best: go to Marietta and find this woman.

The cheapest airline ticket I can find online is over five hundred dollars. I put in my credit card information but am not allowed to complete the transaction. JJ comes into the room and sees me slam my hand on the desk in frustration. Next to the computer he deposits a plate that holds a cup of hot chocolate and a peanut butter and jelly sandwich, no crusts.

He mimics my hand slam. *"What's wrong?"*

"I have a very strong lead to follow in Toby's case but I have to get to Atlanta and my credit card was rejected."

"Doesn't the Department pay for your flight?"

Crap. He's still under the impression I'm on active duty, instead of a suspended cop acting like a loose cannon.

"Sometimes when I'm in a hurry I pay for it myself and CPD pays me back."

I cringe at the bald-face lie I tell my father but I don't want news of my suspension to worry him further. With Evie upstairs all banged up he has enough on his mind.

"My credit card's maxed out. I spent a lot of money on my move." At least that much is true.

He puts down his tea, reaches into his back pocket, and withdraws his wallet. *"Here, use my card."*

I start to protest but he keeps jabbing it at me and I finally take it.

"The Department pays you back and you pay me back, okay?"

He sits down and watches me book a flight for the next day. I leave the return date open-ended, not knowing how much time I'll need down there. The options for a rental car and motel are offered and I add them, pushing the thought of the accrued debt from my mind. I print out my boarding pass and motel reservation information and shut down the computer.

Half my sandwich disappears in two bites and then I remember what I want to show JJ. I hand him the copy of the sketch Toby drew at Pacific Garden Mission when he first arrived in Chicago, and recap what I learned from my visit there.

JJ stares at the crudely drawn picture, then signs, *"So maybe Toby was from somewhere else?*

"That's my strong lead. He might be from Georgia."

JJ gazes at the picture a little longer, then hands it back but I shake my head. *"You keep it."*

He gets up and pins it to the bulletin board above the desk.

"JJ, I'm curious about something I remember from when I was a kid, when you and Toby celebrated your birthdays together."

JJ nods at me to continue.

"We always went to the lake first. You know, on Sixty-third Street? You'd bring us kids with you and Toby so we could run up and down the beach. We thought it was weird the way Toby laughed and splashed in the water, sometimes even with his shoes on. Why'd he do that?"

JJ smiles at my recollection.

"The first time I took him out for his birthday, I wanted to treat him to lunch at a real restaurant. It was a small thing compared to the way he saved my hands from the machine. But I wanted to do something. So there was a nice place not too far from ARC, close to Lake Michigan. When Toby saw the lake he started gesturing and getting excited. I tried to park at the

restaurant but he made it very clear he wanted to go to the lake, so we drove over there. He ran to the water and splashed around in it, got all wet, laughing the whole time. I kept trying to get him to go to lunch but he wanted to stay at the beach, so we did."

JJ laughs and shakes his head at the memory.

"We got back to ARC late and the case manager wrote us up, but Toby was so happy it was worth it to me."

"So going to the beach became part of your birthday gift to Toby?"

JJ nods.

"After six months in the training program I left ARC. But when I went back the next year to take Toby out for our combined birthday celebration, the first thing he did was gesture like this."

JJ splays his hands out in front of him and draws opposing circles in the air.

"I didn't understand what he was trying to tell me. He kept pointing and pointing and for some reason it finally hit me that he wanted to go back to the lake. When we got there, he jumped out of the car and ran to the water, hopping up and down, laughing like a little kid and splashing water on both of us."

"Why do you think he liked the lake so much?"

"I don't know why, really. But after we were done he'd use that gesture I showed you before, remember?"

I watch JJ lay his right hand over his heart. His scarred hand pats a few soft beats.

Goose bumps trill up my arms and prick the hair to attention. Toby's motion captured in the birthday cake picture, Franki Cramer describing the same motion as part of their "little ritual" when Toby sent money to Georgia, and now JJ repeating the identical gesture in connection with the lake—each one a reminder of a place Toby loved.

Home.

20

Saturday morning

Before leaving my parents' house the next morning to go back to my studio and pack for my late afternoon flight, I call Abandonato. I tell him about Evie and the break-in.

"Other than stitches and a concussion, I think she's okay. JJ's angry he wasn't here to take care of business."

"Guy's got to protect the castle. She's lucky she only got beaned. You going to stay with them for a few days?"

A logical question. I don't know how to answer. I don't want to tell Abandonato about going to Georgia until I can produce, in his words, "something solid." I dither with a noncommittal sound. "Mmm. Hey, before I forget. Did you get anything from Rameeka's phone records?" On his end I hear paper rustle in the background.

"Rhonda pays for Rameeka's cell phone and was cooperative in handing over a print-out of the calls made and received last week. Last Saturday at ten p.m. Rameeka did get a call from the Lincoln Hotel. It fits what she said."

I actually feel warm all over hearing that. Another piece falls into place and puts me closer to an accurate reconstruction of the night of Toby's murder.

"But the call she received is from the hotel phone," says Abandonato. "So it's another dead-end, at least for tracing CW directly through his cell."

"Still."

I add a stop at Lincoln and Peterson to my list of things to do before going to Midway Airport.

"Some scuttlebutt you've missed," he says, his voice doing a little jig.

"Yeah? What're you waiting for, a press conference? Give."

"The Prick and Caitlyn? Engaged."

"No shit?"

Although I know from Koz's descriptions and photos that his daughter is an adult, what I picture is a teenager he brought to one of our department picnics back when I was a rookie. Ten years ago. "So she's what, in her twenties?"

"Twenty-seven. Works as a lawyer in a big firm downtown. My source says she's pressuring Koz to groom the Prick for lieutenant to replace him after retirement. She wants them to be, and I quote, "a power couple.""

"Which explains why Koz wants Carrera to have a successful close on Toby's case. Shit."

"Koz keeps pressuring me to leave the rest of Toby's case to Carrera."

"But you're not, right? I mean, we're working this together."

"I got two orders from him. The first one, and don't shoot the messenger here, is to remind you that you're on suspension and need to bring in your gun and badge ASAP. He's pretty pissed at you."

Three days ago I left the department with my badge and gun. Koz took longer to notice and to call me out about it than I thought he would.

"Can you stall him? Tell him I'm out of town until next week. I'll turn them over as soon as I get back." Asking Abandonato to tell Koz a pretend lie feels odd, since it's actually the truth.

"How about I tell him the truth? Your mother has been attacked at home and you're going to stay with her until she's better."

"Or you can say that," I agree.

This is doubly odd, because Abandonato is going to tell Koz a lie while I pretend it's the truth.

"Thanks for covering for me," I say, hoping to put an end to the subject. At this point I'm so confused that I decide whatever he tells Koz is unimportant. Either way results in the outcome I want—I'm not turning in my badge and gun until I catch CW.

"You said Koz gave you two orders."

"He wants me to focus only on the baby case. It keeps getting deeper."

I want to talk more about Toby but Abandonato's case intrigues me. "How?" I ask.

"Autopsy came back on the baby—kid was drowned, not shaken. Marks on the body show someone with thin hands and long nails. There are bruises, pressure marks on the chest, and eight individual cuts higher up on the shoulders."

I picture a woman's hands holding down a baby's body under water, her long talons curving over the shoulders and biting into soft flesh. "The mother," I say, my voice quieter than usual because I'm almost speechless at the sick visual.

Abandonato grunts his agreement.

"And get this. Crystal leaves her nails long. Totally unaware that these would be evidence. They're holding her at County."

"Along with her brother, Johnny Diamond?" I ask, still shaken at the thought of a mother purposely drowning her own infant.

"No. He's bonded out and busy rounding up the best defense lawyers he can find. For both of them. The boyfriend's still in critical condition but talking. If he dies, the alderman's back in jail with his own murder charge."

I tune my voice to sound like Shirley Temple. "What a nice family."

As nauseated as I feel over Abandonato's case, I savor his responding laugh. I miss our daily bantering. We regularly analyze the worst human behavior we see and manage to understand it some of the time. But even though we catch these sickos, it's not always possible to figure out what drives them to commit murder in the first place.

"What do you have for Crystal's motive?"

"Still working on that. She's in custody based on the evidence. Don't know what brought her to the point of drowning the kid. She was pretty riled when Johnny put her boyfriend in a coma. She's very torn up about him. But not the baby."

"Were they living together?"

"I like the way you think. The boyfriend moved out on her a few weeks ago, hasn't seen Crystal or the baby since. Denies being there on the day she says she left him watching the baby. Guy seems genuinely upset about the drowning. He's living with another woman who got back from New York yesterday. I'm on my way to see her now."

The pieces of Abandonato's weird case reconfigure into a whole, giving me a sudden, grisly possibility for the mother's motivation.

"Crystal kills her own baby to set up her boyfriend for murder, simply because he left her for another woman."

Another grunt from Abandonato. "That *is* how it looks. She's a crazy bitch if it's true. Bet you're glad you're on a break, don't have to deal with this."

"Almost," I say.

We're both quiet for a moment, taking in what has to be the new number one on our Top Ten Worst list.

"So," he says. "Anything new I can take to Koz to make Carrera look like more of an idiot? Wait, is that even possible?"

Now it's my turn to laugh out loud. But I hold back the information about going to Georgia and the possibility of finding Toby's family. If Koz is already going with Carrera's assessment and hanging two murders on the hapless Walter Washington, I still have a lot to do to change his mind. And it has to be unassailable.

"I did get the sketch of CW, thanks for that," I say. "When I showed it to JJ he said CW looks a little like Toby. Makes me think even more there's a connection between those two, family or something. It would explain some kind of motivation, even though I haven't found it yet."

"If anyone can, it's you. I'm at Ms. New Yorker's place. Got to go." He clicks off.

Back in my studio I unearth a backpack for my trip that's larger than the one I use for every day. My cell registers an incoming text. Daphne.

"What happened to mom? Is she ok?"

I explain the break-in and Evie's stubbornness about leaving the back door unlocked.

"Concussion and some stitches. She's gonna be ok."

"I can't come home."

I know my sister wants to help but she started her job only a few months ago. The job market's tight enough for hearing people, even tighter for deaf people. She'd probably lose her job if she asked for a leave of absence. I assure her I can cover things here and keep her updated about Evie.

But after we finish texting, I experience a recurring resentment toward my two sibs. Both are single, both have great jobs in faraway cities, and I'm left here to take care of Mom and Dad.

I shake off my pity party and throw two pairs of jeans in my backpack, unsure of how much to take with me. I figure Marietta is a small town, and if Otha Lee Worthy is still alive it won't take long to find her. If she's dead, my stay will be even shorter. I make sure to pack my notepad and folder with my case notes on Toby, including Rameeka's sketch. During the flight to Georgia, I plan to review everything and write out a timeline with a hypothetical reconstruction of events.

An unidentified thought nags at me, something I'm supposed to do today before leaving for Georgia. I find the napkin with Franki Cramer's scribble and remember I want to check with her about Otha Lee Worthy's exact address. When the young teller comes on the line I identify myself and ask for the address. Franki Cramer speaks in a whisper.

"Can't talk. Boss right here."

Suddenly, her volume increases and she speaks in a polished, professional tone. "Yes, ma'am. Would you like me to send you information about our bank in the mail?...That's fine. Your address please?...1425 Locust Street? And your zip?...So it's in the city. Okay, I have it. Do you have any other questions I can answer at this time?"

I jot down the address in my notepad and flip it shut.

"Thanks, Franki. This is a huge help. Take care."

"You're welcome. Glad I could help." I can hear the smile in her voice.

I finish packing a few toiletries and add a cereal bar, banana, and sunflower seeds for the flight. My cell rings and when I pick it up I notice the battery is almost depleted. Damn. I grab my charger and add it to my backpack as I answer the phone.

"Hello, Detective. This is Rhonda Hartman calling. Rameeka's sister?"

"Yes, hi. What can I do for you, Ms. Hartman?"

"I'm—I need to, well, Rameeka came back to me but she didn't stay. She's gone," she says. Her voice wavers. I wait for more but she doesn't say anything. I'm about to ask for clarification when I hear a muffled sob.

"She—she told me about her friend Kandy and I'm so afraid, Detective. I'm afraid for my little sister's life. But she won't listen to me. I tried to get her to stay and she blew up at me. She thinks I'm trying to control her but I don't want this crazy man to get her." At this statement she breaks down.

I hoist my backpack over my shoulder, lock the front door of my studio and walk down the three flights accompanied by her crying.

"I understand what you're going through," I say. All too well. Thinking about what might've happened to Evie scares the crap out of me even though I'm way more used to this kind of stuff than Rhonda Hartman.

"Ms. Hartman, Rhonda, I'd like to assure you that this creep is not in Chicago, but it's really a guess. A good guess, but, well, understand what I mean? When I saw Rameeka I told her to stay with you, too."

At my words, Rhonda Hartman jumps into overdrive, wailing on the other end. I toss my backpack onto the passenger seat, buckle up, and head west on Devon to catch the expressway at Peterson.

"Ms. Hartman?"

More sobbing.

"You've got to help her! She helped you—she gave you a description of that man. You've got to keep her safe. Please, Detective, please!"

"Listen, there's no way I can help her right now. I'm on my way to Midway to catch a flight to Georgia."

And I don't have the authority to provide even nominal protection to Rameeka while I'm suspended. "What about hiring some muscle to protect your sister?"

"I did in the past but Rameeka gives them the slip, says I'm controlling her. And she knows you, likes you. Besides, you have every reason to keep her safe."

I can see why Rhonda Hartman is a lawyer and I understand her impulse to want to protect her family. But I've got to jump on the leads I'm following, not get caught up in her family drama.

"Look, I can't right now. I'm on my way to the airport and—"

"Take her with you. I'll pay her way. I'll pay you. Anything you need. I've got money. Please get her away from here so that maniac doesn't find her."

The mention of money gets my attention. JJ shelled out a chunk of change for me to go to Georgia and would expect it back within a month, but I'm flat broke. My mortgage and rent are both due in two days. Rameeka needs help and I need money.

Sounds like a win-win all around.

21

Late morning

I hate rationalizing my next move. But Rhonda Hartman's two grand in cash—stowed in my backpack that sits on my car's back seat—goes a long way toward making me feel better about what I'm about to do. The only problem? Rameeka refuses to go along with the program. What a surprise.

"Look, it's only for one or two nights," I tell her. "In Marietta you can chill at the motel, stay in bed and sleep, get rid of that obnoxious cough. I've got a good lead to follow so I'll be out of your way. You'll have *room service,* for chrissakes."

I cross my arms and hug my winter jacket closed to ward off the cold breeze coming in my car window, which is rolled halfway down to talk with Rameeka. She leans against my side of the car and clutches her ample Kate Spade bag to her body, the way a woman would hold a newborn.

"I don't want to get on no airplane. Them things crash all the time, scare me half to death."

"Didn't anybody ever tell you flying is safer than riding in a car?"

She pouts at me in response.

"Rameeka! What the hell is wrong with you?"

I count on my fingers to amplify my points. "One, you're scared shit-less CW's going to come after you. Two, your sister tries to protect you but you turn up your nose at her. Three, *I'm* offering to protect you. And you're only worried about the *airplane*? I don't have time to waste on your bullshit. Get in this car. Right now."

She takes her time but she and Kate Spade get in.

We pull up to the Lincoln Hotel and I tell Rameeka I'll only be a minute. "Lock the doors," I say, a familiar refrain these days.

I walk to the entrance and eye the huge neon light with a large arrow pointing to the hotel. Subtle. The place screams cheap rooms and quick assignations, providing the transience and anonymity sought by hookers and those on the downward slide.

I explain to the desk clerk what I'm looking for. He says he has little computer information he can share.

"You understand what I'm saying, Detective?"

I roll my eyes at the guy. "Yeah, you strive to be discreet with your clientele because this is such a fine establishment."

My sweeping gesture takes in the lobby, not redecorated since its probable opening in the nineteen-fifties.

His doe-shaped eyes narrow in a look of disgust at my sarcasm. Or maybe it's from the smoke curling from the cigar stub clamped in the corner of his flabby mouth. Three days without cigarettes and my sense of smell rebels at the stink.

He shakes his head, withdraws the cigar stub from his mouth and talks to it.

"Naw. You got me all wrong. See, what I'm telling you is these people pay cash, most of 'em. Hold on."

He prints out a short report and hands it to me. The hotel guests in October show only a few who paid by credit card. No one from Georgia or with the initials CW.

"Look at this and tell me if you've ever seen this man." I hand over Rameeka's sketch and the clerk studies it.

"Him? Oh sure, I remember him. Short guy. Built like he spends most of his time in the gym." He glances down at his own considerable belt overhang. "This guy was here for the weekend, that's it. Checked in on Friday and left Monday morning." He hands back the sketch.

"So he didn't pay with a credit card?"

"Naw. He came in and plunked down enough cash to rent the room for a week. He didn't need to use no card. Cash is king," and at this he has the nerve to lean in and wink at me.

I pull back and give him a dirty look. "He register a car?"

The clerk snaps his fingers and pulls out a stack of cards the guests fill out if they park in the hotel's lot. He flips through them and finally extricates one, handing it to me.

A chill runs up my spine as I hold the card CW filled out. But in the space marked *name* he'd written President, and under *address* he'd put 1600 Pennsylvania Ave. The spot for the license plate number holds only an illegible scribble. The card is useless for any hard information, except for possibly establishing CW's whereabouts while in Chicago.

The clerk is happy to hand over the card, which I seal in an evidence bag in the off chance CW's fingerprints might be detectable. I jot down the clerk's name and tell him I'll be in touch.

I return to my car—no Rameeka. But I've been in the hotel for, at most, five minutes. She can't have gone far. Our flight leaves in about three hours. I head west on Peterson and give myself fifteen minutes to find her. Otherwise the two grand goes back to Rhonda. I need that cash.

With fourteen minutes gone I see her sitting on a park bench in a small oasis that serves up one tree and a patch of grass. I pull over, hop out, and go sit next to her.

"I ain't going to no Georgia. Don't want to fly on no airplane." She crosses her arms in a huff and looks away from me.

I want to be sympathetic but there's no time. "I don't know why your sister tries to save your ass. You are the most stubborn person I ever met. Christ!"

Rameeka mumbles something to herself, apparently sassing me back but not loud enough so I can understand her. Her tone is enough.

I look at my watch and feel the pressure of time running out. There's a lot of distance to be covered and I want to get to Marietta, not dink around with this hooker with no self-esteem and lousy social skills. I have to think of something quick or my win-win turns into a lose-lose.

When we pull up to my parents' home Rameeka starts to protest again.

"What? What's wrong now?" I ask.

"You see any black people in this neighborhood? They ain't gonna want me in their house. You gotta be crazy bringing me here."

Point taken.

"Okay, I agree with you on that. But a deal's a deal, Rameeka. Five hundred bucks, cash, if you stay here and keep an eye on things while I'm gone. You promised."

She heaves a big sigh as if this is the hardest task anyone has ever given her. "I want my money now."

"Yeah, and I want to look like JLo. Not happening for either one of us today."

At least she cracks a smile at this.

"Come on, I'll introduce you to my father."

"How I know you got the cash? This car don't look like you got much."

"God, you are the most exasperating person—"

I reach behind me and yank my backpack into the front seat, pull out the envelope Rhonda gave me, open it, and flap the wad of one-hundred-dollar bills in her face.

"Okay? Believe me? Now let's get going. I have a plane to catch."

22

Noon

"You know your mother will never agree to this," this meaning a belligerent hooker with magenta hair staying in the guest bedroom. Or maybe he's annoyed that we showed up without any warning.

"Evie's knocked out with pain pills and won't be awake for another twelve hours," I say. "She should stay in bed anyway, not walk around with a concussion."

JJ gives me his patented patient look but says nothing, meaning I haven't convinced him. Rameeka sits on the couch and watches us sign, her head bobbing back and forth as though JJ and I are involved in a game of catch. I check my phone.

"Look, I have to get to Midway. My plane leaves in less than two hours and I don't have time to argue. R-A-M-E-E-K-A," I spell, making up a sign name for her on the spot—the letter "R" pulled in a downward motion on my lips, initializing the sign for red.

"Rameeka is staying here until I get back from Georgia. I don't want you and Evie to be alone after what happened." As good a reason as any.

"Can't FA watch our house while you're gone?"

My father: the master of logic and common sense. Under ordinary circumstances my partner would be happy to volunteer for such duty. But Felice Abandonato doesn't know I'm going out of town to follow a lead I withheld from him. He thinks I'm staying with my elderly, vulnerable parents like any good daughter would, especially a cop daughter.

"FA is out of town too. He's on a big case."

Now I've lied twice to my father in less than twenty-four hours. And it's true that the more you do it, the easier it gets.

"Please, please do this for me. Rameeka is in danger and needs to hide here while I'm gone. This is really to help her."

JJ straightens up at this. *"She's in danger? Can't her own family help her?"*

Before I can answer he follows up with another question, his face projecting alarm.

"Are we going to be in danger because of her?"

I put my hands on his shoulders and give a quick squeeze. *"No. No. It's a long story. Remember the picture of the man I showed you? The one who killed Toby?"* I add a quick description of CW and JJ nods.

"He might be looking for her," I slide my eyes toward Rameeka, trying to be subtle about the fact that we're talking about her. JJ raises his eyebrows slightly in affirmation.

"But he'll be looking for her over by ARC. There's no way he'll know she's here."

JJ's entire demeanor changes. He stands up straight and puffs his chest out a bit. The worried look on his face dissolves and he smiles.

"She can stay here, no problem. I'll explain it to your mother. Go. Go to the airport. I'll watch your friend."

We hug. Then JJ beckons Rameeka to follow him to where she'll be staying in the guest bedroom at the back of the house.

Protecting the castle.

23

Late afternoon

It's near dinnertime by the time my flight lands. I retrieve my rental car and get on the road. The dense traffic around the Atlanta airport gradually thins as I head northwest toward Marietta.

I lower both front windows, allowing the heavy, sweet-smelling air to assault my senses. The countryside is lush and a deeper green than the landscape at home. Birds seem exotic and brightly colored compared to the pervasive gray pigeons in Chicago. I shrug out of my winter jacket, already sweating from the humidity.

I enter the town square and sniff out a doughnut shop. The sweet scent triggers my hunger so I order three double-chocolate doughnuts and a large cup of black coffee.

When I push away the empty plate, I dwell in a bit of self-loathing about how many calories I ingested. But substituting sugar for nicotine right now is preferable to picking up a cigarette. I get a refill on the coffee and show Otha Lee Worthy's address to the teenage boy behind the counter.

"Locust Street? Yes ma'am, not far from here." He gives me directions and even though I bristle at the *ma'am*, I thank him.

Outside the air-conditioned shop I roll up my shirtsleeves, uncomfortable in the lingering heat of the day. The business area quickly becomes residential, and as promised, Otha Lee Worthy's street is not far. However, her address is not among the modest homes I pass. Locust comes to a dead end at a grassy hill at least twenty feet high.

I pull over, get out of my rental, and approach a woman who is trimming her shrubs.

"Excuse me, can you help me?"

The woman squints at me through the gathering dusk as I extend the piece of paper with the apparent faulty address.

"I'm looking for this address but it seems that Locust dead-ends before it gets to this number." The woman takes the piece of paper and studies it, then smiles.

"Oh, yes. This is further down," she points in the direction of the hill where the street dead-ends. "But you can't get there from here. The city dump is right past this landfill and then Locust picks up again."

I find the woman's soft southern drawl oddly comforting as she describes how to circumvent the landfill and the dump. I thank her, turn the rental around, and pull away.

Locust does appear again on the wrong side of the landfill, but no grassy hill blocks the view of a sprawling trash heap. A rampant stink blooms through my open windows, the result of a downwind position from the dump. Ripe. Seagulls scavenge the mess.

If the location and the house itself are any indication, it's obvious Otha Lee Worthy is poor. The one-story wooden structure topped with a tin roof is little more than a shack. A stunted crabapple tree sits alone in a cramped front yard that sprouts nothing more than an overgrown patch of weeds and a little grass.

Above the rusty door-knocker hangs a black wreath. Although I've never seen anything similar, I realize it can represent only one thing and my mood takes a dive.

I tap the wooden door with my knuckles and wait, but when nothing happens I resort to the loud metal rapper. At last the front door opens. I look down at the face of an elderly black woman with short-cropped white hair. Small pearl earrings dot her ear lobes.

"Good evening. May I help you?" She smiles up at me.

"Yes, ma'am. I'm looking for Otha Lee Worthy. Would that happen to be you?" She flicks on the porch light and takes my proffered piece of paper with a hand that trembles.

"Oh, goodness no. Sister Otha has passed to the great beyond. She is with Jesus now." The woman nods her head with conviction and hands the paper back to me.

I sigh. All my recent leads have come to nothing. I hoped finding Otha Lee Worthy would provide the major missing piece I need to solve Toby's murder.

"Oh, I see. I'm sorry for your loss, Miss...?"

"I am Miss Virginia Paylor, a long-time friend. And do not be sorry, young lady. Sister Otha is rejoicing with the Lord. She knows all and sees all and it is surely a glorious new day."

Her deep brown eyes gleam with a patina of tears as she gazes past my shoulder toward the night sky. I have to remember that I'm in the south, where religion wears its heart on its sleeve and Jesus is alive and well.

She turns her attention back to me. "And who might you be, child?"

"My name is Detective Dana Demeter. I'm from Chicago." I show the old woman my badge. "I was really hoping to talk with Ms. Worthy. When did she die?"

"Bless her soul, she passed two days ago."

I swear silently. So close. "Would you be able to answer a few questions for me about her and her family?"

The old woman looks up at me with the first hint of suspicion. "Well now, that depends on why and what you want to know. You say you're from up north, all the way from Chicago?"

I take one step back, acutely aware my frame and bulk crowd the woman. I slouch in an effort to appear as non-threatening as possible.

"Yes, ma'am. I'm here trying to solve a murder that happened in our city and I think may be connected to Ms. Worthy. What I mean is I think it involves someone she was related to. We know only his first name. Toby. He's the one who was murdered."

I unhook my backpack and begin to search for the folder with Toby's picture.

"No!"

The denial escapes the woman's lips, and her face shifts from suspicious to shock and ends with sad. She looks down at the neat mound of waxy begonias on the right side of the front stoop and slowly shakes her head.

"Dear Lord, help me to understand Your ways. First Otha and now Toby. Both gone. My, my, my." She raises her face to look at me again. "And you're looking into this, trying to find out who killed young Toby?"

"*Young* Toby? I'm not sure—"

"I was there when he was born. In this very house." She turns and points. "I haven't seen him since he left at eighteen so forgive me, I'll always hold him in my mind at that age." She shakes her head again.

"Yes, ma'am."

Miss Paylor dabs a hankie to her forehead. "Goodness, where are my manners? Come in, come in, Detective." She reaches up and guides me by the arm into the warm house, closing the door behind us.

Once inside she ushers me to an old, overstuffed sofa.

"Can I get you something? A coke?"

"A Coke would be great," I say.

"Let's see, there's orange, lemon-lime, and Co-cola," she says. "Oh, and sweet tea, of course."

Unsure of why Coke comes in different flavors, I settle for something I know. Miss Paylor returns and places a glass of iced tea, with a sprig of mint, on the table beside me and sits down. I pull out my notepad.

"Toby is related to Ms. Worthy, then?"

"Yes, child, yes. He was her son."

"And what is your relation to Ms. Worthy, if I might ask?"

"We are—were—old, old friends. We growed up together our whole lives right here in Marietta," her accent rendering it as "May-retta."

"My mother taught a bunch of us children at home because we were kept out of the white schools in those days. Otha Lee and I were the only girls in a group of ten and we became fast friends. Let's see. I'm seventy-six, so that was—good lord—seventy years ago." She says this last part in a rush, wonderment in her voice.

I take a long drink of tea, grateful for its cold bite and sugary sweetness. "Did Ms. Worthy have any family other than Toby?"

Miss Paylor nods her head, smiling. "Oh my, yes. Otha's mother had five children altogether, but two died in childbirth. The two oldest boys left for the north around the time of the Second World War, and Miss Olivia—that was Otha's mother—never heard from them again. It pained her so. After the war Otha wanted to go north too, see what she could do there. She had dreams of becoming a nurse, and she could have, too. She was a smart, smart woman. But Miss Olivia wouldn't let her last remaining child leave out of here, so Otha stayed."

She breaks off her story when she spies my empty glass. "Would you like some more tea, dear?"

I smile and hand over the glass.

While Miss Paylor retrieves the tea I lean back into the dusty couch, yellowed doilies gracing the armrests, and gaze around the room. It's not unlike my studio apartment, one large room serving as both living and dining room with a single narrow bed tucked into one corner.

A picture frame on the table next to the bed draws my attention. I cross over to the table. A black and white photo depicts two boys around age ten in blue jeans, bottom cuffs rolled up, bare chests thrust out, each with an arm hooked around the other's neck. Each clutches a bamboo fishing pole that bookends their pose. They look enough alike to be twins.

I study the two faces and realize I know at least one of them. Toby's smile and bright eyes look back at me from a distant summer when it might have been easier to be deaf, his only challenge catching more fish in a nearby river than his friend in the photo. I cover the top half of the picture with my hand and recognize it as the one found torn to pieces at the crime scene. Miss Paylor appears from a separate room I assume is the kitchen and hands me iced tea in exchange for the photo.

"This is Toby." She points to the grinning boy, confirming my thoughts. "He was her boy, her only natural child. He meant every-thing to her, everything." She indicates the other boy in the picture. "That's him with his cousin Charles. Those two were thick as thieves."

My stomach flutters with excitement hearing the name Charles. CW. Charles Worthy, Toby's cousin. Miss Paylor gives the framed picture a brief hug and gently returns it to the table.

"Those two grew up together, but little Toby had a reserve of patience, not like his cousin Charles. That boy was quick to anger, mm-hmm. Still is. I pray for him, you know, to quiet his temper and learn the way of the peace-makers."

I follow her back to the couch.

"I'm confused. Charles is Toby's *cousin*?"

"Mm-hmm, yes ma'am." The old woman stops and thinks for a moment. "Well, we *say* cousin. But Charles is the son of Otha's dear cousin, Ofelia."

I smile at the pattern I'm starting to see in the Worthy women's names. "So second cousins, then."

Miss Paylor nods. "Charles' mother died when he was ten, so Otha kept him and raised him up like her own, poor as she was."

"No fathers?" I ask.

"None that stuck around. One week after Ofelia bore Charles, his father lit out of town. So she moved in with Otha and her Aunt Olivia here," she gestures around the room, "only on a temporary basis, you see, to get help with the baby. But they both ended up staying."

I look at the main room and imagine how crowded it would be with three women and a baby sharing the space. "Was Toby born yet?"

Miss Paylor's face lights up. "He came along less than a year after Ofelia moved in here with Charles. Miss Olivia was livid with Otha for having a baby at eighteen—and so ashamed! It's not like today, women having babies whenever they want and not needing a husband." She stops and crosses her arms.

"Listen to me talk," she continues. "Husband? From what I understand, these days they don't even need a *man*. Clinics supplying women with the, uh, the stuff to become a mother. But Miss Olivia didn't approve of that nonsense, and I must say neither do I. My goodness, no."

"So who was Toby's father?"

The old woman looks directly into my eyes and produces a wide smile. "Well now, that's a question kept the gossips in this town jawing for a long, long time." Her eyes shift toward the ceiling and take on a glazed appearance.

I watch her in silence, drink more tea, and wonder if she's going to answer my question. The craving for a cigarette appears out of nowhere. I shift around, uncomfortable with her delay and eager to get the information I want.

"Miss Paylor? Who was Toby's father?"

The old woman's eyes focus on me. "What's that, child? Oh, Toby's father? We never knew for sure, but I suspect it might could be a young man I was sweet on. But he only had eyes for Otha. She never told anyone if he was the father but she never had any other suitors, either. Three months before Toby came along, he up and left town and headed north, like her older brothers."

"I'm curious about how Toby got to Chicago. Why did he leave Marietta?"

She gives no notice of hearing my question.

"He wanted to marry her, too! Begged her!"

Miss Paylor unclasps one pearl earring and holds it in her hand, tugging repeatedly on the freed earlobe.

"He kept after her for six months until Otha refused to see him anymore. She would not leave the house. She broke that man's heart. What else could he do but leave town?"

I sink lower in the couch, wanting to extricate myself from the woman's prolonged reverie so we can get to Charles Worthy and his present whereabouts. But I admit Toby's history intrigues me.

"So baby Toby came along—not quite full term—and Miss Olivia kept her daughter right here at home, right where she wanted her."

Miss Paylor undoes the other earring and holds both in one hand, worrying them between her fingers and thumb.

"Otha loved her baby boy. But she told me many times she felt trapped here and wanted out to see the world when more opportunities come along for folks like us."

I watch Miss Paylor fumble a bit with the earrings as she pours them from one hand to the other and back.

"You know Toby was deaf and dumb?" she asks.

I wince and shake my head at the phrase still used by so many people who don't think twice about the implied slur. Miss Paylor mistakes my head-shake for a negative answer to her question.

"Prob'ly born that way but we didn't know it until he got past the time young ones 'posed to be talking. They didn't allow him at school with the normal children so Otha kept him with her. She did her best with him but he was never quite right that way. We all knew it. Otha worked long days at odd jobs—taking in laundry, altering clothes, straightening hair for women in our community—but nobody minded little Toby tagging along and helpin' Otha while she worked."

I now understand Toby's strong work ethic, forged at the knee of his ever-toiling mother. But I still don't see how he ended up in Chicago, especially since his mother seemed so protective. I begin to broach the subject again but Miss Paylor speaks before I have a chance.

"Otha didn't want her son to miss out on the world the way she had. She wanted him to go to school, learn some kind of trade, get a real job and support himself, not be stuck in pick-up jobs the rest of his life. He grew up so fast before our very eyes, a baby one day and a young man the next. She worried most about what would happen to Toby when she passed. Lord, what would he do when he was old enough to start thinking about girls?"

She spreads her hands out in front of her.

"No other deaf and dumb children around here, you see."

I flinch again. "So she sent him to Chicago because he was the only *deaf* person here? So he could be with other *deaf* people?" I stress the single word, hoping Miss Paylor will pick up on my disgruntlement with her use of the word "dumb."

Miss Paylor shakes her head. "No, child. Otha didn't send Toby to Chicago. At least, not directly. She did have a cousin who lived in Delavan, Wisconsin, and he knew about Toby being deaf and dumb and—"

"*Deaf*," I interrupt. "Just deaf. Okay Miss Paylor? Please don't say that anymore, deaf and dumb. That's very old fashioned and insulting to deaf people. They're not dumb. Please, only use deaf."

The old woman gazes at the pearl earrings in her hand and slowly pushes each one back into the tiny holes in her earlobes, then attaches each backing. She bows her head formally at me.

"Well, bless your heart. I do apologize," she says, her manner stiff. "I had no idea. It's what we always said."

I wave my hand in a small, downward motion to dismiss my objection and encourage her to continue her narrative.

"Where was I, now?"

"Delavan, Wisconsin. A cousin there knew Toby was deaf?"

"Yes, yes, that's right. He wrote to Otha about the school there, arranged for Toby to be admitted and live there, work part of the time and learn some of the hand language of the deaf and—uh—the deaf people use."

I grin at her.

"It was perfect. Otha was so excited Toby would have an opportunity away from a solitary life here in Marietta, something more than living hand to mouth. He was eighteen when he got on that Greyhound Bus with only his rucksack and enough food for the twenty-four-hour trip. She made sure the driver knew Toby 'posed to meet her cousin in Delavan."

"But he didn't get there, did he? Somehow he ended up in Chicago instead."

Miss Paylor nods. "Mm-hmm, that's a fact. We found out later the bus driver got sick at the Chicago stop and another driver took over. Most likely Toby left the bus and wandered off. When he didn't show up in Delavan, Otha's cousin sent her a telegram—she was too poor to have a telephone. Otha was mighty heartsick not knowing what happened to her boy. She had our sheriff call *you* folks," she nods at me, "to try to find him, but nothing came of it."

And I know what happened after that: Heaven on Earth Mission sent Toby to ARC and they housed him in their group home, putting him to work where he and JJ met. This triggers another question.

"When exactly is Toby's birthday?"

"July first. A summer baby. Every year we celebrated with a trip to the Chattahoochee River where the two boys," she points to the picture on the table, "went fishin' and swimmin.' Then we had us a picnic supper."

She clasps her hands and closes her eyes. "You know, we were dirt poor, not a nickel to spare, but I think about those days and feel happy. We enjoyed simply being on God's earth."

I quickly peg Toby's age at fifty-five, based on his arrival at Heaven on Earth Mission thirty-seven years ago.

Drinking my sweet tea I consider the woman's wise-hearted words in silence, happy that JJ's accidental gift to Toby for his birthday resembled what he enjoyed as a child. It was as if his finding Lake Michigan righted some sort of cosmic imbalance for the lost man in a strange city. And I re-experience some shame for how my sibs and I made fun of Toby when we were young.

Miss Paylor opens her tired eyes.

"Otha blamed herself when Toby got lost. She wanted him to have what she couldn't, going to school and such, and instead he disappeared. When Toby sent his first letter with money in it, Otha was like to die!"

Her hands land in a soft pat on her knees and then raise up to sound a single clap, emphasizing her excitement.

"She was so happy to know he was even alive. And the money meant Toby had a job, like she hoped. He sent her a money order every month. From Chicago! You could count on it. But Otha never spent that money. No. She had me collect her mail and deposit Toby's money in the bank, saving it for him. That Living Trust was our little secret."

I sit up straight hearing this. Toby had worked for over forty years. His initial money orders were probably small, not nearly as much as those later, but still. With the consistency of his mailings and bank interest accruing over almost forty years' time, Otha Lee Worthy must have built up a significant amount of cash for her son.

Then something else occurs to me. What if, when Otha died, she left CW out of the inheritance? That, at last, suggests what might have provoked CW to attack Toby—anger and greed. I jot down this main idea in my notes.

"How was Otha sure Toby would get the money she'd saved? I mean, did she know where he was in Chicago?"

Miss Paylor dips her head and presses her hand to her forehead. "Dear Otha. She was in poor health and preparing to meet the Lord. I moved in with her early this year to tend to her last days. She gave Charles the task of finding Toby in Chicago."

An unfortunate choice.

"Otha had to give Charles a bit of a carrot to get him to go."

"I'm sorry, did you say carrot?"

"Yes. An incentive. Charles balked a bit at Otha's request. So she gave him a thousand dollars for his trouble, but he became angry at her for some reason."

A thousand dollars isn't exactly chump change, though. Could CW have known about the Trust?

"Why do you think Charles got angry?"

"Puzzling, isn't it? Like I told you before, Charles has a quick temper. Perhaps he didn't want to take her money because of his pride. And Otha was so poor. Charles supported his auntie financially when she became too disabled to work. He lived here until his job was transferred to the U. S. of A. postal service in Atlanta."

P. O., Atlanta, goes in my notes, my hand shaking with excitement about nailing down CW's details. "And the Living Trust was only for Toby?"

"Yes, of course. It was his money, wasn't it? And Charles doesn't need it. He has a good job. I sat right here when Otha made arrangements with him to go to Chicago."

"Is it possible Charles could've seen Toby's letters, known about the money he sent Otha? I mean, he worked at the post office, right?"

"That's a fact, but no, Charles doesn't deliver mail. He's a handler—drives all over the county gathering mail from post boxes or people's homes. He's not tall but my, he is strong. Miss Otha had me collect her mail every day directly from the post office in town and bring it to her."

"And you would deposit Toby's check in the bank every month? Charles didn't know about it?"

"As I said, Otha trusted me. It was our secret."

She gets up and retrieves her purse from the kitchen counter. She pulls a paper from within and hands it to me. It is a short letter from the First Bank of Marietta stating that Otha Lee Worthy and W. Lee Nelson are co-trustees of a Living Trust. Toby Worthy is listed as beneficiary, followed by the number of the account.

"From what I understand, Otha made our sheriff the co-trustee to handle matters if she passed before Charles found Toby."

"The sheriff?"

"Oh, she's a distant cousin to Otha but she passes for white." Her eyes twinkle. "There's a lot of cream in her coffee, yes there is."

I get permission to keep the letter until I can track down the sheriff, and I'm pretty sure I know the answer to my next question.

"Who gets the money if the beneficiary dies?"

"I don't know, child. Otha gave me that letter to hold onto until Charles returned with Toby, but now," the old woman's voice quavers, "I am so grateful Otha did not live to know what a terrible thing happened to her boy. Thank you, Jesus." She clasps and unclasps her hands.

And if CW is the beneficiary of Toby's inheritance, like I think he is, Otha didn't have to experience that particular grief, either.

"Where is Charles, Miss Paylor? Have you heard from him?"

"No, nothing yet. He left here, let me think, almost two weeks ago. Yes. Otha died exactly ten days after Charles left. Oh, he'll be so upset about this family news. First his auntie, and now Toby."

I make a noncommittal noise at her statement. So it took CW a week to find Toby before he murdered him. Assuming he's been in Chicago or on the road for another week, I wonder when he will return to Marietta to "report" to his auntie. I get CW's Atlanta address from Miss Paylor and add it to my notes, flip my notepad shut and paper-clip the folded letter to it.

"You've been a tremendous help, Miss Paylor. I appreciate your time." I hold up my glass, empty for the second time. "And the tea."

"Anytime, child, anytime. I hope you catch the godless person what did this."

"That's my only goal right now. One more thing. When do you expect Charles to come back?"

"I have no idea. Otha had only the name of Toby's bank to give Charles as a starting place for his search. And Chicago is such a large city."

"I'll be here in Marietta for at least another day. If Charles does show up, would you call me?" I hand her a business card and look around the room. "Oh. You still don't have a phone here?"

"Otha didn't. But I'm a little more modern." She pulls a cell phone out of her purse. "At my age, you never know when you might need to call someone for help."

"You don't happen to have Charles' number do you?"

She shakes her head. "Until Otha passed I didn't realize I had no way to contact him. I told myself, Virginia, you've got to keep up or this world is going to rush right by you. That's when I purchased this phone." She holds it up for me to admire. "But I don't have anyone's number in it yet. Would you show an old woman how to store one in this contraption? How about your phone number?"

I take the phone and fiddle with the menu for a minute to understand what to do, then show her how to store and save my number. As I hand her the phone, I caution her not to say anything about my visit if she hears from Charles or even to let on that she knows Toby is dead. She immediately understands the implication.

"Surely Charles isn't a suspect, Detective?"

"Unfortunately, everyone who knew Toby is under suspicion, which is why I have to talk to them all. It helps me if people's answers are spontaneous."

She nods her understanding and promises me she will call when or if Charles shows up.

Having spent over an hour in Otha Lee Worthy's dimly lit and stuffy home I feel relieved to sit in my car, windows rolled down, and look at a sky full of stars.

I desperately want to smoke. I want the menthol drug deep in my lungs while I consider what I learned from Miss Paylor. Today marks almost three full days since I had a cigarette, but I don't feel proud of myself, only pissed off that three days of deprivation seem paltry and pathetic. I stuff two pieces of gum in my mouth and make it a priority to pick up more sunflower seeds in town tomorrow, having demolished my stash on the plane ride here.

I study the surrounding area with a critical eye. The odiferous dump in the background is the only "development" in this area. There are no other homes save Otha's tin-roof shack.

Toby's mother had lived in abject poverty, yet she banked every penny he'd sent her in the hope she would give him a better life than she'd experienced. I could never be the selfless mother she was, but I understand the impulse. Like Miss Paylor, I'm relieved Otha had not lived to learn of the death of her son. Nor would she have to live with the tragic irony that the money she'd saved for him ultimately caused his death.

I pull out my cell phone, my instinct to call Abandonato and update him, but the screen shows no service available.

24

Sunday morning

Instead of a local police department, Marietta's citizens fall under the jurisdiction of the county sheriff's office, which covers a large part of northeast Georgia. Sheriff W. Lee Nelson is out of town and won't be back in her office until Monday morning. But when I call her she agrees to meet me for an early breakfast so I can explain my mission. I have to cool my heels until tomorrow.

The motel I checked into last night is situated on the edge of town, offering "conditioned air" and "in-room phones." I briefly think about Rameeka staying here and laugh when I remember I promised her room service. She's definitely better off at my parents' house. At least my meager room offers more privacy than I expected. The motel consists of thirteen separate units in all, spread out in a lazy, horse-shoe shape.

I spend most of the morning in my hut watching old movies on cable. Twice I start to call Abandonato and twice I disconnect. The reality that CW isn't in Marietta, at least as far as I know, puts a damper on the excitement I felt yesterday at being so close to nabbing him. And I have no clue as to when he'll return. I'm also concerned about Rameeka and whether CW is still prowling around Chicago. I want to talk to my partner and get his ideas about what he would do in my shoes. But I hesitate discussing CW with Abandonato yet, because what I have is a good start but nothing to brag about—like my not smoking for three measly days.

After a lukewarm shower, I throw on jeans and a fleece top. While I down a cup of instant coffee, I check my phone and find Abandonato sent me an email with Carrera's report attached, as promised. But when I try to open the attachment it doesn't budge.

Outside, I cross the expanse of grass between my unit and the one housing the motel lobby. Inside, a kid behind the desk is working on his laptop.

"Excuse me. I don't suppose this place is big enough to have some kind of business center for the guests?"

He grins at me. "No, ma'am. But we do have wi-fi, if that's any help."

"It is, but I can't get an attachment to open on my phone."

I give his Mac a pointed look but he doesn't take the hint and returns to what he's working on. I clear my throat and he looks up.

"Five bucks for five minutes so I can try to open this attachment?"

"Ten bucks for as long as you need and you got a deal." He grin is wider this time.

I pull out my wallet, hand over the money, and he passes the laptop to me. "I see big things in your future."

"Yes, ma'am." At least he's polite while he rips me off.

I settle in at one of the small tables used for the gratis continental breakfast the motel serves—packaged muffins and more instant coffee—and hop online. The attachment opens with no trouble and I ask the kid if my ten bucks includes printing something. He allows how it does. I print out the report and return the computer.

I make a lunch run to a Burger King about a mile up the road from the motel. As I jog from the car back to my one-room cabin, a sudden cloudburst drenches me. When I get inside, the soggy sack carrying my lunch begins to rip open but I catch it in time and lay the Whopper and fries on the desk. My effort to eat healthier will have to wait until I get back home.

I start to strip out of my wet clothes when my cell phone rings. I grab it, hoping it's Miss Paylor with news of CW.

"You got to get me outta here—now. Your mother's an evil woman, all up in my face."

"Rameeka? What's wrong?"

"What's wrong? Ain't you mean what's right? I don't know that hand language but I know a fight when I see one."

"What are you talking about? Who's fighting?"

"Your mother. See, I ate some tomato soup and what's left I'm taking upstairs to her. JJ was busy so I'm doing him a favor."

"Okay. So?" I want to ask her how Evie's doing but calming down Rameeka needs to happen first.

"I even put the soup on a nice tray with a spoon and a napkin, some of those salty crackers, too. Sure, 'cause I like 'em crushed up in *my* soup. Thought she might, too."

"You going to tell me how the soup tasted, too? What the hell happened, Rameeka?"

"She screams at me! I go into her room, she rolls over in the bed and sees me and the screaming! Thought I'd have a muthafuckin' heart attack. Tray goes flying, it's raining soup and crackers. I tore outta there. I pass JJ on the stairs and he's going to her room but I didn't stick around for that."

She stops to catch her breath, the recitation of her story amping up in volume.

"Oh, God." I picture large splotches of red soup on Evie's white bedroom carpet.

"So I'm in my room and two minutes later here she comes to my door, trying to talk, waving her hands at me. JJ tryin' to calm her down but she don't listen to his shit. Two 'a them go at each other, so I left outta there."

"What? Where are you? You're supposed to stay with them, Rameeka."

"You shoulda told me your mother don't like black people! She don't talk too good but I know nigger when I hear it. You got to come get me outta here."

I didn't think Evie would even know Rameeka was in the house. The plan was for Rameeka to stay in the guest room on the first floor. With a concussion Evie shouldn't get any farther than shuffling between her bed and the bathroom. My bad luck Rameeka decides to help JJ.

"Listen to me. My mother is sick and should stay in bed. The best way you can help JJ is clean up, do the dishes, stuff like that. Let him take care of Evie."

"Damn right she should stay in bed, getting all up in my face like that."

"Where are you? Did you leave the house?"

No answer.

"Listen Rameeka, we had a deal. You leave the house and no money changes hands. Five hundred bucks waving bye-bye."

I hear a door slam.

"She better not get sassy with me again. Concussion be the least 'a her problems." Rameeka's words are tough but her tone softer.

"Are you—"

"Yeah, yeah. I'm in the house now."

"How's Evie doing?"

"Ain't you listened to one word I said?"

"Okay, okay. She seems to be on the mend. How's JJ treating you?"

"Now there's a person who knows the meaning of respect. Showed me the ABC's so we can spell back an' forth. Kinda fun."

"Good. I'll be back tomorrow but I don't know what time. Could be late, so plan on staying over tomorrow night, too. For sure I'll pick you up Tuesday. Let's say one o'clock."

I hear her sigh but she doesn't argue. We disconnect.

The soggy Whopper and fries are now also cold, so I reheat them in the tiny microwave on top of the room's dresser, then sit down to read Carrera's report.

Pure fiction. Well, almost. It says he interviewed every Campbell House resident when he actually spoke with only one, the day I interpreted for him and Sarah. His tale includes another paltry fact. Washington was stealing from the residents. According to Carrera's logic, Toby discovered the theft, he and Washington fought, and the puny manager overpowered the man of steel.

There's nothing about CW, which Abandonato already mentioned to me. But now I notice there's also nothing about a party or Rameeka or Kandy. Carrera expunged his original report and streamlined it to a truncated version from his imagination.

I can't believe Koz buys this crap. I have to get back to Chicago and straighten him out. Short of hauling in CW, the next best thing I can do is get his DNA so I can prove to Koz he's real, and responsible for both murders.

I text Abandonato to find out if the condoms found at the scene have come back from testing. He responds almost immediately with a negative but then gives me some positive news: the shoebox prints have been ID'd as Toby's and Walter Washington's.

"!!!" I text. "Prick got something right...."

This earns me a smiley face back. "How's Evie?"

I think about how to answer without actually lying to him. "Resting in bed. Keeping eye on her. Gotta go." I click off the app.

So Washington did steal Toby's money, at least what was left after Toby sent his money order and whatever may have been left from previous weeks. And probably after Toby was dead. Though the question remains, when did the manager know Toby was dead? And did he assist CW in the murder?

A more likely scenario is that Washington finds Toby dead after Sarah reported him sick on Monday. He steals the money from the shoebox and retreats to his apartment, unsure of what to do next. Walter Washington knows CW probably killed Toby, but also knows he, too, was in the apartment that night and would be a suspect. A strong suspect.

My fries are cold again but I finish them anyway, then throw away the damp, greasy bags. I crave a cigarette. The long-time habit of smoking while mulling over a problem seems more difficult to shake than the actual addiction to nicotine. Or maybe in addition to.

I drive back to town, scout out some sunflower seeds and a liter of Coke at a local gas station. But as I drive back, cracking and opening the seeds in my mouth and ditching the shells out my window, something Miss Paylor said comes to me. I pull over and call her.

"Yes, hello there. Is that you, Detective? I saw your name come up on my little screen. What a delightful idea to identify the caller before answering." Her voice tinkles with a laugh.

"Yes, it's me, Miss Paylor. How are you?"

"The Lord has given me another day. What can I do for you?"

"I've been doing some work on Toby's case. One of the ways I can tell for sure if Charles was present at the scene is to compare his DNA with some evidence we have."

"Oh, yes. Like on CSI? Miss Otha and I loved that show, loved it. Well, we loved it when William Peterson was on, but after he left we weren't so enthralled. Now Lawrence Fishburne was a fine replacement, but that Ted Danson—"

Shades of Shanti, the manager's fiancée.

"Excuse me, Miss Paylor? Any chance there's something personal that Charles might have left lying around? Like a hairbrush, toothbrush, something like that?"

"Why yes, yes there is. Charles did live here with his auntie until I moved in. When he moved to Atlanta he left behind a small kit of his toiletries for when he visited. I'm sure there's a hairbrush or something like that in there."

"With your permission I'd like to take something back to Chicago for testing. Would you agree to that?"

"If it helps you find who hurt little Toby, by all means. I'm home right now and don't plan on going out any more. I usually retire at nine o'clock and you're welcome to stop by anytime before then."

"I'll be over directly."

"I look forward to your visit, child."

25

Monday morning

By eight-thirty Monday morning the sheriff hasn't shown up for our eight o'clock breakfast. Several cups of coffee slosh around in my stomach, so I signal the waitress to order some food. On her way to my table she stops to talk with a middle-aged woman, whose arrival at the coffee shop is announced by the tipping of a small bell over the door. I watch both women turn toward me, smile in unison and then approach my booth.

"Detective Demeter?" asks the newcomer.

"Yes." I start to stand but she waves me back in my seat.

"I'm so sorry I'm late. I'm Sheriff Nelson. You can call me Wili." She slides into the other side of the booth.

"Dana," I say, shaking her hand.

I hope my surprise at her suburban mom demeanor—slacks and a twin sweater set—doesn't show. I push my ID and badge across the table, which she reads as she orders oatmeal and tea.

"I'll have the bacon and onion omelet," I tell the waitress.

"I wish I could eat like that but my cholesterol is higher than the summer sky," she says, sending my identification back across the Formica table.

My eyebrows inch up. High cholesterol? She looks like she plays tennis every day and never touches anything resembling dessert.

"Your parents country music fans?" I ask.

"How's that?"

"Willie Nelson?"

Sheriff Nelson's steady gaze at me is barely this side of sub-zero.

"Do you have the Northerner's disease, Detective?"

"Sorry?"

"Do you think people from the South are uneducated or ignorant? Does our accent put you in mind of those toothless yahoos from *Deliverance* who raped that white tourist and made him squeal like a pig?"

"My husband is the film buff, not me," I say, and smile in what I hope is an ingratiating manner. I vaguely recall the movie but only from Jimmy's description, not from my personal viewing.

Sheriff Nelson scowls at me. Well, so much for making friends with the natives. My question seems logical to me and not out of line, at least not enough to warrant the response she's given. But I want and need this woman's help and I know how to eat crow.

"Look, can I start over here?"

Her light blue eyes squint at me and then she lifts her chin an inch in my direction, the barest hint of assent.

"It's nice to meet you, Sheriff Nelson. Wili is an interesting name. If I may ask, how'd you come by it?"

"How kind of you to ask, Detective."

Her voice drips butter over elongated vowels.

I smile.

"By the time my parents were in their mid-forties they had given up thinking they could have children. And then I came along. They dubbed me their little princess. Because they were opera buffs I was named after Wilhelmine, the Princess of Prussia, who composed operas in the mid-eighteenth century. Thus, Wili for short."

"And couldn't be further from the country-western singer. My apologies. I see you've gotten the question before."

"If I had the proverbial nickel..."

She lays out her education and experience for me to underscore her point: undergrad in psych and graduate degree in criminal justice, both at the University of Georgia. After ten years in the police department she ran for and became Sheriff four years ago.

"So tell me a little bit more about why you're here, Detective. I understand you're looking for Charles Worthy? Ms. Worthy's nephew?"

I give her a quick synopsis of everything I uncovered so far, ending with the timeline and Kandy's murder.

"Look, I know I don't have a warrant or the authority to extradite Charles Worthy back to Chicago but I'll stake my badge on him being good for both murders."

"What do you want me to do, Dana? Throw cuffs on Charles once he shows up? You know I can't do that. Besides, I don't understand why this Washington's been charged if your evidence against Charles is so damning."

"Do you have incompetent people in your office, Sheriff? Or is it only where I work? The lead detective on Toby's case jumped at the first possible suspect on flimsy circumstantial evidence and didn't investigate any further. Everything I have points to Worthy. Only thing left to do is match his DNA to what we found at the scene."

That and, oh yeah, convince Koz to believe me. I think of CW's hairbrush Miss Paylor gave me last night full of his curly, dark brown hair, now sealed in an evidence bag and enclosed in a box. I can't wait to get it to the lab.

"So again, what exactly do you want me to do?" she asks.

A few strands of hair escape from her up-do. She dunks one finger in her water glass and wipes the errant hairs back in place.

For a split second I envy this woman. I wonder how long it takes her to get ready in the morning. Even though she has ten to fifteen years on me, she's well put together, a shining example of the benefits of high maintenance. Her slacks and peach sweater-set put my worn jeans and t-shirt on notice. And true to Miss Paylor's description, the Sheriff easily passes for a white woman.

"Well," I say, "once Worthy shows up, keep an eye on him? I need to get back to Chicago and convince my lieutenant the wrong guy's been charged and get a warrant for Worthy."

"Fine. But understand that Charles doesn't live in town anymore. He supported his auntie for the past ten years, but she became ill about a year ago and Miss Paylor moved in with her. Charles lives in Atlanta."

I nod at this. "Any connections you can tap into there?"

"I can't guarantee anything but I know a couple of fellas on the force who might do me a favor checking out where he lives."

"That'd be good. But I expect him to come here to report back to Otha Lee Worthy. He doesn't know she's passed, at least I don't think he does. Did you bring your letter?"

The Sheriff pats an expensive looking purse on the seat beside her.

"If you're done," she nods at my plate, "we can go over to the bank. I've already spoken to Grace. She's the manager there and is expecting us."

I pick up the cost of breakfast and we walk to the bank, which turns out to be only a few doors down from the coffee shop. On the way, I voice something that has been bothering me about CW.

"Is there any way Worthy could've known how much money Toby stood to inherit from Otha Worthy?"

"No. Not unless she told him."

"Miss Paylor made it clear that she and Otha kept it a secret from Charles."

"I suppose he could have threatened her in some way. She was a sick old woman, vulnerable."

Anything was possible but it didn't seem like CW would have done so under the circumstances. If he threatened her, it would have alerted Otha to his plan. And that's assuming he knew about the money. From Miss Paylor's description, Otha seemed like a tough old gal who was fiercely protective of her only child. I doubt she would have given up the bank account information to CW.

A woman in a charcoal skirt and white blouse approaches us as we enter the bank. "Morning, Sheriff."

"Good morning, Grace. Beautiful day we're having, isn't it?"

"So beautiful," she positively gushes in response. "I do so love autumn."

She looks at me as though she expects some gushing from me, too. I give her a flat-faced gaze in return, garnering the effect I seek: she leads us to her office.

Once we settle, the sheriff takes out her letter and passes it to the manager. "I'm not familiar with the entire terms of the Living Trust, but I know Ms. Worthy put me in charge if she passed."

The manager scans the letter, nods.

"Yes. I'm sorry for your loss. Ms. Worthy's death certificate arrived this morning from the county coroner. This Trust," she enters a brief spate of data into her desktop computer and reads from the screen, "was established for her son, Toby. He is to receive the entire benefit. As the co-Trustee," she looks at the sheriff, "you simply draw up some papers we can give you, have them notarized, and then Toby can collect his money."

"How long does that process take?" I ask.

"Not long. Generally people choose the Living Trust because it doesn't have to involve the courts or lawyers or probate. I'd say one to two weeks, at the most."

"And how much is the Trust worth?" Sheriff Nelson asks.

"As of the last deposit on October 20th, the Trust was worth $247,000 and change."

The sheriff and I look at each other. She whistles.

I scoot to the edge of my seat, capturing Grace's attention.

"Is there a secondary beneficiary?" I ask.

"Yes. In the event of Toby Worthy's death, Charles Worthy is next in line."

And there it is. About a quarter of a million reasons for CW to murder Toby.

"Would Charles have any way of finding out how much money is in the Trust?" the Sheriff asks.

"No. Not directly from us. Obviously the owner of the account, Miss Otha Lee Worthy, could have told him, or you, Sheriff, as co-Trustee. But otherwise the information is privileged."

"I'm puzzled," I say to Wili, and she shakes her head, too. Now that I know how much money is involved, it is obviously a powerful motive for Toby's murder. But how could it be the motive if Charles had no idea what was in the account? Or even have knowledge of an account, given that Otha and Miss Paylor kept it a secret from him.

"My letter was sealed," says Wili, "to be opened only at Ms. Worthy's death. This is the first I'm hearing about how much she saved. It's astonishing."

"Makes you a believer in compound interest, Sheriff?"

"I'll say."

I grope for something just out of my reach. The last deposit made was on October 20th. I look at the calendar on my phone and see it was a Thursday, possibly Otha's final deposit of Toby's money order—aided by Miss Paylor actually taking it to the bank.

I ask Grace, "How much was the deposit on the twentieth?"

The manager peers at her computer screen. "Four hundred dollars."

Confirms my guess that it's a Toby money order deposit. I turn to Wili.

"I'm stumped at how Charles—"

"And one thousand dollars," Grace interrupts, tapping on her keyboard.

"Which is it?" asks Wili.

"Both. Looks like there was a deposit at nine a.m. when we opened. That's the four hundred. Then a second deposit an hour later. That's the thousand."

And the light shines.

"Sheriff, Otha gave Charles a grand to find Toby. Suppose he also found her letter about the account. It has Toby listed as the beneficiary along with the account number. He deposits the thousand dollars in her account and gets a receipt—"

"—with the account balance printed right on it." Grace completes my sentence and slaps her desk top with both hands.

"Right," I say. "Charles Worthy knew exactly how much Toby stood to inherit."

As Sheriff Nelson and I leave the bank my sense of urgency about finding CW kicks into high gear. I ask Wili to put out an all-points bulletin for him in the state of Georgia.

"Can't do that, Dana. Well, I could but I'm not going to. As compelling as your case is—and please understand, it is compelling—even if I do find him, you said yourself you've got no authority to arrest or extradite him."

I start to interrupt her but she holds up her hand and shakes her head.

"Suppose I do find him and bring him in. I can't hold him more than twenty-four hours. After that, his lawyer's going to poke fun at me and Charles walks. And if he walks, I guarantee he'll be running, even if he is supposed to inherit Miss Otha's money. I know y'all don't have the death penalty in Illinois, but Charles isn't going to risk life in prison."

It pisses me off to admit she's right.

"No. Here's what I propose instead, Dana. You go on back home and do what you have to do, convince your lieutenant, get that warrant. If Charles knows he's going to inherit a quarter of a million dollars, he'll be here soon enough to collect. But I can cause all kinds of delay with the paperwork. You've heard the expression 'shine him on?' That's exactly what I plan on doing."

26

Monday, late afternoon

Back in Chicago I wait at a stoplight where Lincoln, Belmont, and Ashland converge in a three-way conglomeration.

Four young girls pass in front of my Corolla and dash across the street. They each carry a plastic pumpkin holding Halloween loot. Each is dressed as a princess, impossibly pink from head to toe. Or maybe they're channeling Barbie, it's not clear.

But one little girl straggles behind. Her costume consists of blue jeans and a checkered shirt, with a toy gun in a holster. A cowboy hat completes her outfit. Braids trail over each shoulder. Incongruously, she wears sneakers with retractable wheels in the heels. She slides by my windshield clutching an orange plastic bag bulging with candy.

I smile at this laggard, wondering for the umpteenth time what my baby might have looked like, might have become. Would it have been a girl? Would my daughter go along with the giggling pink blur scurrying down the street? Or would she mimic the more independent-minded cowgirl?

One thing for sure, she would not be trick-or-treating with other young girls on the streets of Chicago without Jimmy or me tagging along. Jimmy would have spoiled her and called her Button or some other sappy nickname.

Behind me a car horn blasts. I flinch and punch the accelerator, blinking away sudden hot tears.

At the district office I find Abandonato working the copy machine, duplicating overtime approval sheets and receipts for reimbursement.

"Hey," I say, eyeing him.

He looks tired. Dark stubble peppers his jaw and chin, increasing his haggard appearance.

"How's your mom doing?" he asks.

"I'm not sure. I haven't seen her since I talked to you."

"I thought you were staying with her over the weekend."

"Yeah, no. About that. I've been in Georgia, Marietta to be exact. Following a lead I got from Toby's bank. I found his family, Nuts."

I ignore his initial look of surprise and tell him about my trip, summarizing Miss Paylor's rendition of Otha Lee Worthy's life. Abandonato listens as he continues to work the copier. The moment I finish, the machine stalls and shuts down, a red light flashing on the display screen. He swears and slams his hand on top of the lid.

"What's with the drama?" I ask. "Here, do this."

I step forward and open the front of the copier. "See? Paper jam."

I pull at a large green handle in the machine's guts and slide out a round metal drum, revealing a piece of paper sticking out like a folded fan. I pluck the paper from its trap, close the machine, and punch the start button. It whirs and completes the cycle.

"So I came right here from Midway."

I hold out a small evidence box, sealed and properly annotated, that sat on my lap the entire flight from Georgia to Chicago.

"I got it, Nuts, I got it."

He looks confused for a moment but takes the box.

"Got what?"

"Worthy's DNA. It's in there. Hairbrush full of it. Now we can match him to the evidence at the scene of Toby's murder. Kandy's too, I'm betting. We've got witnesses who can corroborate it and we've got motivation, hundreds of thousands of dollars worth."

Abandonato collects his last copy and paperclips his pile of receipts together, then puts my box on top of the pile and motions with his head for me to follow.

I avoid my former desk chair and sit in one designated for visitors. Abandonato drops into his chair, surveys the large, open squad room, then rolls closer to where I sit. He glances at the box with CW's hairbrush and back at me. His bloodshot eyes look pained.

"Look, Dane. I thought I was pretty clear with you last time we talked. Koz really is done with this."

"I know what you said, but you also told me if I got some DNA evidence to tie Worthy to the scene that would open it up again."

I hear my voice hit a higher register and I sound shrill. I don't want to argue with my partner but I do want him to acknowledge the solid evidence I now have to put Worthy away for murder. I take in Abandonato's exceedingly tired appearance and realize this must be why he doesn't get angry at me for lying to him. After a deep breath I start again.

"You had any sleep since we talked? You look like shit."

"Thanks for noticing." He rubs his hand over his eyes. "The charge against our pal Johnny Diamond has been upgraded to murder. The boyfriend died late last night."

"You've been up all night."

He nods. "The alderman skipped bail and so far we've got nothing. I'm going to catch some sleep and be back in about four hours to work on it some more."

He hands me today's *Sun Times*. The banner headline screams about the missing alderman, Johnny Diamond, with a subheading naming Koz as the bungler of the investigation. I can guess how he's taking it. Before I can ask, Abandonato anticipates my next question.

"And no, I didn't talk to Washington about stealing Toby's money. It's probably the way we figured already and it doesn't amount to anything anyway."

My partner sits forward in his chair, takes CW's box from his desk and hands it back to me.

"Take this. I can't do anything with it. Koz says this is closed, Dane. Washington's taking the rap for Toby's murder."

I try to keep my thwarted expectation from showing, but I'm both astounded and disbelieving that Abandonato would give up.

"But what about Kandy?"

Abandonato shakes his head. "The only evidence tying her to Washington is the steak knife—no prints. The other trace, the semen, doesn't match his and the charge got tossed. Her case stays with the district that found her, not us."

"Even more reason to get this analyzed." I shake the box. "I know it'll match the trace they found on Kandy."

I set the box on my lap and bite my lip. Gazing at the once-familiar open room from the odd angle of the visitor's chair heightens my sense of disconnection from my partner and my job. He's moving on without me, involved in other cases and collaring other criminals. I look at him and try one more time.

"What if I take the evidence straight to Koz, right now, tell him everything I found out. Show him why Washington's the wrong guy?"

Abandonato shrugs at me. "You want to do that? Before meeting with him about your suspension in five days? I wouldn't piss him off. Besides, he's downstate at a conference. Won't be back 'til Wednesday."

"Have you talked to him about this?" I hold up the newspaper, nod at the headline.

"I called him when I found out Diamond went AWOL. The story isn't a total surprise. But the mayor's pressuring him to solve it, of course. Doesn't look good when one of your city's trusted servants beats the crap out of someone and they die."

"Mind if I take this?" I fold the paper, ready to put it in my backpack.

"Keep it." He stands and stretches. "I'm going to turn in this paperwork and go home, get some shut-eye. You going out now? I'll walk down with you."

I shake my head as I stand and look around the squad room. "Uh, no. I'm going to hit the john, see a few more people, then get going. I'll catch up with you later, call you. Enjoy your nap."

I sit in one of the bathroom stalls and consider what to do. Abandonato is right about trying to convince Koz to reopen the case. He'd be furious if I second-guess him, especially if it shows he's wrong. My stomach rolls over thinking about our meeting in a few days. I don't want to tell Koz that I decided to grieve the suspension, at least not until I talk it over tomorrow with our union rep, Colin McBride. But I sure as hell don't want to go to the Employee Assistance Program. I didn't drink on the job and the rest of it is nobody's business.

I skim the story about the missing Johnny Diamond and entertain the idea of contacting someone in the media. I could give them a big story about how the Chicago Police Department has charged the wrong guy with Toby's murder and let the real killer go free.

But I dismiss the fantasy, knowing it's fueled by my frustration at the situation. And meeting or no meeting about my suspension, I don't want to make things worse for Koz.

What I do want is Charles Worthy caught and behind bars for a double homicide. But I have no more authority or ability to make that happen than the average citizen on the street.

An involuntary shiver rattles through me. Tomorrow I talk with Colin McBride and by the end of the week make my final decision about my future with the department.

I leave the stall and pitch the newspaper in the trash. When I study my face in the mirror, the extra weight I carry is evident in my face and neck. My features are thicker and a double chin completes the facial echo of Evie's zaftig mother, Grandma Mimi. If she were in my place, she wouldn't take this shit. She'd march straight into Koz's office and challenge him, call him out to compare the evidence and see who is right.

I exit the bathroom and come face-to-face with Alberto Carrera coming out of the men's john. I stop and regard him, the box with CW's hairbrush heavy in my hand. I can smell the light lemon scent of his cologne. A hand dryer in the background shuts off its noisy whine.

I hate the realization that my last chance to catch CW depends on this now-dapper little man, his new wardrobe improving his appearance but not his coarse language or boorish attitude. He made detective not because of any innate skill or intelligence—he failed the qualifying exam five times—but solely because he sucks up to Koz.

"Carrera. I've been looking for you."

"I don't hang out in the chick's crapper, now do I? What do you want, Demeter? I'm busy." He starts walking back toward his desk and I hurry after him.

"Wait—wait. Here, take this." I proffer the box.

He turns to face me. "What is it?" He takes the box.

"It's a DNA sample from Charles Worthy, the man who killed Toby and Kandy. It'll match—"

"Keep it, Demeter," he says, shoving the box back at me. "Washington's in jail for killing the deaf and dumb guy. We got proof from his jizz at the scene. The knife was his too. Slam *dunk*."

He turns his back on me and starts walking again.

"No, wait. This'll match the other condom at the scene. Worthy's built like Toby, all muscle. You know Washington isn't big enough to kill Toby. The more important thing is that *this* guy," I wave the box, "stands to collect almost a quarter mil from Toby's death. Washington's got no motive."

I wait for the words to sink in, hoping somehow he'll consider what I'm telling him.

He stops but doesn't turn to face me. "A quarter mil? Where's a guy like him get dough like that?"

The money has his attention. I walk to his nearby desk and sit, waiting for him to follow. As much as I don't want to share my hard-earned information with this asshole, the larger goal of capturing CW is foremost in my mind.

Carrera eyes me as he sits at his desk. "So what've you got, Demeter? Wow me."

I lay out what my trip to Georgia revealed about Toby's past, and to my surprise and his credit, Carrera listens. As I finish, I think he must realize my findings have made a mockery of his entire case.

But Carrera leans back in his desk chair, chest thrust out and legs spread wide. He pulls a goofy looking face and laughs out loud.

"So this is all you got? What is it with you and Abandonato, always trying to one-up me? He pissed because I told him to fuck off, that I'd solve this case myself without him or you? Well guess what, Demeter? I did solve it and Koz says case closed. And last I heard, Koz is still the boss and you're still on suspension. So get the hell away from me with your DNA."

Carrera draws air quotes around the last word. His gaze covers me from top to toe and then back, smirking when he looks me in the eye. He mimes tilting a cup to his lips.

"You think you got the answer, Demeter? Then go tie one on and celebrate." He turns to his computer and begins to type.

Even as a sharp retort makes its way to my lips, my heart sinks. I feel numb and extremely tired. Convincing the Prick was a desperate move, my last resort, but I gave it a shot. It's clear, even to me, that though I've completed my best work and identified the real murderer, it makes no difference. I can't persuade anyone to consider the sure-fire evidence or motive, leaving Charles Worthy a rich man getting away with murder.

27

Tuesday morning

November has rolled in on a strong wind from the north. My studio is freezing. I have a couple of hours before my meeting with Colin McBride, our union rep, so I head downstairs to find Sandor, hoping he can do something about the lack of heat.

I get only as far as the second floor landing before finding the hallway blocked with boxes stacked floor to ceiling. Two skinny guys wrestle with a couch balanced on the railing and wedged into the wall. I retrace my steps to my studio, cross through my messy room, and exit my back door, leaving via the back stairs.

When I reach the first floor, I knock at the back door of the manager's apartment. Sandor's wife tells me he's gone out front to mulch the bushes before winter closes in.

On my way through the alley to the front, I pass a metal dumpster bumped up against the back of the apartment building. A large green thing, it overflows with the detritus of a life, stuff someone doesn't want to pack here and unpack again in a new place. Piles of clothes drip over the edge and lay scattered around the container's base.

I kick at the pile of clothing and my foot hits something solid. Curious, I bend down to uncover what's beneath the discarded wardrobe. A hand appears, then an arm, and finally the back of a man's torso. I push aside the remaining clothes. His inert body feels warm. I search for the carotid in his neck and find a pulse. A crusty black gash of dried blood creases his forehead and the overwhelming stink of booze and vomit waft up at me. The guy is out cold.

Sandor appears at the end of the alley and walks toward me, gesturing at the garbage overflowing from the dumpster and saying something I can't quite hear. I motion for him to hurry up and come over. When Sandor sees the unconscious man, his hand shoots up to cover his mouth, his eyes large with fear.

"Sandor, call nine-one-one. This guy needs help."

"Yes, miss, yes. Who is this, please? Do you know this man?"

"No. He's some guy who drank too much and passed out. Looks like he hit his head on the dumpster when he went down. Go call nine-one-one, okay? I'll stay here 'til they come."

The Emergency Medical Technicians arrive within fifteen minutes and shove the unconscious man into their wagon. Both EMTs confide that the drunk is well known to them. In the previous week they picked him up twice in this neighborhood—one day passed out on the sidewalk, another day draped across someone's birdbath.

"He's been ticketed for Drunk and Disorderly and has a court date. Not much else we can do but pick him up and let the ER deal with it. Again."

I thank them and turn to climb the three flights up to my studio when I spy Sandor watching from his kitchen window overlooking the alley. Remembering my cold studio I first stop at his place.

When he opens his door to my knock there's a sad smile on his face.

"This is bad, yes? A man who drinks so much he is out of his head?" Sandor takes off his Cubs cap, scratches his balding head and gestures toward the dumpster. "So much mess! I must clean."

I hurry after him as he quick-steps away from me and heads for the dumpster.

"Wait, Sandor. I need to talk with you about my studio."

He continues toward the trash and begins cleaning up the discarded clothing and garbage. I catch up with him and explain the lack of heat. Sandor promises he'll be up within an hour to bleed the radiators.

On my way to meet with Colin McBride I stop at the bank and deposit a thousand from Rhonda's cash and the check from Jimmy for his half of the mortgage, which finally arrived at my new address while I was in Marietta.

Of the remaining thousand from Rhonda, I keep half for Rameeka and the other half to repay JJ's loan. I don't want to be on the hook for owing him money. Already in the bank by direct deposit is my end-of-the-month paycheck from CPD.

So even though my rent, mortgage and assorted bills are covered for October, I feel minimal relief—I'm barely squeaking by. The reality of losing my regular paycheck frightens me.

I arrive in the reception area of the CPD union offices half an hour late for my ten o'clock appointment. Colin McBride leads me back through a maze of cubicles to his tiny office.

"Jeez, Col, can we both fit in here at the same time?"

He laughs. "Well, at least I can close this door and muffle some of the craziness out there."

He opens a folding chair and places it next to his desk so I face him. Two filing cabinets scarcely fit in the same room. A small tray table with a pot of white flowers sits in front of a solitary window to his left. Outside, a pigeon flutters onto the windowsill.

I sit and apologize for being late. "I've been working on a murder case —a friend of my father's—and I got to bed pretty late last night."

He gives me a puzzled look and picks up a file on his desk. "You're working a case? The report says you been on leave with pay since last Thursday."

I explain the situation with Walter Washington being charged and the information I uncovered now pointing to CW.

"I'm only working some threads that have, uh, been left loose. Not working in any official capacity."

"And of course you're passing the info you've uncovered to the lead detective?" he asks, perusing my file.

Until yesterday I would've answered Colin's question with a lie, but since spilling everything to the Prick, my answer is the simple truth.

"You bet."

Colin McBride nods absently, seeming more intent on my file than my answer. Finally, he closes the folder and lays it on his desk, then looks directly at me.

"So. You're here for two reasons. First, you're out of compliance with the new regs regarding weight limits for officers. Then there's the more serious issue of having a measurable blood alcohol level while on the job."

"Jim, that's a load of crap. I didn't drink *on* the job. I only had a little—"

He holds up his hand to stop my harangue. "Look. I'm not here to judge whether or not these are legitimate charges. I'm here to advise you on what we can do—if anything—to support you in the process."

I shift in my chair, not meeting his gaze.

"Now, on the issue of your weight the new regs are quite clear. You've attended the QuickLoss Clinic for their program and have," he takes a quick peek at the folder, "gained weight instead of losing it."

I feel my face flush at his words, embarrassed at my failure to lose the despised weight. I stare down at my thighs now straining Jimmy's XL sweat pants. I consider telling him about Jimmy, the miscarriage, and finding some solace in food, but remain mute.

"I know Koz is willing to have you on desk duty until your weight lines up with the new regs. Hell Dana, half the department's dealing with being overweight. It's not like you're alone in this."

"You *are* alone when your partner's the world's perfect specimen of a man. For god's sake Col, the guy hates doughnuts." I shake my head, immediately feeling chagrin at my outburst. "Hell, I'm a lousy cop dumping on Abandonato like that."

I start to tell him about the last six months but stop, seeing his eyes glaze over. He's only interested in solving the problem, not what caused it in the first place.

"I have Dr. Hwang's business card. I promise to work with her privately to lose weight now that I flunked the department's weight loss assistance program."

I say this as contritely as I can muster, considering I have no intention of consulting the doctor.

Colin McBride nods and makes a note in the file. "Shoot me an email and let me know when you're going to start with her so I can update this," he says, tapping the folder. "The second issue is more troubling,

Dana. Did you get the results of the Breathalyzer test Koz administered?"

The white flowers in the pot on the tray table to my right arch toward the window in a vain search for sunlight. Outside, the city and sky comingle to form a gray backdrop, which almost camouflages the pigeon as it paces on the window's brief ledge.

"You know it's not good," Colin continues. "You blew a point oh-seven, just under the legal limit. Right there you've violated the department's policy on zero tolerance toward drugs and alcohol on the job. You do have some options, though."

I stop flower gazing and turn my attention back to my rep.

"There are two choices here. The Employee Assistance Provider can assess you for alcohol abuse and th—"

"God, you too, Colin? Look, I don't have a problem with booze. The night before, I was sick and drank some sherry to take the edge off, help me sleep. The next morning there was probably still some in my system and Koz smelled it on me. I wasn't drinking *on* the job and never have. Hell, there are a lot of dicks that start the day at the saloons and keep a steady stream going through the day. I've seen it. What about them?"

He holds up both hands as if to ward off my volley. "The difference is you got caught. I'm not saying it's fair. I'm saying that's the way it is."

"I don't get it, Col. I had booze in my body, yes, I admit that. But I can't make my body get rid of it any faster than it can, right? I'm working a murder case that's close to my family, working it a lot more diligently than that prick Carrera. He's put the wrong guy in jail and charged him with two murders he didn't commit."

My voice has taken on the high-pitched squeak I hate when I get angry.

"I came to work last Wednesday because of this case. I happened to be a little hung over. A *little*. Big deal. Isn't that like being sick? I mean, I come to work when I'm sick and I come to work when I'm a little hung over and for that they think I'm an alkie and want to send me to a shrink? Shit. I think I should get a pat on the back for working under duress."

I take a deep breath and cross my arms over my chest.

He opens his desk drawer and brings out a small glass ashtray grimy with the remnants of old ashes. He places the receptacle between us on the desk and pulls out a cigarette.

"You smoke, right?" He asks this as he lights up and inhales. "Feel free to join me."

"Actually, I've been smoke-free for seven days now."

"Oh, sorry. I'll—" He starts to tamp out his cigarette in the ashtray but I wave him off.

"Enjoy." I pull out a stick of gum.

"Christ, Colin. You *know* me. I wasn't actively drinking on the job and I haven't had a drink since being suspended. Not one drop. Doesn't that count for something?" I rub my sweaty palms on my pants.

"I'm not an alcohol counselor, okay? I can't tell you what constitutes a drinking problem. That's what the EAP is for. Why don't you go have the assessment, talk with them and see what they say? If you don't think you have a problem, you probably don't. If you haven't had a drink for almost a week the assessment should be a breeze. The worst they can do is send you to treatment, right? Rough life. Thirty days off with pay in a nice place where they cook and clean for you."

He draws deep on his cigarette and smoke spills out of his mouth as he chuckles.

I frown, refusing to be cajoled. "You said before that there's two choices, the EAP and what else?"

"Ordinarily, the union is allowed to automatically grieve any suspension. In your case we could do that, however I have to caution you that you would lose your pay status. Right now while you decide what you want to do, Koz has you suspended for ten days *with* pay. If you refuse to go to the EAP and want the union to grieve the suspension, you would stay on suspension but *without* pay for the entire procedure."

He takes a deep drag, the smoke exploding from his nostrils in thick streams. He stubs out the cigarette but a small ember glows on the end and emits a small stream of smoke.

"A couple of things about that, Dana. One, it's a drawn-out process, could take up to six months. Two, I can tell you right now that you will not win. Period." His eyes never waver from my face.

I look down at my lap where my clenched fists are balled on my thighs. He's pushing me toward one thing and one thing only: treatment for alcoholism. He already decided I can't handle booze based on one lousy Breathalyzer test, then joined lockstep with management.

"Let me tell you about a *drunk*, Jim."

I recap the story of the guy passed out by the dumpster behind my building.

"I'm not that guy. And how is it you know I would not win, period?"

"Dana look, I'm not the bad guy here. I'm on your side. The public's attitude right now is anti-drug and that includes the drug alcohol. Too many people being killed in car crashes due to drunk driving, too many gangs shooting innocent victims in their drug wars. People are sick of it. The zero-tolerance policy is exactly what it says. The department is not going to make any exceptions, especially when the grievance process is open to the public."

The small ember on Colin's discarded cigarette butt burns no more, the smoke gone. He puts the ashtray back in his desk drawer.

"I'm sorry, Dana. The wise choice here is to see the EAP and stay on the payroll. If this goes to grievance, you'll lose for sure and be fired."

So that's it. I don't know what else to say to convince Colin to see this my way. My hopelessness morphs into quick anger.

"What I do on my own time is my own business. No one's going to tell me I have to stop drinking. Hell, they're already trying to regulate my eating and smoking, isn't that enough? Screw them, Col. I'll quit drinking when the other juice-heads do."

I cross my legs and avoid Colin's gaze. My attention again is drawn to the plant in front of the window. Tiny, white starburst flowers pepper the slender green stalks.

"You know you don't have to make a decision about this until," he glances in the folder again, "November fifth. That's this coming Saturday. Why don't you take the next four days to think about it? Talk with some people who took the alcohol assessment. I got a few names of co-workers willing to share their EAP experiences. It might help."

My stomach roils with acid.

"Hell, no. I don't want anyone else knowing about this."

How could Colin think I'm a drunk?

"I never, ever drank on the job like those morons who call themselves cops but spend the day cadging free drinks from saloon to saloon, up and down and across this city. Their supervisors never question *their* whereabouts. And what about the cops who shake down gangs for drugs? They snort and smoke whatever they can shake loose, high day after day. How can you associate me with those mopes and losers?"

I stand up abruptly and my chair tips sideways into the small tray table holding the white flowers. I grab at the ceramic flowerpot but it slides away from me and breaks open on the tile floor. The pigeon on the sill startles at the commotion and flaps away.

"Shit. I'm sorry, Col." I bend to pick up the pieces.

"Leave it. Go home and think about your future, Dana. Call me."

28

1:00 p.m.

My stomach growls as I drive to my parents' home to see how Evie's doing and pick up Rameeka. I missed breakfast, and a check of the time shows that lunch is late, too. I try to shake off my anger at Colin McBride but it stays with me, refusing to be assuaged or compartmentalized.

I feel lonely again. Lacking daily contact with my partner feeds my sense of isolation and the knowledge that I now shoulder my problems alone. Abandonato and I used to spend eight hours a day, often much longer, in the pursuit of solving homicides. Along the way we discussed our personal worlds. We shared opinions, solace, and support, and at times challenged each other—deepening our bond during the three years of our partnership. I don't want to talk to strangers about whether or not I should go to an EAP. I want to talk with someone I trust.

But first there's the small matter of rescuing a put-upon prostitute at the home of my parents. And I'm anxious to see how Evie's mending. When I pull up in front of the house Rameeka is sitting on the front steps clutching her overnight bag on her lap. She runs to my car before I'm out of my seatbelt.

She jumps into the passenger seat and makes small shooing motions with her hand.

"Let's go, let's go. I don't want to be stayin' here a second longer."

"Nice to see you, too."

"Yeah, hi and all that. You got my money? I'm ready to get back to it. Don't want no part of that mean little woman any more."

She shakes her head as she glances at the front door of my parents' home, her standout magenta hair seems brighter than the last time I saw her.

"You're talking about my mama, you know." I think teasing will bring her around a bit, but she looks genuinely afraid of Evie.

"Don't care. She put me in mind 'a those, what you call 'em? That animal fights snakes? Grabs ahold and never lets go, shakes and shakes the life outta those muthafuckas. Mongoose, yeah. That's your mama, a mongoose."

I bust out laughing. Rameeka isn't too far off with her description of Evie, especially an angry Evie.

"You've got a choice, Rameeka. I can give you your cash now and you're free to go, or you can wait here in the car until I go check on my parents and talk with them for a few minutes. Then I can give you a ride back."

"Walk to the bus in this neighborhood? Girl, I'd have to be high to even think about doin' that. I'll wait on you. But give me my money so's I can count it while you're gone."

I fork over the cash and go around back to the kitchen door. Locked. I perform a small fist pump, relieved. JJ comes to the door as I'm about to use my key. He looks happy to see me and we hug. I remark on the door being locked.

"I locked it but your mother doesn't like it."

"How's Evie doing?" I gesture at the area on my head corresponding to the area of her stitches.

"Better, better. She's still dizzy and I try to make her stay in bed or at least lie on the couch. But you know your mother. She wants to be up and walking around doing things." He lists a few of Evie's many activities.

Before I can ask if she's in bed, the subject of our conversation swishes into the kitchen, her full-length robe cinched at the waist. I open my arms and engulf her with my hug. Her grip around my middle is strong for a moment but then she pushes me away.

"Don't ever do that again! Never! You can't decide who stays here." She teeters a bit as she yells at me, so I steer her to one of the kitchen chairs. Then JJ and I sit down at the table.

"Looks like you're feeling better," I sign. *"You bawled me out with no problem. But I also notice that the back door is L-O-C-K-E-D."*

I can't resist pushing her nose in it a little bit by slowly fingerspelling the point of contention instead of using the sign.

"What's wrong with you bringing that, that nigger to our home?"

Evie starts crying as she signs the offensive word. JJ scoots his chair close to hers and puts his arms around her. She sobs into his chest.

So here it is again, my mother using the N-word. Granted, she lives in an all-white neighborhood, but she has black friends at church and in many of the deaf social activities she pursues. During my growing up years I never saw her use the demeaning sign.

"Why is she so mad because Rameeka is black?" I ask JJ. I copy the derogatory sign and show my puzzlement at seeing her use it.

"She didn't remember the attacker was a black woman until she saw Rameeka in her room. She thought the woman came back to hurt her again."

Now I really feel awful. When I took Evie to the hospital after finding her crumpled on the floor, she couldn't remember anything about the person who hit her. JJ sees the look on my face and tries to console me, signing with one hand while keeping his other arm around Evie.

"It's not your fault. You were trying to help Rameeka. And I watched out for both of them while you were gone. After your mother gets a little better, she can go to the police and describe who hit her."

JJ helps Evie to her feet and walks her out of the kitchen. I hear the stairs to the second floor creak as they make their way up to the bedroom.

I love my father for his ability to find an up side to a situation when I see only the negative. He's telling me that Rameeka being in their home is a good thing because it jogged Evie's memory about her attacker. Ultimately that might help my mother identify the woman.

I get up from the table, pull out the envelope with the cash for JJ, and start to write a note on it when he comes back into the kitchen. I hand it to him.

"For the airplane ticket. I'll have the money for the motel and car next month."

He takes the money and tosses it on the table. *"Evie wants you to drive us to Toby's funeral."*

This is news. Either the autopsy is scheduled or already done, which means Father Mik can perform the funeral.

"The funeral date is set? When is it?"

"Next Monday," he counts on his fingers, *"the seventh. Ten o'clock."*

"Sure. No problem."

"Sit down, sit down. Tell me about Georgia. What did you find out about Toby?"

I think of Rameeka waiting in the car, so I don't want to drag this out. I also feel crappy about the ongoing lie I maintain with JJ about working on Toby's case, as if I'm still on active duty. I beg off going into any detail about what I know but let JJ know I did find Toby's family.

"CW is his second cousin. We're still looking for him."

As if on cue my cell phone rings, and Wili Nelson's name shows up. I hold up one finger at JJ as I answer.

"Dana? Wili Nelson. Charles Worthy quit his postal job in Atlanta two weeks ago. My guys questioned the neighbors but he hasn't been seen in that time, either. There's no response at his home."

"Okay, thanks. I guess no surprise there. Appreciate the follow-up, Wili. You'll let me know when he blows into town?"

"Sure. How are you coming with the warrant?"

"Still working on it but things are looking good on this end." My facility for telling outright lies keeps improving with practice. "Keep in touch."

I sign off and tell JJ I have to go, not wanting to leave Rameeka waiting any longer. He makes me promise to give him the entire story of Toby's life when I have time.

"But I know you're busy with work. Come over whenever you can and we can talk."

I flash the "I Love You" hand-shape, give him a quick hug, and leave.

As we drive north along Lake Shore Drive, Rameeka notes how the cloudless sky and November sun conspire to render the water a stunning aqua color. "Looks like the water in them magazines about Bahama vacations."

Instead of continuing north I exit downtown and head for Michigan Avenue.

Rameeka starts squawking. "No, no, no! Ain't going to Rhonda's. Turn this car around."

"Rameeka, why don't you stay with your sister? You're homeless!"

"Ain't homeless. Stayin' at the shelters. Might even get me a hotel room with this money." She shakes the envelope I gave her.

I slow to a stop at a red light but before I can argue further she jumps out of my car and disappears into a stream of people on the busy sidewalk.

29

6:00 p.m.

I walk into the Elite to meet Abandonato for dinner. At the counter, a few older men sit on maroon leather stools and watch fake wrestling on TV while nursing draft beers.

I should take a picture with my phone and text it to Colin with this message: "These guys are the alkies." They look like they've been drinking since the middle of the day. I never had a drink that early, for chrissakes.

Chris brings me coffee and a basket of Greek bread, the crust thick with sesame seeds. I order avgolemono—lemon rice soup—and down several pieces of bread while waiting for my partner. He arrives twenty minutes later apologizing for making me wait, but I wave off his excuse.

"No problem. I had my appetizer and now I'm ready for the main course."

I give the waiter my order: two large skewers of souvlaki on a bed of rice, green beans in garlic and tomato puree, and pita bread. Abandonato orders a large Greek salad, dressing on the side and iced tea. I take his pita bread when he tries to send it back.

"Losing the weight, how's that going?" he asks, when I start in on the second pita. His words sting. I put the bread down and push my plate to the side.

"Fuck you, Nuts," I say softly, shaking my head. "This is the first thing I've eaten today."

The last twenty-four hours crowd in on me—Colin McBride, Rameeka, my parents, my unheated studio, the little cowgirl, even the drunk passed out by the dumpster. All of it without nicotine or booze in my system. I feel raw.

"Can we talk about my meeting with Colin, not my diet?"

I pick up the offensive pita bread, fold it in half and take an obnoxiously large bite.

Abandonato holds up his hands in surrender. "Hey, I'm not the one on suspension for not following the regs here."

I gaze at Abandonato while the waiter brings food and refills our drinks. My partner of three years, perfect in every way, doesn't drink alcohol, or smoke, or eat anything unhealthy. He runs marathons, keeps his short frame in top condition, and even gels his hair into submission. This stern self-control typifies his tenacious attitude on the job. Felice Abandonato has the highest solve rate for homicides in the department. I am right behind him in those stats. We collaborate and compete on every case. But god, he can be annoying in his perfection.

Only a few weeks before we began working together, Abandonato's fiancée literally left him at the altar. But he's never talked to me about it. It's easy to imagine how a woman would be put off by a man with such self-control. I love it in him as a detective, though his critical eye on my personal failings is less than welcome.

"Colin McBride wants me to go to the EAP. For an assessment. For drinking."

There. I said it, put it out there for his reaction and analysis. For some reason the shame I felt when I left Col's office resurfaces, along with my misplaced anger at him.

"If I do it—the EAP—I'll still be suspended with pay. But if I decide to grieve it, then no pay. And it could take up to six months."

Abandonato listens. His deep brown eyes focus on me. He says nothing. I don't want to tell him the rest of it, don't want to risk speaking the words aloud for fear of breaking down in a crowded restaurant, don't want to tell him that Colin McBride said I don't stand a chance of winning the grievance, that I would lose my job.

Abandonato moves imperceptibly closer to me and with a slight nod of his head I feel as if he embraced me. My uneasiness drops and I'm able to share the rest of Colin McBride' dire prediction. As I end, I pull an unopened pack of cigarettes from my pocket, purchased on my way over to the Elite.

Abandonato's eyebrows rise when he sees the Kools. He relaxes into the booth's faux leather backing and picks up his glass of water, draining it in one long swallow.

"I think McBride is right. Why not talk with some of the people who've been there, gather information? We're detectives, remember? That's what we do."

I smile at his gentle chiding, grateful he hasn't said anything about the cigarettes.

"Besides, if you're trying to decide whether to choose between being suspended with pay or without, isn't it obvious? Always go with the money."

No surprise he would say this. Abandonato supports his elderly parents, and money worries are second nature. He'll choose the safe thing even if it means giving up something else, something meaning-ful. Abandonato points to the Kools.

"It's an addiction. You stopped, what, three, four days ago? And you're right back at it."

He gestures at the large platter in front of me that holds two bare wooden skewers and a few grains of rice. "Food, nicotine, booze, it's all the same. Couldn't hurt to talk to someone about it."

"I stopped *seven* days ago. And I haven't opened these yet."

I flick the pack with my middle finger, like shooting a marble. I feel worn out hearing my partner echo McBride's advice. My hope fades that he will buttress my own stance. Abandonato's opinion hasn't helped me find a solution, only made me uneasy and anxious again. I don't want to think any more about the job or the suspension or the EAP or the injustice of the Breathalyzer test. And Abandonato's dismissive words have put an end to any further input I want from him. But I nod at him as if considering his counsel.

"Besides," I say. "I'm working Toby's murder. If I go to the EAP and they throw me in treatment, I'm out of the loop for thirty days. You're busy with Johnny and Crystal Diamond, and the Prick's got the wrong guy in jail. Leave him on his own and god only knows who he arrests next."

Abandonato shakes his head. "Collared Johnny Diamond early this morning."

I lean forward.

"You'll love this," says Abandonato. "On a hunch, I staked out his mother's place. She's been making the long drive from Pullman to the county lock-up pretty regularly to visit Crystal. But it turns out mom doesn't have a—"

"Driver's license," I say, finishing his thought. "No shit? *He's* driving her back and forth? The guy's got balls, big ones."

Abandonato leans forward in the booth and laughs. "Driving a car with tinted windows, very dark tinted windows. And he got away with it for a while. So the alderman's in the slammer for beating Crystal's boyfriend to death and Crystal's in the slammer for murdering her own baby to set up her boyfriend for running around on her. You couldn't make this up."

"Yeah. Exactly why I don't watch reality TV. There's a couple of things I want to ask you. JJ told me Toby's funeral is scheduled for next Monday. Is the autopsy done?"

"Don't know. Let me check." He pulls out his cell phone and makes a quick call. "It's scheduled for tomorrow morning at ten. Body will be released to Father Mika...Mika...." He stumbles over the name.

"Miklasevich, which is why most people call him Father Mik. I'll give him a call." I keep the rest of my plan to myself knowing Abandonato's take on Toby's case being closed.

"Did you get anything on the BOLO?" I ask.

"Carrera cancelled it late yesterday. Since he thinks CW doesn't exist, there's no need for a BOLO on a mythical person's car."

"You two still partners?"

Abandonato shakes his head. "Koz is spreading the wealth. The Prick's rotating in for anyone on vacation or leave. Right now I'm on my own."

"That's good, then."

"No. No, it's not. Yes, it's better than tolerating the Prick. But I want *us* back to how we were."

My anger flares at Abandonato for a moment, because it feels like he's abandoning Toby again. I think he doesn't really care about Toby's case—or my suspension, for that matter—only that they affect his comfort level.

"It is what it is," I say, using a bromide I know Abandonato hates. "Look, I wish I could assure you I'll be back soon so we can start solving cases again. But I can't."

I watch Abandonato pick up his paper napkin and begin tearing it in thin strips. I'm leaning heavily toward telling Colin McBride to grieve my case. But when I remind myself that my possible resulting suspension will impact Abandonato the most, my anger at him dissipates. And even though I've been lying to a lot of people lately, I won't lie to Abandonato anymore. But before telling my partner anything, I want to talk to Jimmy and then make my final decision.

The waiter comes by with the check and lays it on Abandonato's side of the table. He picks it up and we head for the cashier. When I try to give him money for my half, he shakes his head.

"On me."

By the time I return from our dinner, available street parking near my studio is non-existent. I park two blocks away. I climb out of my car to make the walk home, but before I can close the driver-side door, my cell rings. "Unknown caller" comes up on the screen.

"Demeter."

"Detective?" Rhonda Hartman's quiet voice on the other end.

"Hi, Ms. Hartman." I assume she's calling about Rameeka and I'm not thrilled to tell her I've no idea of her sister's whereabouts.

"How is everything? Are you still in Georgia with Meeka?"

"Uh, no. I got back late last night. Your sister was afraid to fly, so she stayed with my parents while I was gone. And she was fine there."

"Oh, that's wonderful. She's still with your parents, then?"

I hate to burst her bubble of relief and am tempted to let her think Rameeka is still with JJ and Evie, at least until I can locate that stubborn hooker again and maybe convince her to go back to the Hancock.

"About that, Ms. Hartman. I picked up Rameeka this afternoon and tried to drive her to your place. But she skipped out on me before I could stop her."

The soft voice turns clipped and cold.

"Detective, I paid you two thousand dollars to protect my sister. And you lose her after three days?"

"Hey, I didn't *lose* anyone. She jumped out of my car in the middle of downtown traffic. I couldn't exactly park and run after her." I'm steamed, especially at the implication I somehow ripped her off. "And I gave Rameeka five hundred bucks of that money, you know."

"You what? You gave that much money to a stone cold drug addict? Oh lord, what was I thinking hiring you?"

This brings me up short, and I hate to admit it but she's right. Rameeka probably scored as soon as she got away from me.

"Look, I understood our deal was for me to take Rameeka with me to Georgia. She wouldn't fly so I did my best to hide her in a safe place until I got back. But now I am back and I think that ends our agreement."

"I see. And tell me, Detective, have you found the man responsible for the murder? The man who will go after my sister unless I can get her off the street?"

I slam my car door and begin power-walking to my studio. All of my frustration wells up at CW still being on the loose and at my inability to catch him or convince the powers-that-be to go after him. My voice becomes much louder than Rhonda Hartman deserves.

"I can't do anything about that," I say. "She's a stubborn—she's too stubborn to listen to anyone." Calling Rameeka a bitch almost slips out but I catch myself in time.

Why am I yelling at her sister, a woman who only wants to keep her safe and not turned into another crime statistic?

I arrive at my building and let myself in. "Listen, I do have Rameeka's new cell phone number, if you want it."

"Of course I do. Hold on a moment."

While she searches for paper and pen, I empty my mailbox and climb the three flights to my studio. Inside, I drop, exhausted, into the chair at my desk and wait for Rhonda Hartman to return. When she does, I pass along the number and assure her I'm doing everything in my power to nail CW.

"But I can't make Rameeka come back to you. That's up to you."

"What do you mean? I—"

"She said you're always on her to get right with Jesus, if memory serves me."

Silence. Long silence.

"Think about it, Ms. Hartman. I'll try to keep an eye on her area, encourage her to patch things up with you." I click off from her call and, not wanting to have any more contact with people today, turn my cell completely off.

My progress tracker reproaches me, still sitting on my desk where I left it before going to Georgia on Saturday. I look it over, feeling depressed and surprised at the same time. My eating was for shit on the road and I haven't thought about exercise at all, much less done any. But it's Tuesday night and I haven't smoked or touched booze since last Wednesday.

I smack the fresh pack of Kools against the desk a few times, filter side down, to tamp the tobacco tighter. An old habit I learned from the girl who gave me my first cigarette and showed me how to look cool while smoking. Packing the tobacco tighter seems to intensify the flavor and make the smoke more satisfying. I want to smoke in the worst way after this shitty day and yet at the same time I want to throw the pack out the window. But I've held off for a week. I leave the Kools on the desk and decide to get rid of the day with water therapy. I take a shower.

Feeling better, I come back to my desk and check my cell to make sure the battery doesn't need recharging. Turning it on shows a message from Jimmy that must have come in while I had it shut off. The message is brief and pointed.

"Dana? Jimmy. Listen, I wanted to let you know I'm staying in L.A. At least for now. I might transfer to LAPD. We need to talk but don't call me tonight, I'm into something."

The first inhalation is wonderful and awful—the giddy, buzzing, light-headed feeling I love and missed is once again mine. Nicotine surges into my bloodstream followed by the tarry taste that fills my mouth and makes my tongue feel furry. Relief.

My temporary euphoria devolves into defeat, because once again a paper tube of tobacco controls me. This failure feeds my self-pity over my conversation with Abandonato and the message from Jimmy. I mull over the progress tracker. My hand shakes as I cross out the column indicating how many days I did not smoke.

My memory serves up the smell and look of the drunk passed out in the alley this morning. I take a deep drag on the Kool. I don't want to admit how much that guy rattled me. I clutch the tracker tighter in my hand and concentrate on the fact that I haven't had a drink since last Wednesday.

"And I'm not going to have one today," I say aloud, trying to sound decisive. No booze for six days, seven if you include today. I light a fresh cigarette from the one just finished, then make a wavering check mark in the drinking column to mark another day dry.

30

Wednesday, 9:00 a.m.

Other detectives bitch about the smell of the morgue but the bodies creep me out more. They are everywhere, and not only in the refrigerated drawers. Gurneys of them abound. The sheet-draped bodies, some covered in a hurry, expose purple toes or a hand slipped loose and gone quiet. I'm much more comfortable with the deceased when I encounter them at the kill scene, where they are part of the entire puzzle I'm trying to understand. When they surround me in the morgue I have the odd fear one will sit up and scare the shit out of me. Well, not really, but I do feel creeped out.

The Medical Examiner is about to start Toby's autopsy and I ask to view his body before she proceeds. The pathology suite looks like an operating room except for the obvious absence of any life support equipment. Toby lies on a metal table where drainage gutters run along each side. His body is modestly covered from the waist down with a white sheet that contrasts sharply with his black skin. Some decomp has taken place making his body bloat, but his muscular chest bears the marks I most want to see for myself.

The file photos of Toby that Felice had shown me were bad enough, but seeing Toby up close makes me nauseous. His body catalogues twenty-seven separate stab wounds. CW hadn't wanted to merely kill Toby, he wanted to vent rage over Otha Lee Worthy slighting him in favor of her son. I thank the doctor for allowing me in.

"Could I get a copy of the autopsy report when you're finished?"

"Sure. Email okay?"

It would be if I had access to my CPD account. I tell her I'm having trouble with my email and ask her to send it to Abandonato.

Upstairs, Father Mik is waiting and we make our way into the main area of the Office of the Medical Examiner to investigate cremation services for Toby. We sit to wait for the pathologist and Father Mik asks me how Evie is doing.

"Pretty well, considering. I saw her yesterday and JJ was having a hard time keeping her horizontal. She's got a concussion."

"Will your parents be able to come to the funeral on Monday?"

I nod. "I'm their chauffeur. Do you need me to interpret?" I assume that in addition to my deaf parents, other deaf people from ARC will attend Toby's funeral.

"That's very kind of you to offer, but no. ARC is hosting a memorial for Toby on Friday that the clients can attend, and they will use their staff interpreter. Then of course I'll be signing the mass, so we won't need an interpreter for that."

The unspoken message? I would know he signs the mass if I attended church once in a while. Immediately I feel embarrassed over my internal criticism of Father Mik, a benign man who would not stoop to innuendo to criticize me for skipping church. My mother is the one in charge of the chastising department. I duck outside for a quick cigarette.

The pathologist appears half an hour later apologizing for the delay. "You're arranging to have the body cremated privately?" she asks Father Mik.

"Allen Rehabilitation Center is the deceased man's guardian. Because he was a member of my church, ARC asked me to discuss the details of his cremation with you. I am uncertain whether you can do that service here or are we to arrange for a private means?"

"It depends. Was Mr. Worthy indigent?"

Father Mik looks at me. I shrug and turn to the doctor. "It's tricky. Mr. Worthy stood to inherit a sizeable amount of money from his mother but he was murdered before she died. Mr. Worthy never received any money. It reverted to his next closest relative, so I would say yes, he qualifies as indigent."

"If he has family who can pay for the cremation, we require that to be done."

I shake my head slightly, grimacing at the irony as well as the impossibility of making Charles Worthy pay for Toby's cremation. "It's complicated, Doctor. We have no way to contact his next of kin."

"I'm sorry. We can provide cremation services only if the deceased was indigent and has no other means of payment."

My aggravation at the doctor's intractability begins to surface when I feel Father Mik's hand on my arm.

"I think I can arrange for ARC to pay for the cremation services privately since Toby was their charge. That won't be a problem," he says.

"Fine. Go to the clerk's office down the hall and present them with this form." The doctor hands him an official looking document. "Then fill out the paperwork she gives you and that will take care of the body transfer. You can also ask for a list of possible crematories to contact."

Father Mik asks whether he'll need a death certificate for the cremation.

"Yes, you will. Normally you have to go through the County Clerk's office, but I can streamline it for you, Father." She types some data into her smart phone and peers closely at the screen. Frowns. "It appears there's a hold on the death certificate, which means I won't be able to access the file to print it."

For a moment, Father Mik and I exchange puzzled looks. But then Wili Nelson pops into my mind. I wonder if the sheriff from Marietta has worked some magic on her end to prevent CW from getting a copy of the death certificate. She did promise to shine him on. If CW can't provide the bank with proof of Toby's death, he can't collect the money as secondary beneficiary.

"Does it say who authorized the hold?" I ask.

Father Mik nods at my question. "It would be good to know so I can petition that person for a copy of the death certificate. I will need it for the cremation."

The doctor makes several swipes on her phone and reads a surprising name. "The person in charge of the case ordered it, a Detective Alberto Carrera."

I shake my head and bite my lower lip. What is the Prick up to now?

I quickly assure Father Mik I can get a copy of the death cert from Carrera, but mentally I'm floundering for a logical explanation for the Prick's maneuver. I consider talking to Abandonato but discard the idea in light of our conversation yesterday. Gotta talk to Koz.

I drop Father Mik off at St. Nick's and head over to the office to see Koz. Veda stands near her desk, her outfit shouting at me from the nineteen-sixties. She sports a lime-green mini-skirt and paisley blouse, along with fishnet stockings to complete the look. When I approach, she gives me the once over.

"My, my, my. Look what the cat dragged in. You in that hangover shape again, Detective? Or is your outfit something you threw together from the last church rummage sale?"

I look down at my sweater awash in pilling and slacks in need of an iron and feel chastised. Veda's outfit strains credulity but at least it matches and does look new. I decide to ignore her comment.

"Is Koz in? I have to talk to him. It's important." I grip the box holding CW's hairbrush.

"Yeah, he's in. But he's booked until four. Come back then." With raised eyebrows and a smirk, she says, "I can't *wait* to see how that goes."

Veda knows I know what she's talking about, but since I can't think of any smart-ass come-back, I walk away.

At four, I bypass Veda's desk without a glance and knock on my boss's door. Without waiting for an answer I walk in. Koz stands at his filing cabinet with a manila folder in his hand. His face tightens when he sees me.

"Demeter. Come in."

I close the door and perch on the edge of one of his guest chairs, then put the box holding CW's hairbrush on the chair next to me.

"Koz, I have to talk with you about this. It's very important."

"If this is about Carrera's case you are out of line."

He puts the folder on top of the filing cabinet and takes a seat behind his desk. Still pissed at me. Crap. Abandonato's recent warning flits through my mind. Do I really want to make Koz angry when it's only two days until we meet about my suspension?

"I know you think that, Koz. But what I've got is solid. Carrera's got the wrong guy. Give me five minutes to run this down then you decide who's right."

Koz gives me a look I can only describe as pity mixed with anger.

"I already decided. This case is closed, Demeter. Charges have been filed."

"But Koz, please listen—"

"*Me* listen? That's rich coming from you, Demeter. Let's have the gun and badge. On my desk. Now."

He makes a beckoning motion with his hand, then jabs his index finger on the desk.

This is not going the way I planned. Not at all. I stand and detach my shoulder holster, laying it on his desk with my badge. But apparently he isn't through chewing me out.

"And how about when I left you a voice mail message, *last week,* telling you to lay off Carrera's investigation. Cease and desist? Any of this ring a bell?"

Does he really want an answer or is this rhetorical? I try my best to look contrite but I don't think he's buying it.

"This is personal, Koz. The guy who was killed, Toby, he was my father's friend. When I saw how much Carrera was screwing up I had to do something."

"And you did. According to him you tried to ruin his investigation. I don't expect you to like Carrera, Demeter. Hell, I don't even expect you to get along with him. But I do expect a level of professionalism you haven't shown. Period."

This is too much.

"Are you holding up Carrera as the standard for professionalism?"

Koz holds up his hand toward me—palm out—and shakes his head.

"I don't want to hear any more. Consider yourself warned. Any more interference and I'm writing you up for insubordination. We're done."

He has a right to be pissed at me but I can't believe he won't even listen to what I've uncovered.

"Do you really want another headline like the one with the alderman? This is going to blow wide open, Koz, and it'll fall on you because Carrera's charging an innocent guy and the real murderer has killed two people and is running around free."

"Let me worry about the media." His voice is quiet.

I decide not to press the issue. At the door I remember something.

"I need a favor, Koz."

His face reddens and the volume of his voice increases. "What's the female equivalent of having balls, Demeter?"

For the second time I wonder if he's being rhetorical or if he really wants to know.

"Sorry. Toby's cremation and burial can't proceed because of Carrera. For some reason he has a hold on the death certificate."

A perfect example of how he fucks things up, I want to add. But I bite my professional tongue and finish in a hurry. "Any help you can give the priest with that would be much appreciated. I'll email his address to you."

Koz gives me a level stare and I duck out before he can say no.

31

Early evening

The last item I pick up at the grocery store is a carton of Kools, which I toss into my shopping cart. I wend my way toward the checkout and stand at the back of a long line of people picking up last-minute items. I keep thinking about Koz's stubborn refusal to hear me out and his blind support of Carrera. By the time I get home and put away my groceries I have the body of an email formed in my mind, ready to bang out.

First I send Father Mik's email info to Koz. Then I realize I left the box with CW's hairbrush in Koz's office: my subconscious working overtime. So I write another email outlining everything I found out since JJ visited me on October 25, eight days ago, to report Toby's death. I beg Koz to submit the hairbrush for analysis and compare it to the DNA evidence found at both murder scenes.

In a burst of what-the-hell-do-I-have-to-lose, I once more make this personal for him. By tying up this loose end he won't find himself the butt of the media's scorn when it comes out Carrera is wrong about Walter Washington. With so many guys serving life sentences in Illinois being exonerated by DNA testing, years after their convictions, it seems prudent to straighten out this issue before Washington goes to trial.

My main concern is not exonerating Washington, though, or even protecting Koz's reputation. I want CW. I send the email to Koz, with a blind cc to Abandonato, not expecting any response.

I eat grilled cheese and a bowl of soup for a quick dinner, then light a cigarette and debate the phone call I need to make. I already know Abandonato's take on my meeting with Colin McBride, but Jimmy's opinion matters to me most. Problem is, I'm still pissed over the message he left yesterday—afraid of what it might mean about us. I take a last, long drag and douse my cigarette, then speed-dial his number.

"Yeah, Gennaro."

"Jimmy, it's me."

"Good, good. You got my message?"

"Yeah, Jimmy. Listen, that's not why I'm calling. I met with Colin McBride yesterday."

I explain everything to him, lay it out. He isn't surprised that my non-compliance with the regs on weight and smoking put me on desk duty. That sums up our last conversation. But my suspension for drinking shocks him.

"It was a bullshit call. No way was I drinking on the job."

"Sure, D., sure." The words are there but his tone is less than supportive.

"So, I'm seeing Koz Saturday to give him my decision: either the EAP or grieve it with the union."

I disclose the fact that if I grieve the charge it will be without pay. And seeing as how I have no savings to get me through a possible six months, the burden of our finances will fall on his shoulders.

"Seems like a no-brainer to me, D. We have to go with the money."

God, he sounds like Abandonato. Money's the important thing. Never mind that I'll be sequestered with a bunch of losers for thirty days confessing my sins.

"I am not a drunk, Jimmy. I haven't had a drink since Koz tested me. It's been *eight whole days*." I look at my progress tracker on my desk and it verifies my stance.

"Okay, so what's Koz say to that?"

"I told you, I don't see him until Saturday."

Isn't he listening?

"Right, right."

"So? What do you think?"

"If you grieve this thing we've got no money coming in. And I'm out here. Not sure about my job right now, either. Why not try the EAP? I mean, it couldn't hurt."

"Couldn't hurt you, you mean. California far enough away from me, Jimmy?"

"Jesus, D. You take offense at the slightest thing. What I mean is you were pretty down after, you know, the baby. Couldn't hurt you to have some R and R, talk to a shrink, and get paid while you're doing it."

Christ, now he sounds like Colin McBride, making alcoholism treatment sound like a stay at some resort.

"I'm not going to treatment. I don't have a problem with booze. And going to a thirty-day program for juice-heads to talk to a shrink about my miscarriage seems pretty ass-backwards."

"Hey, you asked me what I thought. With our bills, both of us need to bring in money. If the only way is through the EAP then I think you should go."

"So I'm just a paycheck to you. No concern about my feelings and what's going on with me. You don't want me to interrupt your precious time in the sun."

I hear him crack open a can in the background. Beer? He slurps whatever he's drinking and clears his throat.

"We've got to have both our paychecks to make it. And I can tell you this, Dana. If you don't go to the EAP, I won't be coming back."

∼

A FEW HOURS later I motion to the bartender.

"The same again." My third boilermaker. I'm starting to feel relief but my conversation with Jimmy still replays in my mind. The bartender places the shot and draft in front of me and looks at whoever's behind me, tapping me on the shoulder.

I turn to face a startlingly handsome guy who has to be at least five years younger than me. He looks familiar but I can't place him.

"Detective?"

"Yeah. Demeter. Dana Demeter."

I hold out my hand feeling a little foolish, not sure of the current dating scene protocol. A beat later I realize he must know me or at least know who I am.

"Right. Marty Czychowicz. Mind if I sit down?"

He motions to the stool next to me. I look around the bar, which at midnight holds only the serious drinkers or those working night shifts. Not crowded by Howard Street standards. I see a lot of empty tables where he could park his ass. I realize, again a beat late, he only wants to talk. Glad I didn't embarrass myself thinking this is a come-on.

"Uh, sure."

I give him a hard, sidelong look as he settles his tall frame on the stool. At last my memory serves up this guy's stats: he's the rookie partnered with Nick, the moocher who never shows up on time for the doughnuts Abandonato brings in.

"Okay, Marty. What're you drinking?" I motion to the bartender and point to my new friend.

"I'll have what you're having."

The bartender picks up my empty after I gulp my shot and I point to Marty, order a double round. "So the Emergency Communications Center was too boring for you?" I ask.

"Hell, no. Just the opposite. Something's always popping there. It's—I got tired of sending other cops out. I was always imagining what it must be like for them. Took me awhile to get it, but I realized I wanted to be where the excitement was. You know, at the scene. Especially the ones with the bodies. I wanted to find out what happened in the rest of the story."

We drink in silence for a short while until Marty gets to the real reason he's chosen me for his drinking buddy.

"So tell me about Abandonato."

His voice is harsh and his demeanor puts me on edge. I turn on my stool to face his profile but he stays hunched over his beer, eyes down. Before I can ask why he wants to know about Abandonato, he speaks again.

"I don't know much about him, only he's one of those long distance guys. Marathons. And he's got the best solve record. Guy must be smart."

He says this with such wistfulness I realize he isn't angry at Abando-nato, more like an admirer from a distance, so I relax.

"You nailed it. He is smart. And dedicated."

Too bad he has an asshole partner who can't admit she's wrong, who is ready to give up a great partnership because she doesn't want to kowtow to a stupid departmental policy.

Marty nods at my assessment of Abandonato and smiles. "I thought so."

We drink some more in silence, listening to the jukebox play mostly old country-western from the Patsy Cline era. Marty switches to Diet Coke. To conserve my money, I cut back on boilermakers and order a draft beer.

"You like being a detective?"

His question seems sincere but I'm not in the mood to discuss my personal problems. I don't mind talking to this hunk of a man, but don't particularly want to be reminded of the job I love but might lose.

"Being a detective is, is..." what?

My thinking has deteriorated into that slow blur, which happens after I drink hard liquor. It's weird. In my own mind I actually feel I'm thinking a lot clearer than usual, but when I articulate those thoughts I hear my voice as a slowed-down tape recording. He looks at me, eager and interested in what I'm going to reveal about the inner workings of a detective's mind.

"Being a detective fucks you up," I say at last. "It takes over your life so you don't have any life, just working The Case. No husband. No chil-dren. Disappointed parents. Excuse me."

I slide off the stool and go outside to smoke. Instead of invigorating, even the cold air feels oppressive.

When I go back in he's still there, a fresh round waiting. "Okay, Marty, one more round. But then I'm outta here."

"So, Abandonato. I'm—"

For some reason his hero worship of Abandonato grates on me and I don't want to hear any more.

"Look, you want to start a Felice Abandonato fan club, be my guest. But don't ask me to join, okay?"

He gives me a hurt puppy dog look. "Koz assigned me to him starting next Monday, that's all I was going to say."

"Oh. Well, he'll be a lot happier with you than that prick Carrera."

Marty snorts at my mention of the Prick, which earns a smile from me.

"You know him?" I ask.

"Between you, me and the bartender? That guy is...is the, what's the opposite of a really good detective? He's the anti-Abandonato, yeah." He drains his Diet Coke. "That's another one of the stories I didn't get to see the end of."

When he doesn't fill me in any further, I nudge him with my elbow. I always like to hear stories supporting my low opinion of Carrera.

"So don't leave me hanging here, Marty. Spill."

He turns on his stool to face me and I swing a bit toward him, our knees almost touching. "I'm partnered with Carrera since last Friday, so today's what, Wednesday? Yeah. On Monday, we're driving around, shootin' the shit and we get a call from a patrol cop who's run down a BOLO. Carrera's BOLO. On a murder suspect. So we go screaming over there and cop's got the guy, big Afro, short but built, cuffed against a white sports car."

The story is mildly interesting until my blurred brain connects the dots of the suspect's physical description and car.

"CW. Christ."

I take a deep breath and let it out slowly. So Charles Worthy is still around, still in town, since this happened only two days ago.

Marty pauses, signals for a glass of water. I push my glass forward for another draft, then motion for him to hurry and pick up the narrative.

"So I stand there 'cause I'm supposed to watch and learn what Carrera does, you know, how he treats the suspect and everything. He talks with the guy for a few, then tells the patrol cop to un-cuff the guy."

I almost drop my beer, somehow knowing what Marty's going to say next but afraid to hear it.

"Get this. He orders me and the other cop to get lost. I'm thinking, Carrera's by himself with a possible killer and he don't want backup?"

Crap. I make Marty repeat everything. He describes CW and his car perfectly. Carrera rejects CW as even existing, yet when confronted with him in person, he lets him go. I'm sick at the thought. And pissed that Carrera does this only to maintain his version of Toby's murder.

Marty asks me if I know the rest of the story.

"Yeah. It's short. Carrera cancelled the BOLO and thanks to him, a two-time murderer is on the loose."

I stand up to leave and stagger a bit. Marty catches my elbow and ushers me outside. But instead of walking me to my car he hails a cab and stuffs me inside.

"You can't drive, detective. Get your car tomorrow." He pulls out some money and hands it to the driver.

I don't like being treated like a child but I have to admit part of me enjoys being taken care of by this handsome guy. Marty gives the cab's roof a couple of thumps. Jeez, he even knows Abandonato's mannerisms.

At home I shuck off my clothes and take a hot shower. Afterwards I sit at my desk with a piece of paper and a pencil, trying to figure out what Marty's new information tells me. I'm too drunk to make sense of it. Coffee is no help.

When I wake at four a.m. to use the bathroom, my brain is less scrambled and I realize Rameeka needs to be warned about CW. My call goes straight to her voice mail and I leave an urgent message to call me.

32

"Nothing new here," I say, tossing the autopsy report back on Abandonato's desk. He picks it up and skims through it, sipping his morning tea. "But thanks for letting me use your email." I smile, happy to be back with him to spill what I've learned about Carrera—until I spy Marty crossing the room and making a beeline for the doughnut box on the desk in front of me.

"Detectives," he says by way of greeting. He kind of ducks his head at Abandonato before taking a dive into the box, resurfacing with a doughnut in each hand. "You mind?" he asks.

Abandonato shakes his head. "The sooner they're gone the better, as far as I'm concerned."

I'm uncomfortable in Marty's presence, knowing the last time he saw me I was drunk enough that he had to put me in a cab. But he says nothing about Wednesday night, and instead takes a bite of one doughnut and then a bite of the other, less for comparison than to lay claim to both.

"See you Monday, Detective Abandonato. Look forward to working with you." He nods at me. "Have a good weekend." He walks back to his desk before either of us can respond.

"That guy there is the president and charter member of the Felice Abandonato Admiration Society," I say.

"Just my new partner."

"Yeah, so I found out a couple of nights ago," I say without thinking.

"What, you two on a date?" Abandonato chuckles as he says this.

I laugh a little too long at his joke. I don't want to tell him I spent most of yesterday morning in bed, hung over, berating myself for picking up a drink after being dry for one week. Don't want to tell him I had to take the el up to Howard Street so I could retrieve my car because I was too drunk to drive home the night before.

"He told me something really weird about the Prick." I relay the scenario of Carrera responding to the BOLO on CW, and then letting CW go.

"I mean, he cancelled the BOLO right after that. Right? Monday, late afternoon?"

Abandonato nods. "Right. But I thought he cancelled because he didn't believe CW existed. He's got Washington locked up—literally and figuratively—for Toby."

"Yeah. But that's not all. He put a hold on Toby's death certificate." I run down my trip to the morgue with Father Mik.

My partner sits up in his chair and frowns at this piece of information. "Have you asked Carrera about that?"

I shake my head. "Haven't been able to yet. I gave JJ a break yesterday and babysat Evie for most of the afternoon. The short version of Evie's recovery? She kept trying to get out of bed and do things around the house and I kept ordering her back to bed."

Abandonato shakes his head and grimaces.

"Besides," I say. "Carrera won't talk to me. Koz is pretty pissed at me, too. I was hoping you could help me make some sense of it."

Abandonato gets up and walks across the squad room to Marty's desk and talks to him for a few minutes, then comes back and sits down.

"Prick's out of town for a three-day weekend. I don't get the death certificate thing. Why would he put a hold on it? First he acts as if he doesn't believe CW exists, but when the BOLO actually brings him face to face with CW he lets him go." Abandonato's face is a mass of puzzled lines.

I shrug. "Well, Carrera thought Washington made up CW. To take the focus off himself."

Abandonato nods. "Right. And the Prick doesn't know about Toby's trust money, which makes CW's motivation a lot stronger than Washington's. Maybe that's why he let CW go."

I feel my face grow hot. "I told him about the money."

Up until now, as Nuts and I worked this case, I felt good and whole, as if I was still an active detective and we were partners. This is a glaring example of us not working together seamlessly, the kind of glitch that didn't happen prior to my suspension. Abandonato rarely looks surprised, is unflappable by most standards, but my bit of news makes him lean forward in his chair and shoot me a wide-eyed stare.

"Don't look at me like that," I say. "After you refused to take CW's evidence to Koz, I took it to Carrera as a last-ditch effort. I figured if the Prick knew the whole story about the money as the motivation he would see Washington's the wrong guy."

Abandonato leans back and mulls this over. "But he let CW go," he says again.

"I figure he doesn't want to give up Washington as his guy. He'd be blasted for incompetence. And if the papers got hold of this so soon after the alderman scandal, the brass would string up Koz along with Carrera and walk away from them both."

We look at each other. Neither of us has any trouble believing Carrera would *think* about letting a murderer go if it meant saving his own ass. Not to mention saving that of his future father-in-law. But would he really go through with it?

"Maybe the Prick figures he can assuage his conscience about Washington taking the fall by putting a hold on the death certificate," says Abandonato. "That way he's keeping CW from collecting his money,"

"That seems to make sense on the surface, assuming of course that Carrera has a conscience."

Abandonato smiles at my jibe.

"But eventually he'll have to release the hold so Toby can be cremated and buried. CW will inherit anyway."

I explain Sheriff Nelson's role as co-trustee and feel frustrated again at not having the go-ahead to nab CW and extradite him when he eventually shows up to claim Toby's money.

"What about Rameeka? Anybody warn her?" Abandonato asks.

"I called her after Marty told me about the BOLO but only got her voicemail. I tried again yesterday but she didn't answer. She's pissed because I tried to take her back to her sister's place. I think she's ignoring me. After I got her voicemail a second time I left her a message about CW possibly still being in town."

I would have preferred telling her directly. I also had considered calling Rhonda to let her know. But since I figured Rameeka wouldn't be with her, I didn't want to put additional stress on the woman. She worries enough about her sister without my adding to it.

At the far end of the squad room the door to Koz's office opens and he walks out with a young woman. Caitlyn. Abandonato and I watch them chat for a minute with Veda. Caitlyn is dressed in a red power suit and four-inch stilettos. A leather purse the size of a pillow is slung over her shoulder.

I don't know much about haute couture but I can smell expensive across the room. This is one high-maintenance young woman. For a split second I compare myself to Caitlyn and again feel lousy about my weight, clothes, and general appearance. I wouldn't want to be her, but I sure would like to have the confidence she exudes in her femininity.

Abandonato emits a low whistle and confirms my assessment. "I see why Carrera is dressing better these days. Competing with other guys for her must be fierce."

Caitlyn heads to the elevators and Koz returns to his office. A minute later my cell phone rings.

"The lieutenant wants to know if you're able to come see him this afternoon instead of tomorrow for your meeting?"

No hello, no identifying herself, Veda launches right into her request. I can see her across the room, phone to her ear, her back to me.

I say, "Hi, Veda," and get up and start toward her desk. "Let's see. This afternoon? About what time?"

"He says about four."

I tap her on the shoulder. She jumps and turns in her desk chair. I disconnect our call. "Four will be fine."

33

Mid-afternoon

I go home, do laundry, eat a late lunch, then head back to the district office. After I climb the five flights to the squad room and start to head toward Koz's office, Abandonato catches up to me. He stays me, his hand on my arm. For someone who is not physically demonstrative, his touch speaks volumes.

"If I'm not here when you get done, call me after," he says.

I haven't yet told him I'm going to grieve the charge of drinking on the job. On the drive back to the office I rehearsed how to tell him but couldn't come up with anything. I hate that I dread his disapproval. What I really hate is the thought of not working with him for the next six months. I can calm my personal money worries by freelancing as an interpreter during my hiatus, but god, I'll miss working with Abandonato—neither of us is happy about our separation.

I pat my partner's hand in response.

My palms are sweaty when I knock on Koz's office door. I think about trying—one last time—to convince him Washington is the wrong suspect and to go after CW. I startle a bit when my boss opens the door. He steps aside to let me in, then motions for me to sit in one of the two visitor's chairs. I sit down. The box holding CW's hairbrush perches on the corner of the desk, a silent reminder I shouldn't give up.

"Koz, I have some things I need to tell you."

"Let's get to it, then."

He walks back to his desk and buzzes Veda in. She sits at Koz's computer and he comes around the desk to sit next to me. I turn to him and begin to speak but he holds up his hand.

"Let me start. Veda, please put in today's date and time we're meeting. The heading will be Detective Dana Demeter, discussion of suspension, etcetera, etcetera. You know."

Veda nods at Koz, having already typed before he gave her directions.

"Now, you've had ten days—amend that to nine days, agreed to by Detective Demeter—to consider two options. The first is that you can see the EAP, submit to an evaluation for drugs and alcohol, and follow their recommendations."

Veda begins typing again.

"If you choose this option, you will be on leave with pay. Your second option is to grieve the suspension through the union. If you do, you will be suspended without pay for the duration of the grievance."

I hear Koz talking but the words fade into a buzz. Outside the window behind his desk, I can see dusk gathering over an eastern portion of the city, ending in a slash of blue that marks Lake Michigan. On the window's ledge pigeons bunch together, their heads pulled down to ward off the chill.

This isn't going the way I want. I hoped before he began talking about my suspension, Koz and I could discuss the email I sent him detailing everything about Toby's murder. I'm certain he will see I have solved the case, that I'm competent and capable. Then I notice Koz has stopped talking and he and Veda look expectantly at me.

"I'm grieving the suspension," I say. I pick up the box and hold it toward Koz. "I need to tell you more about this. Did you read my email about it?"

Koz shakes his head.

"This is the DNA of the guy who is really responsible for Toby Worthy's murder. I stake my reputation on it."

Veda coughs at this last bit and I shoot her a dirty look.

"I have no doubt he's also good for a dead hooker in the Goose Island District, Koz. CW was the last person seen with her."

I rush on, afraid he might interrupt, and enumerate the witnesses who corroborate Washington's story and finish with CW's financial motivation for killing Toby.

"That's it. We've got to move on this or Worthy'll be gone."

As I say it, my voice breaks and tears start behind my eyes. I sound as angry and as desperate as I feel. This is the end of it. I know Koz won't budge. The system is already set in motion to try Washington for Toby's murder. CW is free and will inherit almost a quarter of a million dollars. And I'll be on suspension without pay from a job I love.

Koz takes the box from me and places it back on his desk. I start to rise but he detains me, his hand on my arm.

"Stay a minute."

He nods at Veda and she leaves the room.

"Dana, listen to me. Grieving this suspension is going to get you nothing but fired. Believe me when I tell you that."

"Fired? What the hell good is a grievance process if the outcome is already decided? Why should I be treated like an alkie because of some arbitrary reg?" I clench my teeth hard to keep from ranting further. My tears are gone. I want to fucking scream.

Koz holds out his palms toward me, a motion of appeasement. "Please. Look, I don't want to lose you and your tenacity. I need you here, doing the thorough work you've always done."

He points at the box holding CW's hairbrush. "And do even when you're *not* supposed to. You're second only to Abandonato in solve rates for our district. The two of you together are the best. Think about your partner here. See the EAP."

In spite of myself I feel a brief glow at his compliment, but not for long. My cynicism takes over and I think he's only trying to sway me into doing what he wants. As if I'm some girly-girl like his daughter, who'll go along with the program if offered a new purse, a larger diamond, or in this case, empty flattery.

I grab the box off his desk and thrust it into his hands. "What about the DNA, Koz? Will you run it, match it to Worthy and the condoms? It's outlined in the email I sent you. Did you read it yet?"

Koz shakes his head and puts the box back on his desk. I'm desperate for him to side with me but I can see he's disengaging from our conversation.

I pull out my phone. "I can re-send it to you right now, Koz."

"You don't get it, do you? This isn't a negotiation between us, Dana. You're here to choose how you want to handle the rest of your career. Or whether you even have a career. Forget about Carrera's case and worry about your own problem." Koz returns to his chair behind the desk.

I stand up and lean over Koz, my fist softly pounding his wooden desk and punctuating each word.

"I. Am. Not. A. Drunk."

I struggle between anger and overwhelming sadness. Unable to think clearly and feeling nausea rising in my gut, I stalk out of his office.

Veda holds up a single sheet of paper as I approach her desk, her head turned the other way to avoid looking at me. I snatch the paper from her, scan it quickly and sign at the bottom. I thrust the form back in Veda's direction and let it fall, not waiting for her to take it.

"You'll get a copy of this in the mail once the lieutenant signs it, Detective." Veda's happy voice trills after me but I ignore her delight in my demise and continue toward the women's john.

As I veer toward the bathroom I see Marty at Abandonato's desk, deep in discussion—about the finer points of some case, no doubt. I sit in a stall and let the tears come, stifling the noise of my sobs although a few hiccups still escape. Ten minutes later I wash my hands and splash cold water on my face. I'm not yet ready to meet eye to eye with Abandonato and give him the word about my decision to grieve the charge.

When I leave the bathroom I feel my cell phone vibrate in the back pocket of my pants. I let it go, not wanting to talk to anyone. Abandonato and Marty are still conversing, so I try to be unobtrusive as I approach, quietly collect my backpack from under my former desk, and walk to the elevators.

A short minute later I hear Abandonato. "Dane! Wait up!" He jogs over to where I stand by the elevators, Marty trailing behind.

"I don't want to talk right now," I say. I purposely look at the floor because I can tell Abandonato is trying to make eye contact with me. "Call you later."

My cell phone vibrates again in my back pocket. Irritated, I pull it out and answer it.

"Demeter."

Whoever is on the other end isn't talking. A low hum comes over the line.

"Who the hell is this?"

Again, nothing but the humming noise, then a whisper.

"Help me. You got to help me."

"Who is this?" But as soon as I ask the question I know the answer. "Rameeka?"

Abandonato steps closer to me when he hears her name. I grip the phone tighter to my ear.

"It's me," she says.

Her voice is barely audible, her former bravado a distant memory.

"Where are you? What's going on?"

"CW. He got me."

My stomach drops like the express elevator from the 95th floor of the Hancock. I can hear her crying but trying not to make noise, similar to my tears in the bathroom only a few minutes ago.

Rameeka snuffles. "In his trunk. He gonna kill me."

Marty joins us and the three of us stand close together, a tight circle. I tell Rameeka to hold on for one second and then hit the mute icon to give the two men a quick synopsis. I punch the speakerphone button.

"Rameeka, listen to me—listen! Stop crying. Can you tell me where you are?"

She cries for a minute but manages to stop. "Don't know. It wasn't his car. Fooled me."

I strain to hear her whispers.

"What time did he pick you up?"

"About two. You got to help me." She starts crying again, this time louder.

It's almost five o'clock, which means he could be in another state by now.

"Hold on, don't hang up. Do you hear me? Don't hang up." I take her gulping for a response. I turn to the two men. "I don't know anything about tracing cell phones. You?"

Abandonato shakes his head but Marty lights up like a slot machine.

"Sure. Come on," he says.

He moves to my old desk that is now his—right next to Abandonato's. He takes my cell from me. "Rameeka? I'm Detective Marty Czychowicz of the Chicago Police Department. I need some information from you and we will trace your call, catch this guy. You hang in there, hear me?"

Abandonato and I look at each other and I show my glee over Marty's competence by gesturing both thumbs up. Marty gets the name of Rameeka's phone service, hands her back to me, and goes to work on Abandonato's landline.

"Rameeka? It's Dana."

"Help me," she croaks again.

"We are, we are. Marty's going to trace your cell phone, so don't hang up." I assume this is right. I look at Marty and he's nodding at me as he talks on the landline.

"Is there anything you can tell me about CW's car so we can start looking for you? You said it wasn't his car."

"It's red. No license. New."

"That's good. Hold on." I relay the info to Abandonato. He and Marty huddle.

"I'll stay on the phone with you. Don't talk unless you have to. I don't want CW to hear you."

"He look different—bald, got glasses."

"Good, that's good information. Hold on. I'll tell my partners."

Abandonato wears the focused look he assumes when operating in high gear. Marty has Rameeka's phone company on the line and they've already identified the cell towers picking up her signal. She's almost to the Iowa border. My partner is talking to the Illinois State Police, having explained the situation and asked for assistance. ISP already connected with the phone company and they're dispatching ground and air support to the area.

"How's she holding up?" Abandonato asks.

"Rameeka? We got your signal—we're coming for you. Hang in there."

But instead of a response from her, I realize I don't hear the humming of CW's car in the background anymore. The phone is dead.

34

I disconnect my cell and immediately redial Rameeka's number. It goes directly to voicemail.

"Marty! I've lost her. I think her battery died."

I picture Rameeka huddled in a dark car trunk scared to death, CW speeding away from us to god only knows where. Marty raises an index finger to me as he finishes talking on the phone. He hangs up, gives me a big smile, and comes over to where Abandonato and I stand.

"No worries. She's got GPS on her phone and it doesn't matter if it's on, off or dead. ISP's got a clear signal on her and they're moving in. We're good."

My partner and I bump fists, then simultaneously give Marty identical slaps of approval on the back of the head in recognition of his quick work. I'm giddy at the prospect of catching CW and, of course, saving Rameeka. The three of us hustle over to Koz's office to check out the protocol for CW's extradition.

Veda has already left for the day and Koz's office door stands open. He's at his desk packing some files into a briefcase as Nuts gives a quick knock before we enter.

"Lieutenant," says Abandonato, "we're in the middle of a kidnapping and need information from you."

Koz looks at me briefly as if surprised I'm still in the office but then turns his attention to my partner. Abandonato and Marty give Koz the rundown on Rameeka's kidnapping. Abandonato then surprises me and states that CW could be a strong suspect in Toby's and Kandy's murders, and briefly restates what I told Koz earlier. When did Nuts change his mind about all this? And when was he going to tell me?

Koz squints his eyes and looks at Abandonato, then at Marty.

"Has Demeter here swayed the two of you to her way of thinking?" Before he lets either of them respond he continues, "I'm going to say this one more time, for everyone's benefit, and it better be the last time I have to say it. This is Carrera's case and *Washington* is the one being charged with murder."

Koz gives me a measured look. "And it's staying that way." He goes back to packing his briefcase.

Abandonato gestures at me using both hands in a patting motion, a gesture meant to mollify me for the moment so I don't argue with Koz. I nod and look away.

"Message received, sir. But what about extradition? This guy's almost to Iowa. Do we go out and pick him up? And what about the woman in the trunk? We have to bring her back, have her press charges, take her statement."

"Coordinate it with ISP, see if they'll bring the two of them back. If they refuse, check with the district where he first picked her up, see if they'll cooperate. Do not, I repeat, do not go out there. This has nothing to do with Homicide."

"Christ, Koz! This has everything to do with Homicide."

I blurt this out before my partner can stop me. "Why do you think Rameeka called me?"

Koz gives me a puzzled look and I know for sure he didn't read my email, doesn't have a clue who Rameeka is.

"Rameeka—the woman in the *trunk*. CW kidnapped her and he *will* kill her because she's the only one left to connect him to Toby's murder. And Carrera *had* CW but he let him *go!*" I throw both my arms up to punctuate my point.

Koz goes to another filing cabinet and retrieves more files, pointedly ignoring me.

Since baiting him about Carrera gets no response, I try a different tack and hurry to Koz's side.

"Rameeka's sister is a hotshot lawyer, lives in the Hancock. I'm sure she'd be grateful if you treat her little sister well."

I'm hoping Koz picks up the implied message that the opposite will be true if he doesn't treat Rhonda Hartman's little sister well.

Koz walks back to his desk and I scurry after him. He begins to put the files in his briefcase but stops, and I think I've hooked him. "What are you saying, Demeter?"

I glance at Abandonato. He stands with his arms crossed in front of his body, Marty copying his stance. Not happy with me, not at all.

"Same chapter different verse of what I said earlier, Koz," I say, pressing on in spite of my partner's body language. "You'll get positive press about saving Rameeka and catching her kidnapper. That would make the brass happy, right?"

"She isn't in our jurisdiction, Demeter. I thought I was clear about that."

"But her sister could—"

Abandonato crosses the room in quick steps and grabs my arm, pulling me out of the office. Marty follows behind.

I wrench my arm free. "What'd you do that for? I'm trying to—"

"I know what you're trying to do. But pick your battles with Koz. He isn't in any mood to be finessed here."

"You kowtow to him too much, Nuts. 'Message received, sir.' Shit, he's got to be challenged on this. What's with you, anyway? You surprised the shit out of me telling Koz that CW is a still a strong suspect. Then you back right down."

Marty looks uncomfortable with our arguing, moves back toward his desk. Abandonato watches Marty for a moment, then motions for me to follow him. We move around the corner away from Koz's office to an empty desk and sit.

"I was trying to gauge his reaction, see if he'd listen. But he's got his mind made up."

My disappointment with Abandonato's handling of Koz must show on my face.

"Look," he says, "at the very least, CW's going to be charged with kidnapping. We've got him cold on that, okay?"

Grudgingly, I nod.

"But you've got to let it go on Toby."

I know he's right but I can't accept it. The reality of my situation hits me hard. Grieving my suspension truly means there's nothing left for me to do.

As Abandonato and I walk back to his desk I realize I still have to tell him about my earlier meeting with Koz. It'll have to wait until we have more time, until I'm able to sort out what I want to say.

I sit at my old desk for a minute, Marty somewhere else, and experience the final disconnect from Abandonato. Even my once-familiar chair feels foreign to the contours of my body, as if someone larger has forced it into an unknown, uncomfortable shape.

Marty shows up and walks toward us, talking on his cell phone and nodding his head in a staccato beat.

"Okay, okay, yep, right, okay. We'll be there." He clicks off his phone and punches his fist once in a downward movement.

"What've you got?" says Abandonato.

"ISP nailed him—blocked the freeway with their copter and didn't even have to give chase. The guy gave up! Woman's okay physically but hysterical. When they pulled her out of the trunk she lunged at the guy and started beating on him. They let her get in a few licks before pulling her off!" Marty laughs and Abandonato joins in.

The thought of Rameeka doing any damage to CW is humorous, but I hope landing a few punches—however ineffective—gave Rameeka some satisfaction.

"ISP offered to fly them here in the copter, said it would take a half hour tops, so I agreed. That was okay," Marty asks, "wasn't it?"

Abandonato looks at me and raises his eyebrows, a small smile giving way to a grin.

Together we both say, "Sure."

35

6:00 p.m.

I 've never been near a helicopter as it lands. Sounds like I'm surrounded by Hell's Angels. Abandonato, Marty, and I huddle close to each other on the helipad of County Hospital, which the Staties use occasionally instead of Palwaukee Airport out in the 'burbs. Chopper blades whip the already cold wind colder. When everything comes to a halt, the side door opens and an ISP trooper jumps out. He wrestles a handcuffed man with a stocky body onto the pad.

At last I am face to face with the man I've pursued for the last two weeks, a man who strongly resembles Toby. CW wears no coat. Up close I see he does have a well-toned physique. His short-sleeved shirt reveals muscled arms that gleam in the bright lights of the landing pad and end in barbell-size fists cuffed behind his back. Even though Toby was strong and tough, I can believe CW has the strength necessary to overpower his second cousin.

The trooper guides CW away from the helicopter toward us. Abandonato moves forward slightly with Marty, badge out, and identifies himself.

Marty cuffs CW a second time, then the trooper removes the original cuffs, reattaching them on his belt. As this exchange is going on I walk over to the helicopter and try to see inside. All I can make out past the pilot's head is a thatch of magenta hair. I walk around to the other side and open the door.

Rameeka looks awful. Whatever makeup she put on this morning is mixed with dirt and tears or has rubbed off. Her hair stands straight up but not because she styled it that way. The paramedics must have worked this magic to get at what I guess is a wound because it's hidden by a large gauze pad covering the left side of her face.

Her purse is missing, she has no shoes, and wears some light blue hospital socks inadequate for the cold. I hold out my hand and help her from the seat.

"Thanks," she says as she scoots forward and comes to a standing position next to me.

"You okay?" I ask.

Rameeka peers at me like I'm the slowest kid in the class.

"I look okay to you?" She pats her hair but it's a feeble attempt.

"Right. Stupid question. How are you doing?"

"Got a headache big as a bus," she says, dabbing her fingers lightly on the pad taped to her head. "And I'm cold. Lost my coat." I imagine her coat in the trunk of CW's car. She eyes my winter jacket and I feel overdressed in jeans and a sweater, compared to her micro-skirt and tube top.

"Here." I hand over my jacket and she wraps it around her body, folding her arms and hunching her shoulders forward in an effort to warm up.

Rameeka and I head toward Abandonato, Marty, and CW to get out of the way of the helicopter as the pilot prepares to leave. She walks a bit behind me, my body her shield. The five of us stand and watch the chopper rev its rotors and lift into the night sky. As soon as the loud chopping noise recedes CW speaks to me.

"You got nothin' on me for my cousin."

I lift my chin slightly and stare at him through squinted eyes. I want to pour out everything I have on him for Toby and Kandy's murders, run down the proof of what I have uncovered, and tell him he's going away for a long, long time. I want my father to be proud of me for nailing the guy who viciously murdered his friend. But a few hours ago I gave up my authority to make anything happen. My hands are as bound as CW's.

"When I was a kid we used to say 'Guilty dog barks first.' Ever hear that expression, CW?"

I wish my comeback had more snap to slap on him, but at least Rameeka snickers behind me. With my frustration level at an all-time high, it's nice to have one appreciative onlooker.

"That skinny runt manager at Toby's house did him in! Stole his money and did him in!" CW shouts, as if we need to hear him over the long-gone helicopter.

"Save it, Worthy. This isn't about your cousin. This is about kidnapping Rameeka," says Abandonato, nodding in our direction.

"Kidnappin'? Kidnappin'? Who, this skank? Didn't kidnap her. She stole my wallet after our business transaction, know what I'm sayin'? And nobody steals CW's wallet. Tryin' to teach her a lesson, officer. Put her in the trunk and we went for a little ride. I was gonna let her out after awhile."

I'll give him this, he's good. He sounds genuinely put out that we think he kidnapped Rameeka.

"We're taking you over to the Goose Island District where you'll be charged with kidnapping," says Abandonato.

Rameeka comes to life with that pronouncement, stepping forward and getting in CW's face.

"Oh yeah, muthafucka, you being charged. I'm chargin' you. Try to kill me? Your black ass goin' away for a long time." She turns to Abandonato for confirmation. "Right?"

"Yep. A long time."

I hook my arm through Rameeka's, both of which are planted squarely on her hips as she gives CW what-for. I give a gentle pull. "Come on. Let's go get you checked out downstairs," I say.

As I start to move away she coughs up some phlegm and spits it squarely between CW's eyes. CW howls. Because his hands are cuffed behind his back he can only whip his head from side to side in a vain attempt to dislodge the gob of phlegm dripping down his nose.

Marty and I both laugh.

"I'd say that's the least you deserve," says Abandonato, all business. He pulls CW toward the exit. "Let's go."

36

11:00 p.m.

Rameeka sits in the passenger seat of my car as we creep east from County Hospital toward the melee that is Friday night in downtown Chicago.

"Bulls' game must've let out late," I say.

A full moon shines like a fluorescent light on her dark skin. We spent the last three hours in County's Emergency Room where Rameeka checked out fine on the physical end of things. The district cops questioned her and the FBI made a brief appearance, taking her statement and strongly encouraging her to press charges against CW, which she did. CW is being held without bond at Goose Island, the area where he first picked up Rameeka.

Rameeka shivers and her teeth actually chatter. I close the slight opening of my driver's side window and turn up the heat.

"Cold? Or nerves?" I ask.

"I just can't, you know, stop jitterin' inside. Thinkin' about what that man was gonna do to me."

As if to prove the point her body does a minor tango, her dangle earrings tinkling in the after-shock tremor. She's given me back my winter jacket but I offer it to her again.

"Unh-unh," she says, shaking her head. "Heat feel good, though. Thanks." The bumper-to-bumper traffic edges forward.

"We would've made better time *walking* to your sister's place," I say, trying to elicit a smile from her.

Rameeka looks out her window, quiet.

"You going to call your sister before we get there? It's pretty late to surprise her if we show up without calling," I add. I light a Kool and Rameeka bums one from me.

I hand her my lighter.

"I've never seen you smoke," I say.

"Me? I don't smoke. But now seem like a good time to start."

A non-smoker wouldn't understand her sentiment but I get it, one hundred percent. Rameeka inhales and immediately doubles over with a cough. I crack my window for relief from the smoke-filled car and the heat blasting from the vents. I'm sweating while she shivers.

Rameeka screws the cigarette into the corner of her mouth and pulls out her cell phone to call her sister, or so I assume. Suddenly she starts laughing. She takes a heavy drag of the cigarette and tosses it out the window, exhaling smoke from her nostrils in two thick streams. A few seconds later she starts sobbing.

I pat her awkwardly on the shoulder and let her cry it out, not sure what triggered this emotional jag. Traffic picks up to a faster creep and I see we're approaching Michigan Avenue.

"I—I'm outta my wits." She hiccups. "When we was talkin', you and me?"

She bangs the cell phone against my dashboard.

"And this damn cell phone died? I knew I was one dead ho. I been on the streets, been beat up, even knifed once. But this? Ain't never been so scared in my life."

She blows her nose. Her voice drops to a whisper. "And it's my own damn fault."

"I understand your fear but I don't get why you're blaming yourself for being kidnapped."

"Did what Rameeka wanted to do. Didn't listen. My sister been telling me, you been telling me, hell, my *life's* been telling me: 'stay safe, hide out at Rhonda's.' Stubborn bitch, that's me." She hums a short tune unfamiliar to me.

I think about relaying Abandonato's earlier advice to me about picking one's battles but feel like a hypocrite. I pull my cell from the back pocket of my pants and hand it to her. She calls Rhonda and makes contrite noises, asks meekly if she can stay with her for a while and even promises to go to church.

Handing back my cell, she sighs. "That's that."

I elbow her lightly. "Church, huh?"

"Don't let Rhon know you heard that." We both laugh.

I turn north on Michigan Avenue and head toward the safety of the Hancock Building, joining the thousands of other people downtown not currently at home and asleep.

37

I don't get on Lake Shore Drive the next day until almost sundown. It's time to talk with JJ about CW's arrest and fill him in on what I found out about Toby's family and his early life.

When I arrive, the front of the house is dark, though I'd use the kitchen door anyway. So I traipse around the side to find the back yard empty of Halloween decorations, looking bare and somehow older in the thin light of the security lamp. Through the kitchen window I see Evie with her back to me attending to something on the stove. My key in hand, I try the doorknob, and when it yields I feel a flare of irritation.

I slip inside and approach Evie from behind, pinning her with my arms. I let her squirm a few seconds before I let go. She turns around and starts to beat on me with the pancake turner that she's using to cook bacon but stops when she sees it's me. The utensil drops to the floor.

"I can't believe you left this door unlocked!" I make my signs large and aggressive. *"You got hit on the head already. You want it to happen again? Or maybe worse?"*

She mimes my pinning her. *"Why did you do that? You think scaring me will make me do what you say?"* Evie steps away from me, rubbing her upper arms.

I stop and look at her, small and vulnerable in her housecoat, her long braid coiled around her head. Her question brings me up short. Why *did* I do that to her? I feel like a parent trying to keep her child safe, only in this case the child is sixty-six years old and not willing to be bossed around. I start to apologize but she's not having any of it.

"This is my house! If you don't like this," she indicates the door with both palms sweeping up and down in a dramatic flair, *"you can leave!"*

In response I go to the door and throw the deadbolt home. Evie stoops, picks up the pancake turner and tosses it in the sink. She returns to the stove where the bacon is starting to smoke and pulls the frying pan off the burner.

Our argument reminds me of my recent disagreements with Koz and Abandonato, only I see my mother's continued insistence about the door as foolish stubbornness, whereas I see my continued insistence about CW as hardworking perseverance. It is clear, however, whose genes I inherited.

I sit at the kitchen table and wait for her to finish assembling a BLT in progress. She brings the sandwich to the table, sits down, and starts eating as if I'm not here. The bacon smells great and I realize I've had little other than coffee and cigarettes during the day.

"Your sandwich looks good," I sign.

Evie continues to ignore me and eat, but after a minute she points to the stove. I take this as marking a truce and make myself a sandwich thick with extra bacon.

"Where's JJ?"

"Your father's getting some exercise instead of sitting in his lounge chair watching TV. He's bowling with his friend Pete."

I'm relieved but also frustrated to hear JJ isn't home. I don't want to face him and relay the news that even though CW has been caught, he won't be charged with Toby's murder. But at the same time I want to unburden myself, detail for him everything I've done to find CW and solve the case. I swear under my breath.

"Don't swear in this house. I can lipread a little bit, you know."

God, I can't get away with anything around her. This increases my resolve not to tell her about my suspension. Evie would only worry. And worse, she would come down hard on me for grieving the suspension. I know what she would say: *You're foolish! Do what your boss says!* This, from a woman who never held a job in her life other than homemaker. There's also the thorny problem of the reason for my suspension. If Evie thought I'd been drinking on the job, her criticism would be swift and sharp.

I ask her, *"What time do you want me to pick you up on Monday for Toby's funeral?"* Father Mik called me early this morning to let me know Carrera released the hold on Toby's death certificate. The cremation is today and the funeral will be Monday.

Evie thinks for a minute, transfers her sandwich to her left hand and signs with her right. *"You can pick us up at ten. Don't you have to work?"*

I can see her concussion hasn't left any lasting problems—she's back to grilling me like the old days. *"Not until later in the afternoon. I'll come by at ten."*

"Your father will like that. Come earlier so we can get a good seat."

"God, Evie. It's a funeral, not a social event."

My mother stands abruptly and takes her plastic plate to the sink, thrusting it into the dishpan where it lands with a clatter. She turns and leans against the countertop, giving me the same stern look that hasn't changed since I was five.

"When I was growing up I never would have talked to my mother that way. First you scare me and now you're rude. I'm not surprised Jimmy wants to stay in L.A. instead of here with you."

Her words hit home. *"I'm not a little girl, Evie."*

Still, I recognize the truth behind her blunt assessment of my marriage.

"Why do you always side with Jimmy?"

I regret the question as soon as it's out. She gives me a look that says I'm the dumbest thing since Chia Pets.

"He wants you to have a baby. What's wrong with that?"

I stand and bring my plate to the sink. Evie backs up a couple of feet to maintain a comfort zone between us for signing. Problem is, I can't think of how to answer her question because there isn't anything wrong with Jimmy wanting me to have a baby. I want it, too. When I don't reply but instead run the water to wash our dishes, she approaches me and touches my elbow.

"What?" I say, using my voice and forcing her to lipread, although I'm sure my facial expression alone is enough to show my irritation. I plunge my hands into the hot dishwater and begin cleaning our lunch plates.

"You're not being a good wife. You're overweight. You smell like cigarettes. Jimmy doesn't like that."

Evie declines to say my clothes look like they're from a rummage sale and my hair looks like I cut it with kids' scissors. My mother's idea of being kind is to mention only two of my defects instead of four. Abandonato's advice about picking my battles replays its monotonous song.

"I don't want to talk about Jimmy right now." Especially not with you. Soap suds drip down my arms from signing.

Evie takes the hint and leaves me to the dishes. A few minutes later I put on my coat and go into the yard for a cigarette, hoping JJ will return soon. I look at the house of my childhood and wonder when I stopped confiding in Evie.

The answer seems simple: when Jimmy and I married. I picked up the reins of adulthood at twenty, eager to prove myself through achieving as a cop right alongside Jimmy. We made a great duo until it went to shit with my failure to carry our baby to term. Now he's two thousand miles away and my mother sides with him.

I curl up in the Adirondack chair as it gets colder, chain-smoke, and wait for my father.

At nine JJ still hasn't returned so I decide to wait until the funeral to talk with him. I go upstairs to say goodnight to Evie but she's already in bed, and the room dark. I lock the deadbolt on my way out.

∽

AT HOME, I free the ninth can of beer from the twelve-pack I picked up on the way back from the south side. I cried about Jimmy and our baby the entire trip between my parents' house and Louie's Liquors. Our wedding video sits in the DVD player, waiting for me to watch it for the fourth time. I punch the remote and fast-forward to where we exchange vows.

"'Til death do us part," a youthful Jimmy echoes Father Mik's line.

The last phone message I have from my husband puts a lie to that vow. I replay Jimmy's promise several more times before ejecting the DVD and turning it off. I want to call Jimmy to make some sense of why he's staying in L.A. instead of coming home. I hit speed dial and it rings five times. I'm ready to ditch the idea and hang up but he answers, his voice sleepy.

"Yeah. Gennaro."

A hundred things I want to say jockey for position.

"Hello? Anybody there?"

"Jimmy, it's me."

"Oh, hey. It's a little late, isn't it?"

I glance at the cell phone. Two a.m. for me, but only midnight for him.

"Look Jimmy, I want to tell you, talk to you. About L.A. And I'm not going to the EAP. I'm gonna grieve it. But don't worry about the money. I can interpret. I wish you'd come home, you know? Evie's right. I'm a lousy wife."

I open the beer but put it down on the floor. I can't talk. Any more words out of my mouth and I'll be bawling again.

"You're drunk, D."

"Yeah. Mr. Obvious Man."

His laughter surprises me for a moment, but knowing the familiar sound is so far away only reinforces my loneliness.

"Why are you calling me so late? What's wrong, D?"

"I don't know. Everything. My case went to shit, you know? I wanted to talk to you, tell you I miss you. Evie's right. You should have a baby."

He laughs again.

"Stop laughing at me. This is serious."

"You really are drunk if you think I can have a baby."

"No, no, no. You know what I mean. We should, you know—"

"Yeah, I know. I've been thinking about coming home for a visit at Thanksgiving or maybe Christmas, and—"

"Really? That's good, Jimmy. Want to talk to you, see you."

"Listen to me, D. Go to bed and sleep it off. We'll talk more when you're sober. I'm hanging up now. Go to bed."

I hear Jimmy disconnect. I look at my cell and watch the screen accrue seconds and then minutes of my connection to him in California. I lie down on the futon and fall asleep with the phone on the pillow beside me.

38

―――――

Monday, 10:00 a.m.

A t St. Nick's, I finish my first Kool of the day, toss the butt into
the street, and get out of my car. Evie and JJ sit in the back seat,
ostensibly because it's easier to sign with each other, but I think they
get their kicks pretending I'm the chauffeur. I open the door for my
mother who is still giving me a cool shoulder for my stupid prank on
Saturday. JJ lets himself out on the other side and I lock up.

We are a half hour early for Toby's funeral mass. We step into St.
Nicholas Catholic Church, a century-old building recently added to
the Registry of Historic Buildings in Chicago. Cherry wood pews,
grey stone walls, and wooden floors black with time emanate more
gloom than the lights or candles on the altar can overcome. We make
our way to the front of Father Mik's unoccupied church, the first of
Toby's friends to arrive.

I quick-step in front of Evie and face her, sweeping my arm in a large
semi-circle to encompass the empty church.

"You're right. Good thing we got here early to get a good seat." Either Evie completely misses my dramatic eye-roll as I sign my sarcasm or she purposely ignores me.

Instead, she points to a small table positioned in front of the altar. A round, light-colored object about the size of a small hatbox sits on the table.

"See that box? Your father made that. It has Toby's ashes inside."

I take my seat in the front pew between my parents. I tap JJ's knee to get his attention and point at Toby's wooden box.

"It's beautiful. I remember the playthings you whittled for David and me when we were kids," I sign. I mime stringing large wooden handmade beads on a long shoelace.

JJ nods. His hands then describe a wood dachshund with a drawn-down belly like a bowed hot dog, a toy I haven't thought about in years. It was a favorite of mine.

"I still have those toys at home, waiting for the next generation," JJ signs. He winks to make sure I understand that his comment is only what he wishes, not an Evie-like statement of pressure and guilt.

I wink back at my father and pat his large, scarred hands that crafted those much-loved toys. A small bump of hope rises within—Jimmy and I might yet provide those grandchildren.

But my hope is quickly squelched, because I immediately relive my embarrassment about drunk-calling him late Saturday night. He still hasn't called back. Yesterday, recovering from my hangover was my major activity. But I didn't drink the remaining booze—simply poured it down the drain this morning. I debate whether to tell Evie that Jimmy said he's coming home at Thanksgiving, but sounds from the back of the church distract me.

I turn and see two women walking up the long aisle toward us. The lighting is so dim I don't recognize Sarah Gilbert, Toby's apartment-mate at Campbell House, and Jan Marie, his case manager at ARC, until they move closer. I tap each of my parents on the knee and point over my shoulder to indicate the approaching women.

"Do you mind if we sit with you?" asks Jan Marie. She looks uncomfortable in the cavernous church. Sarah exchanges a quick hello with Evie and JJ.

"That's fine; sit, sit." Evie waves them in. She smiles at the two women, then shoos JJ and me farther down the pew to make room.

JJ leans past me and gets the attention of Sarah and Jan, then points to the wooden box. *"I'm glad to see someone from ARC here for Toby,"* he signs.

I notice JJ has transitioned the location for Toby's name sign. The letter "T" resting on his bicep has morphed into a soft tap over his heart.

Evie nods at the women. *"This entire church is empty. We're the only people to show up."*

Her hands splay outward, middle fingers hyper-extended, and swoop around in large circles to encompass the church. This exaggeration of the sign captures her disapproval of people not in attendance. Evie's judgment isn't lost on Jan Marie.

"ARC had a memorial service for Toby on Friday after work. Most everybody went to that," signs Jan Marie.

JJ's face conveys surprise and then hurt at the information. No one, including me, thought to tell him about the service, which I'm sure he would've attended. I make a mental note to talk with JJ again about getting a smartphone.

It's one more reminder that my father is not in step with the ongoing advances in technology that make life easier for deaf people. It's also a sad snapshot of how much my parents are aging. I glance at Evie gaily signing with the two women and feel a rush of love for her. Even though we regularly spar with each other, my connection to her is unbreakable.

JJ leans past me and gives a small wave to Jan Marie and Sarah Gilbert to divert their attention from some gossip Evie imparts.

"Next Saturday we will spread Toby's ashes at Lake Michigan. Will you tell the other Deaf at Campbell House and ARC?

Both women nod at JJ and promptly turn their attention back to Evie, who hasn't stopped signing.

JJ lightly elbows me. *"Your mother tells me you came by Saturday when I was bowling."*

"Yeah. I waited until nine. That's a lot of bowling." It's a familiar tease I use with him because I know he probably went out for a few beers after knocking down some pins.

"We went to the Deaf Club because they were showing a captioned movie. Pete and I went to see it but ended up playing cards. Until midnight!"

JJ looks amazed at this turn of events. I guess staying up past midnight at sixty-four is the mark of an exceptional evening. I pat him on the knee, happy he's able to get out of the house after the scare with Evie. JJ looks at his watch, then asks me the question I want to avoid.

He points again to the carved box with Toby's remains and asks about news of the investigation. When I hesitate answering, JJ misinterprets this and assures me we still have fifteen minutes until the services starts.

"Remember the sketch I showed you of the man who killed Toby? You said he looked like Toby?" I sign this to JJ and he mimes how he crushed the picture into a ball and threw it in the trash. I nod.

"His name is C-H-A-R-L-E-S W-O-R-T-H-Y." I truncate the fingerspelling for the name into the initials "CW" and tap them on the side of my head, explaining briefly to JJ that CW is now bald.

"He's Toby's second cousin. We arrested him Friday." Before I can say any more JJ throws his arms around me and gives me a big squeeze.

"Wonderful! I knew you'd catch him!"

As I hug him back I debate how much more to say. Neither he nor Evie know about my suspension and I'm not going to drop that bomb a few minutes before the start of Toby's funeral. It seems best to leave the troublesome topic on hold until we have at least a few hours to argue about my grieving the charges. And if I know my mother, there *will* be an argument.

But because JJ took Rameeka in and protected her, I want to let him know what a good thing he's done. I give him the abbreviated version of Rameeka's kidnapping and how Marty traced her cell phone, leading to the capture of CW. I purposely turn my body to shelter the story from the three women on my left, telling JJ the information is confidential and not to tell Evie. I don't want anything to remind her of being attacked at home.

JJ's eyes reflect his amazement at the kidnapping story. *"You and FA are a good team, catching CW. Toby can have peace, now."*

I start to tell JJ that CW won't be charged with Toby or Kandy's murders, but then I hold off and reconsider. CW is in custody and that's enough for my father to know. Besides, if I tell him why CW won't be charged, I'll have to tell him about hapless Walter Washington, which would then uncover the fact Carrera is the lead detective for the investigation. That's closer than I want to tread right now. I push away the thought that at some point, very soon, I'll have to tell my father the truth.

"Toby's case is finished."

JJ clasps his hands together, raises his arms shoulder-high and lightly shakes his hands back and forth in a dignified cheer.

JJ's next question shows he still believes my continued charade of being on active duty.

"What are you and FA working on now?"

Before I have a chance to consider my answer, Father Mik enters the church from a side door near the narthex. I tell JJ we can talk later. Father Mik walks up to the small table in front of the altar where Toby's ashes rest in my father's lovely box. He turns and faces us. JJ leans over me and taps Evie on the arm to draw her attention away from chatting and toward the priest.

"Let us begin," Father Mik signs.

39

Tuesday, 8:00 a.m.

The close-up photo in the newspaper of Carrera and Caitlyn is pretty sappy. It's attached to an article in the social section of the *Trib* about them and other young do-gooders at a fund-raising dinner. I read the article while sitting at my now-former desk in the squad room, waiting for Abandonato to show up with my coffee and the ever-predictable box of doughnuts. I'm here to tell my partner in person that I'm grieving the charges against me and that it might result in my being away from the job for six months.

I look at the happy couple's picture again. Carrera and Caitlyn sit close together, his arms around her and her left hand draped oh-so-subtly smack in the middle of his chest. A huge diamond ring blazes like a bonfire on her finger. They gaze into each other's eyes, so very much in love.

I want to puke.

The article's content makes me want to puke even more. In addition to portraying Caitlyn as a whiz kid lawyer, Carrera comes off as a one-

282

man avenger of the mean streets. Wonder how he convinced the reporter not to fact-check his bullshit. I toss the paper onto my old desk. It lands right next to a box that holds the remains of my personal stuff I finished packing a few minutes ago. Across the room I see Abandonato exit the elevator and head my way with our morning stash.

"Hey," he says, depositing a large black coffee in front of me. He drops the box of doughnuts onto his desk and our popularity instantly increases. After the vultures leave, the box empty except for a few crumbs, I pick up the newspaper and hand it to him.

"Check it out."

He scans the article and notes the announcement of their engagement.

"Wonder if we'll get invited to the wedding," I say, grinning at Abandonato.

He chuckles, then looks more closely at the picture. "How much you think that ring set Carrera back? Eight, ten grand?"

"Twice that, easy."

"A woman like that, starting out with a ring like that," he says, shaking his head.

Unsure of what Abandonato is implying, I ask for clarification.

He shrugs. "She's what, in her late twenties? As their marriage continues, seems like she's going to expect a lot more." He taps the paper. "I wonder how the Prick's going to find enough money to keep her comfortable," he says, drawing air quotes around the word "comfortable."

"Or faithful," I say, feeling as mean-spirited as I sound. I'm not jealous of Caitlyn's engagement and future marriage to Carrera, but envy isn't too strong a word for how I feel about the young woman's rosy future, especially compared to mine. Abandonato's comment tugs at me, though.

"Yeah," he says. "Still don't get the attraction between those two. Seems more like an arranged marriage, you know? I see someone like Caitlyn setting her cap for a guy who earns more than a cop. A lot more."

"She *will* get more if Koz is grooming the Prick for lieutenant." But I understand what he means. Caitlyn is way out of Carrera's league. As if the two of us conjured up the Prick by talking about him, he walks off the elevator and comes toward our desks.

"Demeter, what's this? Last rites?" Carrera points toward my packed box of personal items. "Getting ready to leave for good now you're grieving the charge? That's a lost cause. Zero tolerance means zero, zip, nada. No way the union's gonna save your ass."

And here we go again. The man with the inside source once more supplants what I'm preparing to tell my partner. Abandonato looks at me and then at the Prick. If he's pissed at hearing it from Carrera first, he hides it well.

"Pretty cozy with Koz, aren't you? Your future daddy-in-law tell you we nailed CW on Friday for kidnapping?" I say.

Carrera's eyes widen for a second but that's long enough for me to notice and know—Koz *didn't* tell him. The Prick assumes a casual attitude and shrugs. "Means nothin' to me." His words sound unconcerned but his right fist clenches and unclenches at his side.

"It should, Carrera, it should," says Abandonato. "This is the asshole I had the BOLO for. The one you pulled over and then let go."

A picture of Rameeka's bandaged head and messed up face surfaces in my mind and I get angry again. I stand up and lean in toward Carrera, get in his face.

"Yeah, the same asshole who killed Toby and Kandy and would've killed Rameeka if we hadn't gotten to her in time." I drive my index finger into his chest. "And you let him go."

Abandonato stands up next to me. "I've been thinking about that. You letting him go. And you putting a hold on Toby's death certificate."

I join in. "Feeling guilty, Carrera? About charging an innocent guy? So you block CW's ability to inherit his money thinking that'll even things up somehow?"

It feels deeply soothing to badger him. The other cops in the room quiet down and watch our tag team.

"Didn't want the press to look any further into the story of the bang-up job you did on skinny little Washington?" Abandonato echoes my tone of voice with his own snide mimic. "Didn't want Koz to get hung out to dry because of your incompetence?"

Carrera stands mute in front of us, eyes lowered, taking our abuse without a comeback. For a split second I feel like a bully in the schoolyard ganging up on the proverbial shy kid. But then I remember this is the Prick, the one who has nothing but smart-ass remarks and crude gestures for everyone around him. He looks up.

"You two trying to scare me?" He turns to the squad room at large, his voice booming like a ringmaster at the circus. "Dumped-at-the-altar Abandonato and his sidekick, Dana the Dipsomaniac, ladies and gentlemen. I bow to their great detecting abilities."

He turns back to us and bows. The cops who were listening go back to work, having lost interest. Carrera holds up his hands in mock surrender, then drops them to his side and walks away.

We both sit down at the same time. "He sure knows how to take the fun out of a tag team," Abandonato says.

Something about the Prick's quick capitulation sends up a red flag but I can't put a name to why. I turn to ask Abandonato about it and find him looking at me with a sad expression.

"Oh Christ," I say, forgetting what set us off. "It's why I came here today. To tell you about my meeting with Koz. I'm going to grieve the charges, Nuts. I'm sorry you had to find out from the Prick first. *Again.*"

My partner doesn't say anything and we sit quiet for a moment while the squad room starts to buzz with activity.

"Colin McBride said it could take up to six months—at the longest— and then I'll be back. I promise."

Abandonato drinks from his cup of tea, then looks at me. "Just be sure you *get* back, Dane."

I've never felt as unsure of anything in my life as I do about my promised return. I pick up my box of stuff and tell Abandonato I'll call him later, that maybe we can get some dinner after his shift if he's around.

He agrees and walks with me toward the stairs. When we pass the elevators, one opens and a man with a briefcase steps out.

"Excuse me. I'm looking for Detective Abandonato?"

"You found him," Abandonato says. "What can I do for you?"

The man looks at me with a speculative air.

"This is my partner, Detective Demeter." We shake hands and he introduces himself as Lovie Smith, defense attorney. "No relation to the coach," he adds, smiling.

"You look like you played ball," Abandonato says, eyeing the guy's stocky build and strong hands.

"Wrestler, actually. High school all-state champ my senior year, heavy weight. Did some more in college but gave it up. Try to keep in shape with lifting now." He pats what I imagine is a rock-hard stomach. "You?"

"I run," Abandonato says.

Lovie Smith nods.

"Don't let his understated modesty fool you, Mr. Smith," I say. "My partner here has qualified for Boston the past five years straight. His best marathon is a two forty-three. I have to brag for him because he's shy."

The lawyer's laugh is hearty and loud.

Abandonato allows himself a small smile. "But enough about me. What can I do for you, Mr. Smith?"

"Lovie, please. I represent Mr. Charles Worthy. He has asked me to talk with you about a matter related to his arrest for kidnapping."

40

4:30 p.m.

I wait outside the building of the Goose Island lock-up. I pace and chain-smoke until my throat is raw. Abandonato is supposed to meet me here after his shift, sometime after four, but my phone says four-thirty and I'm beginning to think he blew me off. I try his cell again but get voicemail.

The day has dragged since Lovie Smith dropped the bomb that CW wants to talk to Abandonato. He would only say that CW has information he wants to trade for reducing the charge of kidnapping. We couldn't get Lovie to tell us any more than that. The lawyer left after Abandonato agreed to meet with CW when his shift ended. My partner wasn't hot on letting me accompany him to their meeting.

"This isn't official, Nuts. The guy wants to talk, is all. Look, you can't cut me out now. Not after how much work I did."

I sound so pathetic when I whine.

"I wish Koz was here so I could get the go-ahead from him," Abandonato says.

"Come on. This'll be after hours. We're not doing anything official except talk to CW, see what he has to offer. We tell him we—or you, actually—aren't in a position to plea bargain anything, only evaluate his information. A preliminary step."

"One condition. You can't be in the room when I talk to him," Abandonato says.

I'm sure visions of my flying off the handle with Koz are dancing through my partner's head. I don't like the condition he's placed on me but think I might be able to finesse something once we're in the room with CW. At least Abandonato's letting me go with him.

"Okay, sure," I say. "I'll wait until you're finished or maybe they'll have a room with a one-way so I can watch."

And now Abandonato is over a half hour late and I'm hyperventilating trying to contain my excitement. At last his cherry red Prius swings into the lot. He parks and jogs toward me.

"Been waiting long?" he calls as he gets near.

"Just all friggin' day. Come on."

He laughs as I toss my half-smoked cigarette into the street. We push through the front door into the dank building.

The smell of dirty clothes and unwashed bodies hits us as soon as enter the lock-up, a repository for men and women waiting for trial. The building is slated for demolition next year, and will be replaced with a new regional center for lock-ups on the north side of the city. Green paint peels from the walls and missing tile squares pockmark the linoleum floor.

Abandonato speaks to the desk sergeant and he brings us to the squad room. We wait next to a gigantic radiator that must date back almost a hundred years, but in spite of its size, the room remains cold and vaguely damp. I wrap my winter jacket close to my body.

The sergeant returns to show us where he set up CW in an interrogation room. I ask if I can watch the conversation through a one-way but he laughs at me.

"That's much too modern for us, Detective. But what you can do is sit in the next room and eavesdrop. The walls are so thin you'll be able to hear everything."

Abandonato frowns at me but says nothing.

The sergeant brings us to the room. Abandonato enters and I catch a glimpse of CW and Lovie Smith seated at a table, their backs to me. I'm shown an adjoining room, which is about the size of a confessional at church. It must be where they sweat the tough guys who otherwise wouldn't crack. Claustrophobic? You'd give up your mother in five minutes. But as the sergeant promised, I can hear my partner's voice clearly.

"I'm going to record our conversation, Mr. Worthy."

I hear Abandonato talk into his digital recorder, stating the date, time, place, and people involved.

"Don't want no recordin' of this," says CW. "I ain't talkin' if you recordin'."

"Is that absolutely necessary, Detective? What my client has to tell you will be verifiable in other ways. I also assume you will write a statement and ask him to sign it. Maybe you could take notes?"

I imagine Abandonato huffing to himself but going along with Lovie Smith's request. I pull out my notepad and get ready to take my own notes.

"You asked to see me, Worthy. What about?"

"I got information I wanna trade, get my charges dropped."

"There's no way kidnapping charges are going to be dismissed."

"Then you get nothin' from me," says CW.

Well, that's that. I hear some low murmuring and think Lovie Smith must be saying something to CW. I strain to make out his words but fail.

Then the lawyer speaks in his normal tone. "Detective Abandonato, my client has information regarding a police officer who has committed a felony. He has proof. I did tell him his charges wouldn't be completely dropped, but we'd like to share this information and perhaps get some consideration from the court for leniency. My client has never been in trouble with the law."

I want to put my fist through the thin wall and apprise the counselor of the two murders his client committed. Only luck has kept him from being in trouble with the law—so far.

"I can't promise any kind of deal for your client, Mr. Smith. I'm not the arresting officer in this case."

"I understand that, but my client's information relates to a detective in your squad. Since Mr. Worthy knows you, he wants to share his information and have you act on his behalf with the officers who *are* in charge of his case."

I'm all ears. Carrera has to be the subject of CW's information, because he's the only cop CW's had contact with other than Abandonato and Marty. And the Prick's not-so-subtle reaction to the news of CW's arrest produced a tell as obvious as frowning at a bad poker hand. I silently will my partner to blow smoke, for a change, and agree he'll do what he can for CW.

"That's pretty far-fetched, Worthy. Especially knowing what I know about your recent activities. Why would I go to bat for you? I want to see you put away for a nice, long stretch."

We may have been partners for the past three years but I see we have work ahead of us on the ESP component of our relationship.

I hear more murmuring between the counselor and the accused. I think about the Prick's response to the BOLO on CW. Marty said

Carrera talked with CW privately, then let him go. Was Carrera trying to shake down CW for his blood money? He'd held up Toby's death certificate, keeping it away from CW, but now I see it isn't out of any remorse he feels about putting Washington away. Abandonato and I never figured Carrera might somehow try to use the death certificate for himself and score the quarter of a million dollars Otha Lee Worthy painstakingly saved for Toby.

In a flash I pop out of the phone booth and barge into the next room. Abandonato waves me off, mimes I should close the door.

"One minute," I plead, motioning to the corridor.

He comes into the hallway, closing the interrogation room door. "See?" Abandonato gets in my face, his jaw tight. "This is why I don't want you in the room, Demeter. I can handle this. Well, I could handle it if you hadn't broken my rhythm."

I back up a step. "But he's giving us a perfect chance to nail him for murder. Don't you see? The Prick must've threatened CW, told him he could put him away for Toby and Kandy unless he gave up the inheritance money. That's why he delayed the death certificate. CW couldn't get the money without it."

Abandonato listens and nods. "Okay, but how could the Prick access the money? Having only the death certificate wouldn't entitle him to it."

"That's what you've got to find out from CW, what they planned. He's going to flip on Carrera, thinking he can get charges reduced for Rameeka. Look, CW doesn't know we have actual proof against him for murder. Once he offers what he's got on the Prick, we can tell Koz what his future son-in-law's really been up to. Then he'll have to run the DNA on the hairbrush."

In my excitement of laying it all out, I grab my partner's forearm. He clamps his hand over mine in response, then returns to the room.

41

Wednesday, 10:00 a.m.

K oz looks dwarfed between the two stacks of file folders on his desk that frame him like bookends. Abandonato and I sit in the guest chairs facing him, our notes on our laps, ready to report what Koz won't want to hear about our visit to CW yesterday.

"Charles Worthy has made allegations against Alberto Carrera. He says Carrera tried to railroad him for the murders of Toby Worthy and Kandy Kane," says Abandonato.

The coloring of Koz's face changes from pale to dark grey as he looks at both of us. He takes his time before speaking. "Railroad him how?"

"Blackmail," I say. "Carrera told Worthy to turn over the inheritance money to him. Almost a quarter of a million dollars, Koz. He told Worthy if he didn't go along with the shakedown, he had enough evidence to charge him for both murders."

Evidence I uncovered, I want to remind Koz.

"But Carrera's never gone along with your theory of murder, Demeter. What made him change his mind?"

"I did," I say, my lips settling in a grim smile, "although I didn't know it at the time. When I couldn't convince you to test CW's hairbrush for his DNA I gave it one last shot by trying to convince Carrera. I laid it out for him about CW being enraged because Toby had inherited the bulk of the money from Otha Lee Worthy's estate, and showed him that CW had motive and opportunity. Kandy's death was collateral damage, either because she witnessed Toby's murder or was in on it."

Abandonato picks up on the narrative. "I had a BOLO out for CW's arrest at the time. A patrol cop pulls him over and calls it in to Carrera because he was lead. Marty Czychowicz is with Carrera at the time and observes him talking to CW for a little while. Then Carrera orders the cuffs off CW and tells Marty and the patrol cop to get lost. Marty thought it was weird, Carrera wanting to talk to a murder suspect without any backup."

Koz stands and walks the length of his office and back, twice, silent. He picks up the phone and calls Veda, orders coffee. "You two want anything?"

I jump at the offer for coffee and Abandonato puts in an order for tea with lemon and honey. Koz returns to his desk chair and sits down.

"Okay. So far you only gave me the word of a kidnapper against the word of a police officer. Not exactly compelling evidence."

He swivels his chair around to look out the window behind him. The morning sky is overcast and light flakes of snow toss around in the wind.

I look at Abandonato. He raises his eyebrows and lifts his open palm to indicate the notes on my lap. I take a deep breath and continue.

"That's background, Koz. Here's what happened."

Koz doesn't turn around as I speak and I'm actually grateful for it. He's cut me off so much lately it'll be easier to tell the back of his chair.

"Carrera held up Toby's death certificate as insurance against CW collecting the inheritance. Carrera and CW made plans to meet at Otha Lee Worthy's bank in Marietta this past Saturday."

"That's the mother," Koz says. He's following my thread so well it makes me think maybe he *did* read the email I sent him.

"Right," I say. "Only Carrera didn't know CW got arrested on Friday. And by the way, Koz, Abandonato and I both believe CW kidnapped Rameeka with the intent to kill her. She's the last person who could place CW at Toby's apartment that night."

"Well, the last person who's out free," Abandonato adds. "Washington's in jail."

"Yeah, there's that," I say. "So yesterday when Abandonato talked to CW and his attorney, we got final proof about Carrera jacking up CW. CW was booked Friday night at Goose Island and of course they took his phone away. He guaranteed us there would be an unheard message on his cell from Carrera on Saturday. We checked it out and there was a message from Carrera wanting to know where the hell Worthy was. It came in on Saturday morning."

Abandonato adds that he checked CW's cell phone records, which showed the incoming call came from Marietta.

Koz remains in his position looking out the window, his back to us. "Why would Worthy meet Carrera in Georgia? Why wouldn't he take off?"

"Two reasons," I say. "Carrera couldn't access the money alone—that was his biggest problem. He had to have the legitimate next of kin *there* to sign for the inheritance. But Carrera was smart. He didn't shake down CW for the whole thing, he split it: Fifty K for Worthy and two hundred K for himself. That was supposed to be the carrot for CW."

"And the second reason?"

"Simple. CW thought he'd get away with it. He thought he'd get the money first, then split."

Koz is quiet for a minute, then swivels his chair around to face us. "Because Worthy was picked up they didn't follow through with it, so no money changed hands."

I can see Koz fighting to keep Carrera clean in this. I assume his concern for Carrera is really concern for Caitlyn. It must throw him to see us dismantle the case of his future son-in-law and expose him as a corrupt cop. A cop Koz supported, who then hampered an investigation, made a false arrest, and allowed—even colluded with—a suspected murderer to go free. I wonder if Caitlyn will stand by her man or bail out when this hits the papers.

"There's one more thing," says Abandonato. "Dana has been in contact with Wili Nelson, the sheriff in Marietta."

I interrupt Abandonato. "My father asked me to see if I could find any of Toby Worthy's family, Koz." I don't want him to blame me any further for interfering with Carrera's investigation.

Abandonato continues. "Carrera went to the bank in Marietta on Saturday and waited for CW. When CW didn't show, Carrera talked with a bank officer about the procedure for accessing the inheritance money himself using the death certificate. But she confirmed what he already knew: he needed the beneficiary to sign the paperwork. The best she could do was offer Carrera the paperwork, have him get CW to sign it and have it notarized."

I will myself to sound calm even though my insides are jumping. "I called Sheriff Nelson right after CW gave us the information about Carrera. The sheriff checked with the bank and the bank officer confirmed Carrera being there. They reviewed the security tapes from Saturday and have him cold."

Koz sits quietly taking this in until there is a knock on his door. "Come," he says. Veda enters carrying a cardboard tray with our assorted drinks.

"Here's your tea, Detective," Veda says to Abandonato, "but they only had honey, no lemon."

We sip our drinks in silence.

Koz picks up Caitlyn's picture and looks at it for a while, then puts it down. "So Worthy flipped on Carrera thinking he could get his charges reduced for the kidnapping. But he doesn't know you have the evidence against him for the murders, is that correct?"

I nod. And as eager as I am to push Koz to send out the hairbrush for testing, I hold my tongue. I feel my partner's gaze and glance at him. His head dips in an almost imperceptible nod, support as clear as if he'd patted me on the back and pumped my hand in congratulations. My quick smile in return says, *See? I did learn a few things from you.*

Koz gets there on his own, without any help from me. He goes to his filing cabinet by the door and pulls out the box holding CW's hairbrush that Miss Paylor gave to me almost two weeks ago. Koz hands the box to Abandonato, instructs him to send it to our lab for testing, and approves a rush order on it. Even with that it will take almost a week to get the results.

"I'll need Sheriff Nelson's number, Demeter. Internal Affairs will have to investigate this charge. In the meantime, stay close. They'll want to talk with you, too."

"I know this is hard for you, Koz, and I—"

He cuts me off. "You can't possibly know, Demeter. You're not a parent."

To Abandonato he says, "Get that over there today. The sooner this is resolved, the better. We're done."

"Right, Koz." We stand and leave his office.

Back at my partner's desk we each sit for a minute. I finish my coffee but Abandonato tosses his half-full cup of tea in the trash, saying it's too sweet without the lemon.

"Not half as sweet as Koz approving the test," I say. Abandonato groans at the play on words but holds up his hand for a high five, which I deliver with an extra sting.

~

OUTSIDE, a good inch of snow has already covered Abandonato's red Prius. He opens the passenger side, places the box on the seat and retrieves his snow brush from the back.

"Well, I guess this is good-bye for awhile." He uses a two-handed grip to brush snow from the car roof. "Keep in touch." He tips his head toward the box in the car. "I'll let you know how it goes with the results." He clears the side windows in a hurry and comes back to the driver's side, where I stand.

"Good," I say. "And whatever happens with Carrera too, okay?"

His lazy salute hand ends in a clamp on my shoulder. I grip his forearm in return. He slides into the driver's side, flips on his lights, and pulls away.

I jog to my Corolla, get in and start it, letting the windshield wipers, front and back, do the work of clearing the white stuff. I make a mental note to buy a snow brush for the coming winter.

While my car warms up I smoke and relish the feeling of satisfaction at finally nailing CW for the murders of Toby and Kandy. I'm positive the DNA on the hairbrush will match the evidence found at Toby's apartment as well as the semen and prints found on Kandy. And even if they do reduce the kidnapping charges against CW in exchange for his information about Carrera, I'm pretty sure I can persuade Rameeka to testify against CW for Toby's murder, putting him away for a very long time.

I lower my window for a moment and toss the spent cigarette into the curtain of snow. I feel the letdown that inevitably follows the initial adrenaline rush experienced in Koz's office. Even though I finally succeeded in advancing my case, I feel empty instead of happy. It occurs to me that Toby's murder might be the last case I ever solve, the last case my partner and I ever work on together.

Koz, the union rep, Abandonato, and Jimmy all advised me to go to the EAP for an eval instead of grieving the charge. What I continually avoided thinking about now looms large—the distinct possibility I'll be fired as the outcome of the grievance.

If I feel this drained before even starting the process, I hate to think how I'll feel if I can't be a cop anymore, unable to put away scum like Charles Worthy or expose greedy pricks like Carrera. What will my life be like without Abandonato as my partner? Will Jimmy and I, currently separated by a physical distance, grow further apart without the common bond we always shared?

What were Rameeka's words of capitulation about her unwillingness to listen to everyone's advice? Oh, yeah.

"Stubborn bitch, that's me."

I cut off the engine, lock up, and dash back inside to find Koz.

42

Saturday, sunset

The mid-November weather makes it easy to find a parking spot in a lot that in summertime is wall-to-wall cars. The setting sun highlights a small group of people gathered at the far end of Fullerton beach, where a wind churns the lake water into endless snowcaps. Father Mik is easy to pick out, both because of his height and his black ensemble. JJ has one arm around Evie and holds the wooden container with Toby's ashes in his other hand.

I have yet to tell my parents about my suspension. And along with Abandonato, they also don't know I'll be going to the EAP next week for an assessment of my drinking. My partner will, of course, get the news. But I decided to keep my parents out of the loop. I don't need to hand Evie one more reason to berate me, nor could I bear to diminish JJ's pride in me for doggedly solving the murder of his friend.

I glance at my dashboard and the picture taped there. Toby still grins at me from behind his birthday cake.

"Success," I sign to him. Then, *"finish."*

Carefully I pull the picture from the tape, tuck it into the pocket over my heart, and climb out of my car to join the others.

ACKNOWLEDGMENTS

Friends and family have been wonderfully supportive of my writing. My gratitude goes out to Michelle Brooks, Karen Burgess, Mark Burgess, Bob Carty, Karen Graham, Bruce Joleaud, Kathy Joleaud, Luann Keizer, David Keizer, Cindi Mason, and my six brothers and sisters (Mardi Whitehouse, Tina Baron, Walt Whitehouse, Tim Whitehouse, Dave Whitehouse, and Jay Whitehouse). Posthumous gratitude to Dirk Jellema.

My parents, Jack and Fran Whitehouse, were inveterate readers. I'm grateful their example imprinted on me at an early age.

Mark Burgess gets a huge thanks for his cover design which, frankly, makes the book.

Thanks also to Chris Roerden, editor extraordinaire.

ABOUT THE AUTHOR

A. F. (Addy) Whitehouse is a writer and a former Sign Language interpreter who hails from Chicago. She lives with her husband, Bob Carty, in a distant suburb.

For my monthly newsletter and to discover upcoming Dana Demeter mysteries, please visit: www.afwhitehouse.com

twitter.com/addyfran
amazon.com/author/afw

Made in United States
North Haven, CT
04 May 2025